Assessment and Intervention for Executive Function Difficulties

School Based Practice in Action Series

Series Editors

Rosemary B. Mennuti, Ed.D., NCSP
and
Ray W. Christner, Psy.D., NCSP
Philadelphia College of Osteopathic Medicine

This series provides school-based practitioners with concise practical guidebooks that are designed to facilitate the implementation of evidence-based programs into school settings, putting the best practices *in action*.

Published Titles

Implementing Res ponse-to-Intervention in Elementary and Secondary Schools: Procedures to Assure Scientific-Based Practices
Matthew K. Burns and Kimberly Gibbons

Assessment and Intervention for Executive Function Difficulties
George McCloskey, Lisa A. Perkins, and Bob Van Divner

Forthcoming Titles

Resilient Playgrounds
Beth Doll and Katherine Brehm

Ecobehavioral Consultation in Schools: Theory and Practice for School Psychologists, Special Educators, and School Counselors
Steven W. Lee

Comprehensive Planning for Safe Learning Environments
Melissa A. Reeves, Linda M. Kanan, and Amy E. Plog

Assessment and Intervention for Executive Function Difficulties

George McCloskey
∎
Lisa A. Perkins
∎
Bob Van Divner

Routledge
Taylor & Francis Group
New York London

Supplementary Resources Disclaimer

Additional resources were previously made available for this title on CD-ROM. However, as CD-ROM has become a less accessible format, all resources have been moved to a more convenient online download option.

You can find these resources available here: www.routledge.com/9780415957830

Please note: Where this title mentions the associated disc, please use the downloadable resources instead.

Routledge
Taylor & Francis Group
270 Madison Avenue
New York, NY 10016

Routledge
Taylor & Francis Group
2 Park Square
Milton Park, Abingdon
Oxon OX14 4RN

© 2009 by Taylor & Francis Group, LLC
Routledge is an imprint of Taylor & Francis Group, an Informa business

Printed in the United States of America on acid-free paper
10 9 8 7 6 5 4 3 2 1

International Standard Book Number-13: 978-0-415-95784-7 (Softcover) 978-0-415-95783-0 (Hardcover)

Library of Congress Cataloging-in-Publication Data

McCloskey, George.
  Assessment and intervention for executive function difficulties / George McCloskey, Lisa A. Perkins, and Bob Van Divner. -- 1st ed.
    p. cm.
  Includes bibliographical references and index.
  ISBN 978-0-415-95783-0 (hardback : alk. paper) -- ISBN 978-0-415-95784-7 (pbk. : alk. paper)
  1. Educational psychology. 2. Executive ability in children. 3. Learning disabled children--Education. I. Perkins, Lisa A. II. Divner, Bob Van. III. Title.

LB1051.M393 2008
370.15--dc22   2008025199

Visit the Taylor & Francis Web site at
http://www.taylorandfrancis.com

and the Routledge Web site at
http://www.routledge.com

Contents

PART 2 ASSESSMENT AND INTERVENTION

PART 3   CONTEXTUAL APPLICATIONS

List of Tables and Figures

TABLES

FIGURES

Series Editors' Foreword

The School-Based Practice in Action series grew out of the coming together of our passion and commitment to the field of education and the needs of children and schools in today's world. We entered the process of developing and editing this series at two different points of our careers, though both in phases of transition: one (RWC) moving from the opening act to the main scene, and the other (RBM) from main scene to the final act. Despite one of us entering the peak of action and the other leaving it, we both continue to be faced with the same challenges in and visions for education and serving children and families.

Significant transformations to the educational system, through legislation such as the *No Child Left Behind Act* and the reauthorization of *Individuals with Disabilities Education Act* (IDEA 2004), have made broad, sweeping changes for the practitioners in the educational setting, and these changes will likely continue. It is imperative that as school-based practitioners we maintain a strong knowledge base and adjust our service delivery. To accomplish this, there is a need to understand theory and research, but it is critical that we have resources to move our empirical knowledge into the process of practice. Thus, it is our goal that the books included in the School-Based Practice in Action series truly offer resources for readers to put directly into action.

To accomplish this, each book in the series will offer information in a practice-friendly manner and will have a companion CD with reproducible and usable materials. Within the text, readers will find an icon that will cue them to documents available on the accompanying CD. These resources are designed to have a direct impact on transitioning research and knowledge into the day-to-day functions of school-based practitioners. We recognize that implementation of programs and the changing of roles come with challenges and barriers, and as such, these may take on various forms depending on the context of the situation and the voice of the practitioner. To that end, the books of the School-Based Practice in Action series may be used in their entirety and in their present form for a number of practitioners; however, for others, these books will help them find new ways to move toward effective action and new possibilities. No matter which style fits your practice, we hope that these books will influence your work and professional growth.

It has been a pleasure having the opportunity to work with Dr. George McCloskey, Ms. Lisa Perkins, and Dr. Bob Van Divner to develop the second book in the series. In recent years, the concept of executive functions and how they impact the lives of youth, as well as adults, has become prominent in the literature. However, despite ongoing research and the increase of information available on executive functions, many questions remain. For practitioners in school settings, questions such as, "What are executive functions?" "How do we measure executive skills?" "How do executive function difficulties affect learning and behavior in school?" and "What do we do to help students with deficits in executive processes?" remain.

To help answer these questions and others, McCloskey, Perkins, and Van Divner have developed a comprehensive guide filled with innovative views and practical resources. The authors challenge the readers to think beyond traditional perspectives, and they provide a number of ideas that will promote reflection and offer a means for practitioners to examine or reexamine their current practice. This book is based on a thorough review of the literature as well as the clinical wisdom and practical experience of the authors. We believe this book will offer a new understanding of executive functions to the readers and will enhance their current practices in the assessment and intervention of executive functions.

We extend our gratitude to Mr. Dana Bliss and Routledge Publishing for their support and vision to develop a book series focused on enriching the practice and service delivery within school settings. Their openness to meet the needs of school-based practitioners made the School-Based Practice in Action series possible. We hope that you enjoy reading and implementing the materials in this book and the rest of the series as much as we have enjoyed working with the authors on developing these resources.

Rosemary B. Mennuti
Ed.D., NCSP

Ray W. Christner
Psy.D., NCSP
Series Editors, School-Based Practice in Action Series

Acknowledgments

My sincerest thanks are offered to the many individuals who helped make this book a reality, especially the following:

- Drs. Rosemary Mennuti and Ray Christner, who invited me to write this book for the series and offered encouragement and invaluable support throughout the writing and manuscript preparation process.
- Lisa Perkins and Bob Van Divner, who agreed to sacrifice their time to assist me with the preparation of this manuscript.
- Drs. Matt Schure, Bob DiTomaso, and Rosemary Mennuti for their exemplary leadership of the academic community at PCOM and for creating the academic environment that enabled me to pursue this project concurrent with my teaching and research duties at the university.
- Drs. John Breen, Jeanne Gold, and Steven Feifer, who reviewed the original book proposal and provided encouraging feedback to the publisher and to me. A very special thanks to Jeanne Gold, who provided me a forum for discussing the ideas presented in this book with psychologists, educators, and school administrators in numerous workshop presentations that she arranged for me to do at the Putnam-Northwestchester BOCES. A deep debt of gratitude is owed to John Breen, who encouraged me to pursue this project before it was even proposed by the series editors.
- Drs. John Breen and Jack Raykovitz, cherished friends who shared their thoughts and insights about psychology and education in numerous conversations over the years.
- Drs. Joe French, Jim Murphy, and John Salvia, my mentors at Penn State who helped me to develop professional skills and learn the important hard lessons that are part of becoming a school psychologist.
- The many participants of my workshops and the PsyD and EdS students at PCOM. Over many years, they have taught me much and offered information, insights, and challenging questions that have made me work harder

to find answers, clarify perspectives, and improve my skills.

- Dana Bliss, acquisitions editor at Routledge, and the other members of the editorial and production staffs who worked so hard to get this book to press.
- Finally, but most importantly, I would like to thank my wife and my sons, Michael, Nathan, and Matthew, for their patience, love, and support throughout this process. My wife Laurie, a gifted teacher with elementary, secondary, and special education training, has always been there to help me think through difficult concepts and situations and to do the right things for children, parents, and educators. My sons have been a constant source of joy and inspiration over the years. They, and their friends who have spent time in our home, have taught me much about brain development and how children make use of executive functions in their daily lives.

GM

My deepest gratitude goes to George McCloskey for giving me this opportunity to explore in depth a topic of longstanding interest, as well as for his confidence in me, his mentorship, and his guidance. It was through him that I found the supportive community of PCOM, with its talented and dedicated faculty, and luckily became part of a wonderful student cohort. Thanks go to Bob Van Divner, cohort member and co-author, whose strong intellect and skills have encouraged me to work harder. Also, many thanks go to Dr. Rocco Marotta, whose encouragement sent me on this recent didactic path in the first place. Most importantly, very special thanks go to my two daughters and husband: to Caitlin, who has given rich context to the impact of executive functioning difficulties and has served as the primary catalyst for further study in this area, to Kristen, whose expressions of pride in this accomplishment have been a source of great encouragement, and especially to Andy, my husband and my best friend, for his generous and loving support and eternal patience.

LAP

I would like to thank "Nana," "Pap," and my parents for providing me with the foundational self-confidence that has enabled me to persevere and succeed professionally. I would also like to thank Leah, Sevi, and Drew for their patience and understanding when time needed to be dedicated to this project. Many thanks go to Dr. Roe Mennuti and Dr. Ray Christner for their support throughout my time at PCOM, and to Lisa Perkins, co-author, colleague, and friend. Finally, a special thanks to Dr. George McCloskey for asking me to participate in the preparation of this book and for his willingness to mentor me through the PCOM doctoral program, and his continual encouragement of me to utilize my skills to their fullest potential.

BRVD

Preface

The purpose of this book is to provide psychologists and other clinical practitioners with a solid understanding of the concept of executive functions. This includes offering information regarding the methods for assessing individual executive function processes (both strengths and weaknesses), as well as providing effective interventions for remediation and accommodation of executive function difficulties.

The first section of this book is comprised of four chapters used to increase and clarify the reader's understanding of executive functions.

Chapter 1 begins by presenting six case vignettes to engage the reader in a thinking process about the information presented throughout this book.

Chapter 2 offers brief definitions of executive functions and the specific capacities encompassed by this concept. The chapter articulates the similarities and differences between the concepts of executive functions and intelligence, and these concepts are clarified through the presentation of brief case vignettes.

Chapter 3 provides a comprehensive model for conceptualizing how executive functions guide and impact everyday behavior. The model offered here presents a framework for understanding how executive functions cue and direct the use of cognitive, emotional, and motor capacities within four specific arenas of activity (intrapersonal, interpersonal, symbol system, and environment).

Chapter 4 offers a context for understanding the intricacies of executive functions and their role in regulating behavior. The brain regions associated with executive functions and the difference between anatomical structures and psychological constructs is discussed along with the distinct neural circuitry of internally generated versus externally demanded executive control processes. Discussion includes the time frame and trajectory of executive function development, and the relationship of executive functions to other psychological constructs (e.g., working memory). Given the role executive functions have on classroom learning and behavior, we discuss the interrelationship of executive functions and learning disabilities. We briefly discuss the relationship between executive functions and other clinical diagnoses, such as Attention Deficit Hyperactivity Disorder (ADHD), Autism Spectrum Disorders (e.g., Autism, Asperger's Disorder, etc.), Disruptive Behavior Disorders (e.g., Conduct Disorder, Oppositional Defiant Disorder, etc.), and other disorders listed in the *Diagnostic and Statistical Manual for Mental Disorders, Fourth Edition, Text Revision* (DSM-IV-TR; American Psychiatric Association, 2000).

The second section of this book focuses on assessment and intervention strategies for executive function capacities. Chapter 5 discusses general best practice approaches to the assessment of executive functions as they cue and direct perception, cognition, emotion, and motor capacities within the four arenas of activity. This general section is followed by a detailed discussion of administration and interpretation of executive function assessment methods and instruments specific to each *arena of activity* and in the context of a three-tier service delivery model in schools.

Chapter 6 imparts a general framework for categorizing and selecting executive function interventions based on information gathered through the aforementioned assessment process. We highlight the information regarding the framework by presenting an illustrative written case report.

Chapter 7 provides information about general approaches and specific programs that can be used to address executive function problems.

Chapter 8 discusses methods that can be used on an individual basis to monitor response to, and evaluate the outcomes of, intervention efforts focused on improving the use of executive function capacities.

The last section of this book is designed to integrate the information from the previous chapters to aid in the implementation of services to children and adolescents. To accomplish this, Chapter 9 provides the comprehensive case report for a secondary-age child. This case study offers background information, assessment results and interpretations, a case summary and recommendations, as well as describing intervention efforts and the outcomes of these efforts. In addition to providing our concluding comments in Chapter 10, we further discuss future directions in this area as well as specific practice implications when working with children and adolescents.

The accompanying CD with this practitioner's guide makes available additional information resources and materials. The resources found on the CD include:

- Executive function overview handout for professionals
- Executive function overview handout for teachers and parents
- Self-regulation executive function definitions and observable behavior difficulties
- Self-regulation executive function expanded definitions with specific examples within domains of functioning and arenas of involvement
- Executive function structured interview parent/teacher and child forms
- Executive function student observation form
- Executive function classroom observation form
- Comprehensive psychoeducational evaluation reports for two students
- Annotated executive function bibliography
- Collected chapter case vignettes

Part 1

CONCEPTUAL OVERVIEW

1

How Do Executive Function Difficulties Affect Children? *Six Case Study Examples*

In keeping with the goal and theme of this book series—*school-based practice in action*—we wanted to provide a context for readers to apply the knowledge presented throughout this practitioners' guidebook. This chapter will introduce six case vignettes that describe the executive function difficulties experienced by children of varying age. In each subsequent chapter, we will revisit each of these children and discuss case conceptualization processes from an increasingly expanded perspective on the specific executive function difficulties each child is experiencing.

CASE VIGNETTES

Case of Justin

When Justin's parents received his report card for the first quarter of his seventh grade year, they were surprised. Justin had always been a good student and never received less than a B grade on any report card in elementary school. His elementary school teachers never mentioned any signs of learning problems, and state competency tests and standardized group test results consistently reflected above average levels of performance in all areas of basic academic skills. Now, after one quarter of seventh grade, Justin was failing English and social studies, barely passing science with a D, and just hanging on to a C in math. In discussions with the parents, Justin's teachers offered little in the way of insight into the causes of Justin's poor performance in their classrooms. All four teachers indicated that Justin had several incomplete or late homework assignments and generally poor quality of work on projects.

Scores on tests in all classes fluctuated from high A's to F's. His teachers expressed the belief that Justin was capable of doing better work in their classes and getting better grades, and all felt that the main problem was Justin was "not putting enough effort into his schoolwork." Concerned with Justin's increasing loss of interest in school, though unconvinced that a lack of effort was Justin's only problem, his parents requested a comprehensive evaluation "to determine the nature of Justin's lack of academic success and to identify ways to help improve his performance."

The report of the results of a comprehensive psychoeducational evaluation completed by the school psychologist indicated above average intellectual functioning (WISC-IV Full Scale IQ of 118), above average achievement scores in reading and math, and an average score in written expression. Results of rating scales completed by Justin's parents and teachers did not suggest the presence of internalizing or externalizing emotional problems, hyperactivity, or inattention. Based on the results of the evaluation, the school multidisciplinary team concluded that Justin possessed the intellectual ability and academic skills needed to succeed in school and concurred with the teachers that the primary reason for Justin's lack of academic success was "his lack of adequate engagement with class activities and his lack of completion of assigned homework." Justin's parents were encouraged by the team to work with Justin to help improve his work habits and his attitude toward school.

Case of Kevin

Before Kevin stepped through the door of Mrs. Jones' fifth grade classroom, his reputation had already preceded him. An athletic, energetic boy, Kevin seemed to be a magnet for turmoil, and, as predicted by Kevin's fourth grade teacher, the turmoil always had a negative impact on Mrs. Jones' ability to maintain order in her classroom. Of particular concern were Kevin's extreme temper outbursts, which occurred at least twice a week. Once Kevin became angered, he seemed unable to control himself, and he would shout and curse at anyone who tried to calm him down, including Mrs. Jones. After a month and a half of trying to handle Kevin herself, Mrs. Jones asked for help. The school psychologist was asked to work with Mrs. Jones, and this initiated pursuing a functional behavior assessment (FBA). She observed Kevin several times in Mrs. Jones' classroom, as well as at lunch and on the playground during recess. The school psychologist also interviewed Kevin, his parents, and Mrs. Jones, as part of the FBA. Although disruptive behaviors were never directly observed during the FBA, the school psychologist observed and interacted with Kevin during the aftermath of one of his temper outburst episodes, and Kevin was still very agitated at that time. Additionally, all parties interviewed, including Kevin, indicated that temper outbursts occurred frequently enough to be considered a "real problem." In his discussions of these outbursts, Kevin was always quick to justify his behavior as an appropriate reaction to what other students said or did.

The school-based team determined that they would target a reduction in the frequency of Kevin's angry outbursts through the implementation of a positive behavioral support plan. The central focus of the plan involved positive reinforcement of appropriate classroom behaviors. On a chart posted in Kevin's classroom, his teacher indicated the kind of behavior Kevin exhibited during morning classes, lunch, recess, and afternoon classes. For every class period that Kevin exhibited appropriate behavior, he would receive a gold star. If Kevin accumulated five out of the eight possible gold stars by the end of the school day, he received a playing/trading card of his favorite team. The program worked well for the first week, as Kevin earned at least five of eight gold stars and chose a card as his reward on four consecutive days. Beyond the first week, however, Kevin was unable to sustain a positive behavior pattern. Kevin would frequently accumulate three or four gold stars per day, only to see his accomplishments halted by an unanticipated emotional meltdown. The frustration of coming close to but not reaching the goal seemed to have an extremely negative effect on Kevin's general mood and willingness to engage in positive classroom interactions. The idea of changing the criteria for a reward from five of eight stars to three of eight stars per day was discussed by the team. However, the classroom teacher felt very strongly that such a reinforcement schedule would be sending the wrong message to Kevin and the other students, some of whom were already complaining about the "special treatment" that "the child with the worst behavior in class" was receiving. Hearing that the team was unable to reach an acceptable compromise for amending the current plan and believing that an example had to be set for the other children, the school principal delivered an ultimatum—"Evaluate and place Kevin in a class for children with emotional disturbance or Kevin would be suspended if another temper outburst occurred."

Case of Caroline

Caroline is a quiet, shy 15-year-old high school sophomore. While Caroline has been a C student over the years with no apparent learning problems, she is beginning to fail courses due to absenteeism and incomplete homework. Caroline's parents are becoming very concerned about increasing disengagement with school and suspect that she might be getting involved with drug use. On school days, when not closely supervised by a parent in the morning, Caroline is beginning to skip school or arrive late. Caroline tells her parents that she intends to get to school on time, but complains about how difficult it is to get up in the morning. Caroline's parents indicate that she goes to bed at a reasonable hour to ensure eight to nine hours of sleep; however, this does not seem to be enough for Caroline to feel well rested. Complicating matters is the fact that Caroline has been unable to develop a predictable routine for self-care. Her unpredictable occupation of the bathroom at critical times is causing a great deal of tension between Caroline and her brother, as well as her parents, as it disrupts the flow of the household and appears to show a lack of consideration for family members. The few friends that she has have stopped calling her, as she rarely returns their phone calls or initiates contact. Both parents and teachers say she has no "self-discipline," though privately her parents worry that Caroline may be depressed. Caroline herself provides little insight as to what is going on, saying only that she feels "stupid" and that no one likes her. After meeting with Caroline's guidance counselor, who also expressed concerns about the possibility of depression, Caroline's parents scheduled an appointment with a psychiatrist. Based on his evaluation and the reports from school and home and discussions with Caroline, the psychiatrist diagnosed her with depression and prescribed an antidepressant. After taking medication for several months, Caroline's mood improved and her fatigue symptoms decreased noticeably. However, she continues to experience many of the same behavioral and performance difficulties that were noted prior to the start of medication use.

Case of Brett

With a visible shudder, Brett's mother describes him as a "holy terror." At 5 years of age, and much to the chagrin of his parents, Brett is already well known to the local hospital emergency room staff. At the age of 3 years, Brett jumped from a moving swing and broke his right leg. At age 4 years, he broke his left arm while attempting to slide down the banister of the entryway steps in his home. Now in kindergarten, Brett has his classroom teacher in a state of frenzy over a number of situations that occurred. In one instance, while on a field trip with the class, Brett dashed into the middle of the street to retrieve a metal object that had caught his attention. Although Brett is very active and likes to engage in gross motor activities like swinging a bat, chasing the family cat, and jumping down stairs, he tends to avoid fine motor activities. Although Brett can identify letters quickly, understands how sounds go together to make words, recognizes a number of words by sight, and counts quickly and accurately, he struggles greatly when attempting to form letters with a pencil and is very poor with tasks such as coloring within the lines with crayons or cutting shapes out of paper with scissors. In fact, the last time Brett handled a pair of scissors, he managed to open a deep gash in his left palm that required another trip to the emergency room for treatment. Efforts to discipline Brett both at home and in school only seem to make the situation worse. With much exasperation, Brett's mother remarked, "It's to the point where we're afraid to praise him for good behavior; this only seems to draw attention to the behaviors we want him to avoid, and the next thing we know, he's back at it with a vengeance."

Case of Morgan

Morgan is a bright, vivacious, outgoing fifth grader who loves to be involved in many activities. In fact, Morgan's parents are beginning to wonder if her multiple, highly varied interests are at the root of Morgan's "scattered" approach to her academic work. Complicating matters is the fact that Morgan has a reading disability and her spelling and writing skills also are very limited. Morgan was identified as a student with a learning disability in second grade, and since that time she has been receiving specialized instruction in reading, spelling, and writing through the district's special education resource room program. Over the years, Morgan's regular and special education teachers have consistently commented on what they have observed to be extreme difficulties with focusing and sustaining attention, especially when Morgan is required to read or write. Morgan's parents tended to attribute these difficulties to Morgan's resistance to engaging in tasks that are very difficult for her because of her learning disability. Consequently, when speaking with Morgan's pediatrician, her parents always downplayed the AD/HD symptoms that teachers reported to them and that they observed in the home. Morgan's special education teacher seems very knowledgeable regarding appropriate instructional interventions to help Morgan develop her reading and writing skills. At this point in time, however, Morgan's parents are becoming very concerned about how much Morgan struggles when attempting to read or write, and they are beginning to wonder if Morgan's attention and concentration problems are more than just avoidance symptoms and if she is being instructed with the proper teaching methods. With these concerns in mind, Morgan's parents requested that the school provide an updated psychoeducational evaluation.

Case of Alex

Through his early school years, Alex's pattern of development seemed quite normal. At age 13 years, however, Alex experienced an extreme bout of nausea and vomiting during a public speaking appearance required as part of a religious instruction program. From that point on, Alex has experienced intermittent gastrointestinal symptoms, especially during stressful situations. During Alex's late high school years, the physical symptoms began to intensify and occur more frequently. Marijuana smoking became habitual and outbursts of anger and threats of violence were often associated with attempts to confront Alex about his behavior. Consultations with a gastrointestinal specialist and a psychiatrist resulted in trial use of various antidepressants and eventually lead to daily use of Depakote to help maintain a stable mood. Although Alex's problems resulted in excessive absences from school and failing grades his senior year, he was able to graduate and was accepted to study at a nearby university. After high school graduation, Alex's problems began to greatly interfere with his daily functioning. He cancelled a vacation trip with friends because of severe nausea. On the day he was to leave for college, he experienced extreme gastrointestinal symptoms that persisted for several days. Because of his physical reaction that appeared to be linked to the stress of thoughts about living on campus, Alex remained at home and enrolled at the university as a commuting student. College did not go well, and by the spring term, Alex was not attending any of his classes and had to withdraw from the university. This pattern of absences and failure was repeated the following year when Alex enrolled at a local community college on a part-time basis. A serious gambling problem developed and needed to be addressed within the following year. Between the ages of 18 and 22, Alex saw several therapists; however, the treatment he received had minimal effect on his somatic and behavior problems. Although Alex pursued treatment through cognitive behavior group therapy, he missed several sessions and was inconsistent in the completion of between session homework assignments provided by the therapist. Now at the age of 23, Alex is unemployed and not attending school, and he lives at home with his parents. He rarely leaves the house except for an occasional visit with friends. He assumes some responsibilities at home, though his parents find they must monitor him closely to attain compliance with work requests. At the urging of his parents, Alex agreed to undergo a comprehensive psychoeducational evaluation.

Although his parents always believed that Alex was a very "capable" young man, they were surprised to find out that Alex earned a Full Scale IQ of 132 on the WAIS-III. Truly baffled and exasperated with Alex's apparent lack of motivation and inability to engage the worlds of work or school, Alex's parents are wondering what course of action they should take. Although Alex, at the age of 23, has the legal right to make decisions for himself, concerns remain regarding the choices he makes. Alex's parents struggle with their role in his life, often asking themselves: "What should be done when a person who has the right to make all of his own decisions refuses to make any meaningful ones about his life?"

THINKING THROUGH

Do the difficulties being experienced by these children sound familiar to you? Have you encountered children like this in your clinical practice? Reflect for a while on how you would conceptualize assessment and intervention for these individuals and what your impressions are of the reasons for the difficulties they are encountering. In each subsequent chapter, we will provide additional information on each of these

2

Introduction to
Executive Functions

At this point, you might have surmised that executive functions have something to do with the difficulties of the six students featured in our case vignettes; however without a clear understanding of what executive functions are, the specific ways in which they impact learning and production, and the kinds of interventions most likely to help affect desired changes, acknowledging the presence of executive function difficulties does little more than attach an exotic neurospeak label to the puzzling nature of these student's problems. To really make a difference in the lives of students such as those in our case studies, much more than a cursory familiarity with the popular media conceptions of the concept of executive functions will be needed. This chapter will introduce the reader to some basic definitions and distinctions needed to form a context for greater understanding and application of the body of knowledge underlying this intriguing new construct that has emerged from research in the fields of neuropsychology and cognitive neuroscience.

Executive functions is a term that is becoming widely used by professionals and laypersons alike. Like other labels used to describe psychological constructs, the meaning of the term executive functions varies greatly depending on the knowledge and intent of the user. The press has become enamored with portrayal of executive functions as "the CEO of the brain" (Saltus, 2003) focusing attention on the pronounced increase in frontal lobe synaptic connectivity that begins to occur during adolescence, eventually leading to developmental improvements in self-direction and self-control (Stuss & Alexander, 2000).

Research has increased tremendously in recent years on both the function of the frontal lobes of the human brain and the role of executive functions in directing behavior. A search

of the term executive functions in the professional literature
easily yields more than 150 references within the last 5 years.
Additional searches on terms related to frontal lobe structures
associated with the concept of executive functions easily generates three times that number of references. The research on
executive functions and the frontal lobes has been applied to
clinical practice primarily in the area of neuropsychological
assessment. This has resulted in a number of instruments being
developed, including the *Wisconsin Card Sorting Test*[1] (WCST;
Heaton, Chelune, Talley, Kay, & Curtiss, 1993), the *Delis-Kaplan
Executive Function System* (D-KEFS; Delis, Kaplan & Kramer,
2001), the *NEPSY: A Developmental Neuropsychological Assessment* (Korkman, Kirk, & Kemp, 1998), the *Behavioral Assessment
of the Dysexecutive Syndrome* (BADS; Wilson, Alderman, Burgess, Emslie, & Evans, 1996), the *Behavior Rating Inventory of
Executive Function* (BRIEF, BRIEF-2, BRIEF-SR; Gioia, Isquith,
Guy, & Kenworthy, 2000), and the *Frontal Systems Behavior
Scale* (FrSBE; Grace & Malloy, 2001).

Although there has been much interest in the assessment
of cognition and behavior associated with executive functions, the manuals for these assessment instruments typically
provide minimal information regarding clinical interpretation of test results and their relationship to the planning and
implementation of interventions for problems associated with
poor performance on these tests. Of equal importance is the
fact that, to date, only one practical application handbook has
been published that directly addresses intervention for educational and psychological problems associated with executive
function deficits (Dawson & Guare, 2004). Beyond the information offered by Dawson and Guare, clinicians interested in
helping parents, teachers, and clients understand executive
function problems are faced with the onerous task of integrating various elements of the theoretical and research literature
to devise unique interventions. Alternatively, they are faced
with the time-consuming strategy of identifying elements
from current interventions that might be effective with one
or more aspects of executive function deficits. Additionally,
the assessment tools that are currently available tend to focus
on executive function involvement with symbolic material
(working with words, numbers, and abstract visual designs),

---

[1] While increasingly used as a measure of executive functioning, the
Wisconsin Card Sorting Test was originally developed in 1948 as a
measure of abstract reasoning and cognitive flexibility.

resulting in only a cursory understanding of how executive function deficits impact intrapersonal, interpersonal, and environmental interactions.[2]

The popularity of the concept of executive functions, juxtaposed with the paucity of information available on its effective use in clinic, classroom, or home settings, has created a great need for practical resources to guide both professionals and the lay public in the effective application of this important construct to the treatment of educational and mental health problems. This practitioner's guide intends to provide the elements essential for bridging the present gap between interest in the construct of executive functions and practical knowledge of how to apply it to help those in need.

WHAT ARE EXECUTIVE FUNCTIONS?

In the most general of terms, executive functions are often defined as the directive capacities of the human brain (Goldberg, 2001). As mentioned in the introduction to this chapter, executive functions have been referred to in the popular press as the CEO of the brain. Basic definitions of executive functions are often accompanied by an anatomical reference of the location of this "chief executive" as being housed in the frontal lobes of the brain. While such simplified definitions of function and location appear to be well-intentioned efforts to educate the public about executive functions, they place the concept at great risk of becoming as poorly understood a cliché as the popular right brain-left brain misconception wherein the left brain processes language while the right brain processes visuo-spatial abilities (see sources such as Springer and Deutch, 2002, for a more complete account of hemispheric specialization in terms of neuropsychological processes).

To make effective use of the concept, it is important not to think of executive functions as a unitary cognitive process or trait. Denckla's (1996) warning not to turn executive functions into the neuropsychologists' g (i.e., a global, singular construct) should be well heeded, although some recent

---

[2] See the manuals for the aforementioned tests of executive functions. These tests make use of tasks that exclusively require the use of symbol system manipulation for successful completion, including oral responses to test questions or using pencil and paper to complete visuo-motor tasks. They do not directly assess the use of executive functions in interactions with other individuals, in self-control of daily routines, or in interactions with the environment.

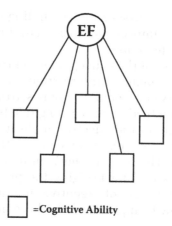

Figure 2.1   Executive Function Capacity as the Conductor of the Brain's Orchestra (i.e. EF as "g").

discussions of executive functions, such as Goldberg's (2001) reference to executive functions as "the 'S' (for smart) factor," might unintentionally lead one to think of executive functions as a unitary, global process. Goldberg, along with Brown (2005), falls into the executive functions as *g* conceptual trap by using the popular metaphor of "the orchestra conductor" to characterize how executive functions direct all behavior, as in the visual depiction of this analogy in Figure 2.1. Using this analogy gives the unintended impression that executive functions represent a single, unitary cognitive control process that directs all thought and behavior. This is clearly not the situation portrayed in the writings of either Goldberg or Brown, nor in most other discussions of executive control processes in the neuropsychological literature. It would be more apt to view the multiple executive functions that govern our conscious perceptions, feelings, thoughts, and actions as constituting a collection of "co-conductors" as depicted in Figure 2.2, each responsible for a separate aspect of the overall production of the orchestra, but each working—ideally—in a highly collaborative manner with the others.

Stuss and Alexander (2000) have addressed this issue very effectively in their writing on executive functions and the human frontal lobes:

> We emphasize that there are specific processes related to different brain regions within the frontal lobes. There is no frontal homunculus, no unitary executive function.

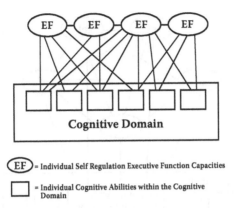

Figure 2.2 Self-Regulation Executive Functions as Co-Conductors of the Brain's Orchestra.

Rather, there are distinct processes that do converge on a general concept of control functions. The idea of a supervisory system is very applicable, if the emphasis is on a system constructed of multiple parts. From a clinical viewpoint, the position that there is no homunculus suggests that there is not a single frontal lobe syndrome with point-to-point correspondence to a homunculus. While a generally consistent frontal lobe syndrome can be found in some patients, this syndrome label describes patients with extensive damage to the frontal lobes often late after injury. (p. 291)

In keeping with the assertions of Stuss and Alexander and other brain researchers, executive functions can be thought of as a set of multiple cognitive capacities that act in a coordinated way. Executive functions are directive capacities that are responsible for a person's ability to engage in purposeful, organized, strategic, self-regulated, goal-directed processing of perceptions, emotions, thoughts, and actions. As a collection of directive capacities, executive functions cue the use of other mental capacities such as reasoning, language, and visuospatial representation. Figure 2.3a depicts how a selected subset of five independent but interrelated self-regulation executive functions can be involved in an integrated manner to cue and direct the use of a single mental capacity within the cognition domain (a cognitive subdomain) such as reasoning with verbal information. Expanding on the concept illustrated in Figure 2.3a, the diagram in Figure 2.3b depicts interconnections

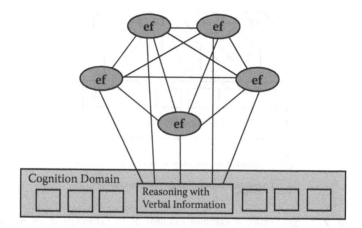

Figure 2.3a   Neural Network Diagram Illustrating Connections Between Five Self-Regulation Executive Functions and One Specific Ability Within the Cognitive Domain of Functioning.

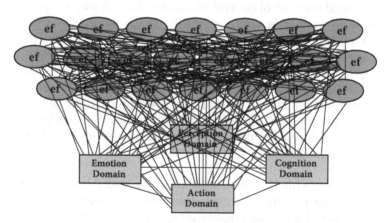

Figure 2.3b   Neural Network Diagram Illustrating Connections Between the 23 Self-Regulation Executive Functions and Four Separate Domains of Functioning.

between 23 different self-regulation executive functions that will be described in later chapters of this book and the four general domains of functioning. The single connections from each executive capacity to each domain of functioning, and even the multiple interconnections of every executive function with every other executive function, really represent an oversimplification of neural connectivity. In actuality, there are multiple connective neural pathways between each executive capacity and each of the various subdomains within each domain of function, as well as multiple pathways between each executive capacity depending on which executive functions and which subdomains of functioning are involved in mental processing at a given point in time. Although a detailed discussion of the multiple neural pathways that connect the frontal lobes with other cortical and subcortical areas of the brain is beyond the scope of this book, a general framework for understanding the ways in which these interconnections vary will be discussed in more detail in later chapters of this book.

While various researchers and clinicians have provided lists of executive function directive capacities, (see Table 2.1 for examples of these listings), and some have attempted to integrate various aspects of executive function control (Barkley, 1997, 2005; Denckla, 1996; Freeman, 2000; Miller, 2001; Taylor, 1999; Stuss & Alexander, 2000), no single reference work, to date, has attempted to synthesize the various writings on executive functions into a single overarching theory of executive control that can be used to guide clinical practice. The next chapter will describe an integrated model of executive functions in greater detail.

- Cueing the inhibition of reflexive, impulsive responding
- Cueing the interruption of, and return to, an ongoing activity
- Directing the focusing of attentional processes, the screening out of interference and distractions, and the sustaining of attention
- Cueing the initiation of effort and judgments about the amount of effort required to complete a task, and the sustaining of a sufficient amount of effort to effectively complete a task
- Cueing the flexible shifting of cognitive resources to focus on new demands or to respond to new conditions or new information
- Directing the efficient use of fluid reasoning capacities
- Directing the efficient use of, and alternation between, pattern and detail processing (knowing when to focus on the "big picture" and when to concentrate on the details, and when to switch between the two)
- Cueing the monitoring and regulating of speed of information processing; finding the right combination of speed and accuracy for optimal performance of an activity
- Cueing the monitoring of task performance for accuracy and efficiency

Table 2.1   Delineation of Executive Function Capacities by Various Researchers and Clinicians

Temple (1997) on defining executive functions:

- The ability to plan ahead and organize behavior across time and space in order to fulfill goals and intentions
- The ability to shift strategies and adapt to changing circumstances
- Planning, decision making, directed goal selection, and monitoring of ongoing behavior
- Also involved in self-awareness, empathy, and social sensitivity

Stuss (1992) on defining executive functions:

- The ability to shift from one concept to another
- The ability to modify behavior, particularly in response to new or modified information about task demands
- The ability to synthesize and integrate isolated details into a coherent whole
- The ability to manage multiple resources of information
- The ability to make use of relevant acquired knowledge

Denckla (2001) "terms used for Frontal (or Prefrontal) Constructs:"

- Freedom from Perseveration
- Temporal Organization of Behavior
- Initiation and Spontaneity
- Inhibition
- Self-Awareness
- Concept Formation/Abstract Reasoning
- Control Over Freedom from Interference
- Manipulation of Representational Systems

Denckla (2001) "Clinical Descriptors—EF Terms from Cognitive Psychology:"

Supraordinate (Higher Order) Processes

- Metacognitive or Metamodal Capacities
- Control Processes (Initiate, Sustain, Inhibit, Shift)
  - Set Maintenance
  - Self-Monitoring and Flexibility
  - Inhibitory Processes
- Integrative Processes
- Sequencing/Organizing Processes

Table 2.1 (continued)   Delineation of Executive Function
Capacities by Various Researchers and Clinicians

Gioia, Isquith, Guy, & Kenworthy (1996) on defining Executive Functions:

A collection of processes or interrelated functions responsible for

- Guiding, directing, managing cognition, emotion and behavior, particularly in novel problem-solving situations
- Purposeful, goal-directed problem-solving behavior

- Cueing the selection of verbal-nonverbal and abstract-concrete processing mechanisms
- Directing motor output and the altering of motor performance based on feedback
- Directing the use of working memory resources—that is, directing the ability to mentally hold and manipulate information
- Directing the efficient and fluent production of language when highly specific production demands are made
- Directing the integration of multiple abilities to produce oral or written responses or products that reflect the level of capacity of the component abilities involved
- Directing the efficient placement of information in long-term storage
- Directing the retrieval of information from long-term storage
- Cueing the engagement of appropriate social behavior
- Cueing the use of cognitive capacities that enable a person to "take the perspective of the other" in order to infer how someone is thinking or feeling at a given point in time
- Cueing the appropriate regulation of emotional control and expression of emotions
- Cueing processes involved in self-observation and self-analysis
- Cueing the engagement of cognitive capacities that enable hindsight and foresight

Within this frame of reference, executive functions are seen only as directive processes. They give commands to engage in processing but do not carry out the commands themselves. Executive functions are not the capacities we use to perceive, feel, think, and act. Instead, they are the processes that direct or cue the engagement and use of the capacities that we use to perceive, feel, think, and act. Rather than being conceived as a single, unitary construct, these executive functions are best viewed as a set of independent but coordinated processes, with amount and efficiency of coordination of efforts varying from person to person.

The concept of independent but coordinated processes is important in understanding how executive functions direct and affect behavior. Because the executive functions represent separate neural circuits, or cognitive modules, there is no guarantee that if one executive capacity is well-developed in a person, all of them will be well-developed in that person. Similarly, even though a person might have many well-developed executive capacities, the interconnections between some of these capacities might not be as well-developed as others, resulting in less coordinated direction and control when one pattern of interrelated functioning is required, but not when a different pattern of interrelated functioning is required. While certain clinical disorders show specific patterns of executive function weaknesses or deficiencies, any person can have strengths and/or weaknesses in any one or more of the different executive functions, as well as variations in the integrity of the interconnections among various executive functions at any given point in time. Assessment of executive functions, therefore, requires a multidimensional approach to identify the specific constellation of executive strengths and weaknesses for any given child or adult.

EXECUTIVE FUNCTIONS AND INTELLIGENCE

Because psychologists, especially school psychologists, are frequently involved in the assessment of intellectual functioning of children and adults, the natural first question that arises in discussions of executive functions is, "How are executive functions related to intelligence or measures of intelligence?" Because of their central role in directing or cueing perceptions, thought, and action, it would certainly make sense that executive functions would be considered to be a component, if not *the* component, responsible for intelligent thought and behavior.

The extent to which executive functions can be considered as "synonymous" or "integrated" with the construct of intelligence depends upon the definition of intelligence that is being espoused. Extremely broad definitions of intelligence subsume executive functions along with just about everything else that contributes to effective learning and production. Consider the definition of intelligence that appears in Sternberg's (2005) *Cognitive Psychology* textbook:

> Intelligence is the capacity to learn from experience, using metacognitive processes to enhance learning, and the ability to adapt to the surrounding environment, which may require different adaptations within different social and cultural contexts. (p. 485)

In Sternberg's definition, the term *metacognitive processes* refers to "thinking about thinking," a term that is widely considered to be synonymous with the construct of executive functions. Additionally, with the emphasis on "adaptation," Sternberg highlights the capacity to effectively direct or cue in a flexible manner the cognitive capacities needed to produce the thoughts or actions most beneficial to the individual at any given time. On the other hand, more narrowly stated definitions of intelligence tend to exclude or significantly reduce consideration of many aspects of mental processing that are the province of executive functions. For example, Terman (1921) defined intelligence as "the ability to carry on abstract thinking" (p. 128).

Many theoretical discussions of intelligence allude to the concept of executive functions, but subsume them under the general heading of problem solving or adaptability. In fact, most of the research in cognitive psychology that deals with executive control processes refers to these mental functions under the headings of *problem solving* or *reasoning* (Sternberg, 2005).

Defining intelligence and measuring it are two very distinctly different enterprises. While theorists can wax eloquently about the broad nature of human intellectual capacities, assessment specialists tend to be more constrained in their thinking, and for good reasons. The development of a measure of intelligence requires an operational, measurable definition of the construct. This practical need places a great many constraints on the nature of intelligence as it is defined and measured by current instruments. As a result, measures of intelligence assess only a small sampling of what is thought to constitute intelligence. This has caused great difficulties within the field of psychology, causing many skeptics and critics of IQ testing to quip that "intelligence is what intelligence tests measure" (Boring, 1923). At best, any single measure of intelligence, no matter how comprehensive in terms of today's standards, can only be considered a very imperfect estimate of some aspects of intelligent behavior. In actuality then, all critical quips aside, intelligence *is* defined by the test that is used to measure it. An inspection of the leading tests of intelligence reveals that they typically do not make any attempt to directly assess and quantify the role of executive function processes, or do so in a very limited manner (e.g., through "supplemental measures"). Table 2.2 provides an overview of several frequently used intelligence tests and their relationship to assessing executive functions.

The nature of best practices in test development also makes it difficult to assess executive function control processes in the context of a traditional standardized test of intelligence. In making a test, developers go to great lengths to ensure that the demands for performing a task are clearly understood by the test taker. This is typically accomplished through the use of a set of standardized directions that are intended to carefully explain to the examinee exactly what should be done for any task included in the test. The better the standardized directions are at enabling an examinee to know exactly what is demanded in the way of cognitive processing for successful task performance, the more these directions reduce the need to "figure out" what must be done. That is, the more deliberate and explicit the instructions, the lower the demand on executive functions to cue or direct processing. In essence, the directions become a substitute for the examinee's executive functions. With the development of the first edition of the *Kaufman Assessment Battery for Children* (K-ABC), Kaufman & Kaufman (1983) effectively further reduced the need for executive function involvement in test taking with the introduction of specific guidelines that allowed the examiner to "teach the test" prior to administration to examinees who were unclear about what they were being asked to do. While these guidelines further ensure that a child understands the requirements of a task, thereby increasing the likelihood of obtaining a valid indicator of the child's ability to perform the task, they significantly reduce any need to engage executive functions to figure out what specific cognitive processes need to be cued for successful performance.

As an illustration of this point, consider the difference between the two sets of test directions below. The first set is very similar to the directions for a task on a standardized test

Table 2.2   Areas Assessed at the Composite Score Level by Current
Intelligence Tests

Test Name	Scores Yielded for Interpretation

Wechsler Intelligence Scale for Children—Fourth Edition (WISC-IV)	• Full Scale IQ Score
	  o Verbal Comprehension
	  o Perceptual Reasoning
	  o Working Memory
	  o Processing Speed

Stanford-Binet Scale of Intelligence—Fifth Edition (SB-V)	• Full Scale Score
	  o Verbal
	  o Nonverbal
	    ▪ Fluid Reasoning
	    ▪ Knowledge
	    ▪ Quantitative Reasoning
	    ▪ Visual Spatial Skills
	    ▪ Working Memory

Woodcock-Johnson III Tests of Cognitive Abilities (WJ-III Cog)—Standard Battery	• General Intellectual Ability
	  o Verbal Ability
	  o Thinking Ability
	  o Cognitive Efficiency

Kaufman Assessment Battery for Children—Second Edition (KABC-II)	• Mental Processing Index (MPI)
	• Fluid-Crystallized Index (FCI)
	• Nonverbal Index
	  o Simultaneous (Gv)
	  o Sequential (Gsm)
	  o Planning (Gf)
	  o Learning (Glr)
	  o Knowledge (Gc)

Differential Ability Scales—(DAS)	• General Conceptual Ability (GCA)
	  o Verbal Ability
	  o Nonverbal Reasoning Ability
	  o Spatial Ability

Cognitive Assessment System (CAS)	• Full Scale Score
	  o Planning
	  o Attention
	  o Simultaneous
	  o Successive Processes

of intelligence. The second set is very similar to the directions of a standardized test of executive function capacities.

Directions Similar to a Task from a Standardized Measure of Intelligence

To introduce the subtest: Say, "Now, I am going to say two words and ask you how they are alike or the same."

Sample item: Say, "In what way are Yellow and Purple alike? How are they the same?"

If the child provides an incorrect response: Say, "Yellow and Purple are both colors. Now let's try another one."

Directions Similar to Those of a Measure of Executive Functions

To introduce the test: Say, "I can't tell you much about how to do this test. Try to figure out which one of these (point to the response options) this one would go with. I'll tell you whether your answer is right or wrong."

Incorrect response to the first item: Say, "Wrong."

Incorrect response to the second item: Say, "Wrong."

Incorrect response to the third item: Say, "Wrong."

Repeat this procedure until a correct response is provided: Then say, "Right."

It is important to note, however, that although the need for executive control capacities is reduced through the use of standard directions and teaching examples, executive functions are often involved in many ways in the performance of the tasks that are used to assess intelligence. Such engagement of executive functions, however, is not guaranteed, and their use tends to vary greatly from one test taker to another. The extent to which executive function processes are involved in task performance and subsequently impact the scores earned on the tasks included on intelligence tests can be objectively determined through careful application of a process-oriented approach to test administration and interpretation (Gioia, Isquith & Guy, 2001; Kaplan, 1988; McCloskey & Maerlender, 2005). The techniques for identifying the contribution of executive functions to intelligence and achievement test task performance using a process-oriented approach will be discussed in more detail in Chapter 5.

For psychologists administering intelligence tests, the important point to remember is that, unlike theoretical definitions of intelligence, the operational definitions of intelligence that have been used to develop tests of intelligence have largely excluded executive control processes as a distinct content domain that contributes to an overall global estimate of intelligence. Therefore, these batteries have not intentionally targeted executive functions for assessment and have not attempted to assess the role of executive control as a part of test performance. As a result, intelligence test scores often do not accurately reflect a child's executive control capacities, nor do they directly provide insight into the extent to which executive function strengths or weaknesses are impacting test performance.

The distinct differences between measures of intelligence and measures of executive functions are reflected in the low magnitude of relationship obtained when these measures are compared, typically producing correlations in the low .20s and .30s (Korkman, Kirk & Kemp, 1998; Perkins, 2009). Executive functions can display a double dissociation from cognitive abilities typically assessed on intelligence tests, such as the ability to reason (either with verbal information or with nonverbal visual material). This means that it is possible to identify individuals who are strong in some executive function processes but are relatively weak in reasoning ability, while at the same time identifying other individuals who are relatively strong in reasoning ability but are relatively weak in many executive function areas.

The distinction between the executive functions that direct cognitive processes and the cognitive processes directed by executive functions (e.g., reasoning, visual perception and discrimination, language, memory, attention, and motor acts) is critical for a clear understanding of the broader picture of a child's cognitive strengths and weaknesses. An understanding of the directive nature of executive functions can add considerable explanatory power to the clinical picture of a child with learning or "performing" difficulties. Consider a situation that many psychologists encounter in their work with students and teachers.

A student is referred for an evaluation because he or she is not performing up to expected standards. The evaluation reveals that the student obtained an overall IQ score of 125, suggesting intellectual capacities well above the average. In disbelief, the teacher suggests that there must be something wrong with the test, the psychologist, or both, because, in the teacher's mind, there is no possible way that this student could be considered that intelligent. The teacher will be able to provide several instances which, in her mind, confirm the lack of intellectual capacity of this student. The teacher might even make reference to another student in the room who was evaluated previously and earned a much lower score on the same test of intelligence, noting that the particular "not so smart" student has no difficulty understanding what is required for a specific task and keeping up with the class, while the "supposedly very smart" student often cannot even figure out how to get started. Whether bluntly or diplomatically stated or implied, the question the teacher wants answered in this situation is, "How can this student be so 'smart' but so 'dumb' at the same time?"

This conversation between a teacher and psychologist should remind you of the prior discussion of the difference between "intelligence" as represented by test scores and "intelligence" as represented by a definition that includes the use of executive function capacities to effectively cue or direct the needed perceptual, cognitive, emotional, or motor capacities at any given time.

While such discussions have often left many psychologists with little more than a credibility gap to show for their efforts, understanding of the role of executive functions in directing classroom behavior can provide the psychologist with the necessary perspective to effectively engage the teacher in a meaningful discussion about what the student can and cannot do well. The Modules 1 and 2 located on the accompanying CD provide handouts for professionals as well as parents and teachers, which offer a helpful summary of the key points of this chapter. Hopefully, after reading the chapters in this book on assessment and intervention of executive functions, you will have several ideas about how to engage in effective intervention strategies in this type of situation. Appropriate interventions may include a consultative intervention approach to assist the teacher in improving instruction by taking into consideration the executive demands that his or her teaching style places on students, or a direct intervention to teach the student how to identify the executive functions being required and ways to effectively engage the necessary executive capacities for successful classroom performance.

CASE VIGNETTES REVISITED

After reading the general overview about executive functions and comparing and contrasting the concept of executive functions with that of intelligence, can you see the six case vignettes from a somewhat different perspective? Consider the additional information gathered on these students after initial attempts to assess and intervene were judged ineffective.

Case of Justin Revisited

Information gathered from Justin and his parents a few months after Justin's school-based evaluation revealed the following:

- Justin often takes a long time to "get into gear" when asked to do things.
- Justin has a lot of difficulty in "sizing up" the demands of school assignments and applying the proper amount of effort to tasks, often thinking that it will take much less time to do work than is actually the case; often thinking that assigned tasks are much easier than they really turn out to be; often thinking that the amount of effort expended was sufficient when in actuality it was much less than needed; and often believing that he did well on a task when in actuality he did very poorly.
- Justin almost always has difficulty stopping an activity of very high interest and "shifting gears" to respond to a request from his parents to engage school-related tasks.
- Justin has a lot of trouble "getting organized" for school. This includes difficulty organizing his notebooks; difficulty organizing his thoughts about school projects, especially writing assignments; difficulty organizing an approach to studying for tests; and difficulty keeping track of school materials such as books, notebooks, announcements, pencils, etc.
- Justin tends to rely on his memory of what is said in class rather than taking notes or reviewing material before tests, only to realize while taking the test that his recollection of what was said in class was not very organized and not detailed enough to enable him to make sub-

tle distinctions when answering multiple choice items or to provide an adequate amount of detail when answering essay questions.

- Justin is very poor with both short- and long-term planning for school tasks. He often starts in on tasks without having everything he needs to get the job done. As a result, he spends a lot of time interrupting work to locate needed materials one at a time. He often fails to bring home books or materials from school that are needed to complete homework assignments. Long-term assignments are completed in a flurry of activity just before they are due.

- Justin is perceived as a very smart boy, but despite his intellectual capacity, he often has difficulty self-generating good solutions to school-related problems. Efficient solutions to problems don't seem to occur to him and he often spends a long time doing things "the long way" or not doing them at all.

- Justin tends to miss or skip over details that are important for accurate completion of homework assignments, projects, and tests. These types of detail errors are especially apparent in Justin's work with math problems.

- Justin's sense of time is very poor when working on academic tasks. He frequently underestimates how long things will take to do and is very poor at knowing how long he has been working on a task.

- Justin seems to have one gear for working on academic tasks—a slow one. Even when encouraged or prompted, he seems unable to speed up his work pace.

- Justin often makes what are usually called "careless" errors on homework assignments and tests, as these errors occur with relatively simple material. Sometimes Justin notices the errors that he makes, but then does not always follow through with correcting the errors he finds.

- Justin demonstrates the ability to do many academic tasks well, but he can be surprisingly inept in his efforts to complete a task in situations where he is called on to perform these tasks without advance warning.

Case of Kevin Revisited

Information gathered from Kevin's parents, teacher, the school psychologist, and Kevin himself after receiving the report of the lack of effectiveness of the school-based intervention revealed the following:

- Kevin frequently misperceives the actions and statements of other children, quickly takes offense from comments or actions that are not necessarily antagonistic, and tends to overreact to these perceived slights.
- Once he gets angry, Kevin seems unable to control his temper and things escalate when other children respond to statements that Kevin makes.
- Once an argument has occurred, Kevin reports that he can't stop thinking about it and it can ruin the entire day for him.
- Although Kevin recalls comments or insults made by classmates during an argument, Kevin is very poor at listening to classmates in normal conversation, often quickly forgets what is said to him, and finds it hard to follow longer conversations.
- Even with emotionally charged events, Kevin often doesn't remember the details of who said what to whom the next day.
- Kevin has very specific ideas for how to perceive, think about, feel about, and do things and usually will not consider alternatives to his own ways.
- Although Kevin openly discusses the difficult situations he gets into, he demonstrates little insight into the problems that his outbursts cause and the effect they have on his classmates.
- In discussions focused on positive problem solving, Kevin demonstrates very little ability to articulate workable solutions for his behavior problems.
- When discussing social interactions, Kevin tends to overfocus on specific words used by other children and misses what their voice intonation and body posture communicates.
- Kevin clearly has difficulty acknowledging and monitoring his own emotional reactions as well as those of others.
- Kevin seems unaware of how his actions affect others and does not seem to be able to anticipate the consequences resulting from his emotional outbursts.
- Kevin finds it hard to say he's sorry to classmates even when he knows he was wrong.

Case of Caroline Revisited

Information gathered from interviews with Caroline and her parents, after several months on the antidepressant medication, revealed the following:

- Caroline has difficulty initiating tasks, even those that she finds pleasurable, unless she is cued by others as to how and when to begin.
- Caroline has difficulty sustaining effort and attention, frequently starting, but not finishing, many tasks.
- Caroline has difficulty in estimating the time frame of getting things done, tending to underestimate the amount of time needed to complete tasks.
- Caroline has difficulty coming up with a plan for completing a self-care activity, showing difficulty with breaking the activity into a sequence of smaller actions.
- Caroline demonstrates difficulty in organizing her belongings, often spending much time trying to locate things at the last minute.
- Caroline has difficulty developing a mature "theory of mind," lacking awareness of the impression that her behavior and demeanor leave with others.
- Caroline has difficulty in accurately describing herself and evaluating not only her performance, but also personal traits and characteristics. She demonstrates little ability to self-monitor and evaluate the effectiveness of her interactions with others. Because of a sense of being "adrift" in such interactions, she is often unable to engage interpersonal skills that she has used effectively in the past, and usually does not make an effort to clarify or correct social miscues.
- Caroline often seems to be in a fog, during which time her emotional and cognitive functioning seems to be "occurring in slow motion."
- In spite of pharmacological intervention, Caroline continues to demonstrate difficulties with tuning into and regulating her emotions, especially as they pertain to her own internal states. She often becomes very upset with herself for not being able to make things be the way she would like them to be, and is usually unaware of how negative her emotions and thoughts have become.

Case of Brett Revisited

Information gathered from an interview with Brett's parents and an assessment session with Brett emphasizing motor activities revealed the following:

- Brett seems oblivious to any possible dangers that the environment might pose.
- Brett shows very little restraint and often "acts without thinking."
- Once Brett begins to do something, he seems to be unable to stop or alter his actions when requested or commanded to do so.
- Brett seems to delight in seeking out those aspects of his surroundings that pose the greatest risk. Everyday for Brett seems to be a high speed adventure; he seems to have one gear—overdrive.
- Nothing seems to hold Brett's interest for very long.
- When Brett becomes involved in an activity, his actions reflect no planning or foresight about the possible consequences of the things he does.
- Brett shows little ability to pick up on details in the environment that would suggest the best way to initiate or complete actions or that would cue him as to possible risks.
- Brett's timing of motor acts is somewhat off.
- Brett often doesn't "pay attention to" his motor movements carefully.
- Brett fails to make necessary corrections to motor routines. These difficulties result in many "accidents" like bumping into other children, knocking glasses off of tables, and breaking less sturdy toys.

Case of Morgan Revisited

Information gathered from Morgan's parents and teachers; Morgan herself, and classroom observations conducted as part of an independent education evaluation requested by the parents, revealed the following:

- On many days, Morgan is in near constant motion. When movement about the room is allowed, she will take full advantage, finding limitless reasons to frequently change her location. If confined to her seat, Morgan still maintains near constant motion including hair twirling, watch adjusting, pencil tapping, etc.

- Despite the seemingly limitless energy and initiative Morgan invests in her extracurricular activities, she is surprisingly reticent and lethargic in her approach to schoolwork involving reading and writing, needing frequent prompting to start and to sustain work efforts.
- Morgan tends to be very tied to the specific strategies that she is taught. She finds it difficult to adapt these strategies to new situations, or to generate new strategies of her own when the ones she knows do not produce the desired results.
- Morgan appears to have a short attention span; she frequently forgets what she was doing; she has trouble remembering things in school even for a very short time (less than a minute).
- Morgan has great difficulty with organizing work for large school projects; she tends to have good ideas but cannot get them down on paper for writing assignments; she starts many tasks, but finishes very few of them.
- Morgan avoids many tasks that require sustained effort, especially those involving reading or writing.
- Morgan is highly distractible in most environments; she is easily drawn away from schoolwork or chores by minor alterations in the environment (soft sounds, movement of any type, etc.).
- Morgan often hands in incomplete work and often does not check her work for errors.

Case of Alex Revisited

Information gathered from interviews with Alex and his parents as part of a comprehensive evaluation at age 23 revealed the following:

- Alex has difficulty initiating thoughts and actions other than those consistent with gratification of desires arising in the immediate moment. Alex attributes much of his lack of initiation to not feeling physically well, stating that he intends to become more engaged with meaningful thoughts and actions when he is feeling better.
- Alex often cannot inhibit perceptions, emotions, thoughts, or actions that lead to the immediate fulfillment of desires or that extricate him from undesirable situations.

In many instances, Alex's unchecked impulses have had serious negative consequences, including arrests for shoplifting and marijuana possession, unauthorized use of family credit cards, and gambling.

- Alex experiences difficulty with the kind of sustained consistency of thought patterns and/or actions that is necessary over a prolonged period of time in order to accomplish short- or long-term goals. Alex recognizes and acknowledges his inability to sustain healthful habits or to finish reading books that he finds interesting.
- Alex finds it difficult to organize his thoughts and actions beyond a brief period of time. Alex frequently loses things that are needed to accomplish tasks and quickly feels overwhelmed and incapacitated when faced with complex tasks.
- Alex demonstrates very little in the way of anticipating how activities or plans will unfold over time and shows little capacity for preplanning to deal with alternate outcomes.
- Alex demonstrates very limited ability to self-direct his reasoning abilities; he frequently does not recognize the need for generating solutions to problems and fails to think or to act in situations where the need for thought or action seems obvious to others.
- Alex demonstrates very poor time management; he often underestimates how long tasks will take to perform, loses track of time when he is engaged in thinking or acting, and generally seems unaware of the need to manage time effectively. For Alex, minutes quickly turn into hours, which suddenly become days, with little or nothing being accomplished despite the best of intentions.

THINKING THROUGH

Does the additional information provided offer greater insight into the possible sources of the difficulties for these six students? Is it easier to see how their behavior and the reactions of others to their behavior are being influenced by executive function difficulties? While it should be apparent at this point that all six of these individuals do have significant executive function problems, the distinct differences in the manner in which these difficulties are expressed should also be apparent. In some cases, the executive function difficulties relate to the cueing and directing of perception or thinking. In others, the difficulties relate to problems with cueing and directing emotions, while in others the problems arise from poor cueing and directing of motor production capacities. The next chapter reviews in detail how executive function direction of perception, cognition, emotion, and motor production (action) varies.

It is also important to note that the type of activities most impacted by each child's executive function difficulties varies greatly. Justin's and Morgan's problems involve difficulties with directing efficient organization, manipulation, and use of the symbol systems that form the basis of education and commerce in technologically advanced societies (e.g., reading, written expression, mathematics, computer use, etc.). Kevin's problems are centered on cueing and directing appropriate cognitive, emotional, and motor capacities in interpersonal relationships. Caroline's and Alex's difficulties involve ineffective directing and cueing of what could be called *intrapersonal capacities*—that is, internal direction and control in relation to the self. While Brett's interpersonal relationships and his ability to master symbol systems such as writing are affected by his executive function difficulties, his primary source of difficulty, sometimes at a life-threatening level, involves his inability to effectively cue and direct perception, cognition, emotion, and motor production in a manner that ensures safe navigation of his environment. The variations in the types of activities affected by executive function difficulties is a key concept in understanding what we refer to as the *arenas of involvement* in which the effects of executive functions are manifested. The concept of *arenas of involvement* will be discussed in detail in Chapter 3.

SUMMARY

This chapter provided the reader with a general understanding of the complex nature of the concept of executive functions as directive capacities and compared and contrasted the concept of executive functions with that of intelligence. The brief case vignettes were used to provide a context for seeing how the concept of executive functions can help to frame case conceptualizations and influence the way we think about the problems that children might be experiencing, to highlight how executive function directive capacities can vary across the domains of perception, cognition, emotion, and motor production, as well as by *arenas of involvement* (intrapersonal, interpersonal, symbol system, and environment). The knowledge gained thus far will be expanded on in the following chapter, as we present a comprehensive model of executive functions and discuss the multiple elements of such a model, as well as continue to expand upon the details of the six case vignettes.

3

Model of Executive
Functions

Elements of six case vignettes were offered in Chapters 1 and 2 to illustrate how an understanding of executive functions can influence the way we think about the problems that children might be experiencing. Chapter 2 provided a general definition of executive functions as directive capacities and discussed the relationship between the concepts of executive functions and intelligence. Chapter 3 will present a comprehensive model for understanding executive functions and discuss how executive control capacities can vary in regard to domains of functioning (perception, emotion, cognition, and action) as well as by arena of involvement (intrapersonal, interpersonal, symbol system, and environment).

A GENERAL HOLARCHICAL MODEL
OF EXECUTIVE FUNCTION PROCESSES
FROM AN INTEGRAL PERSPECTIVE

As noted previously, many different definitions of the mental processes are thought to represent executive functions and the behaviors typically associated with the use, or disuse, of these processes. Although these multiple definitions highlight the complex and multifaceted nature of executive functions, they also illustrate the varying backgrounds and perspectives of the individuals studying and applying the concept (e.g., Stuss & Alexander, 2002; Pennington, 2002). In addition, many researchers study and apply the concept of executive functions without labeling these specific capacities as "executive functions" (e.g., Greene, 2001; Levine, 1998; Posner & Peterson, 1990; Shure, 1992). The perspectives on the mental capacities being referred to here as *executive functions* are quite diverse, but two key dimensions unify all of them. First, they all address, to some degree, mental capacities that direct or cue the use of other mental processes and/or motor responses. Second, they all address functions that have some link to activation of portions of the frontal lobe regions of the cerebral cortex.

Despite the increasing research and clinical application of many executive function capacities, few attempts have been made to pull together all, or even some, of the various strands of research and practice. This has resulted in no overarching structural model being developed that could serve as a single theory of executive control. Building on the conceptual and empirical work of many professionals across multiple disciplines (e.g., cognitive neuroscience and psychology, neuropsychology, developmental and clinical psychology, education, and others), the lead author has proposed a holarchical, developmental model of executive function organization (McCloskey, 2004), which is illustrated in Figure 3.1. This model is proposed as a way to help conceptualize the interplay of the multiple executive capacities that involve frontal lobe neural functions.

As shown in Figure 3.1, this model is structured using five holarchically organized tiers of executive capacity. The first three tiers are directly involved with daily self-control functions, with the first of these tiers being a unitary construct labeled *self-activation*. The second tier, labeled *self-regulation*,

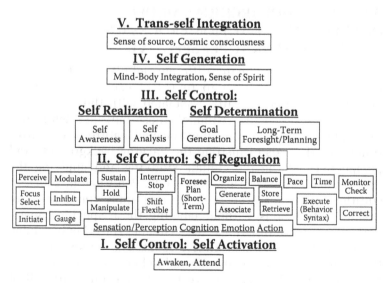

Figure 3.1   The McCloskey Model of Executive Functions.

is a collection of multiple directive capacities that are primarily responsible for direction of day-to-day activities. The third tier includes two general executive capacities, each of which is carried out through two subordinate executive functions: (1) *self- realization through self-awareness and self-analysis* and (2) *self-determination through goal generation and long-term foresight/planning.* The final two tiers represent development of executive capacities that push beyond the direction of day-to-day functioning. These tiers direct the impetus to consider deeper questions involving consideration of the purpose and meaning of life and the articulation of a personal philosophy of life, termed *self-generation*, and the desire to experience the unitary nature of existence from a perspective outside the notion of a "self" through an experience of "unity consciousness," termed here *trans-self integration.* To highlight each of the tiers and the executive functions within each, we will discuss each within the context of the six cases introduced in Chapter 1.

Self-Activation

As proposed in this model of executive functions, *self-activation* has to do with how our executive capacities wake up from sleep. In the case of Caroline, she finds it difficult to get up in the morning even though she consistently sleeps for 8 to 9 hours each night. Caroline herself has observed that it often takes more than an hour or two after waking before she feels like her "brain is working right." During this time, she seems to be in a trance and does very little. When asked what she is thinking about during this time, Caroline's response is "not much." In contrast to Caroline, Brett is almost always the first member of his family to wake up in the morning, and he quickly ramps up to his relatively limited normal state of executive control. Although Justin struggles with school, rising in the morning does not present a problem for him, as long as the volume of his alarm clock is on its loudest setting. For Kevin, he tends to awake in a poor mood and requires "delicate" handling for at least the first 15 to 20 minutes after being wakened by his mother. He is always dressed and ready to leave home on time, although his moodiness often accompanies him to school.

Research has documented that most persons are lacking in executive control for at least a short period of time when roused from a deep sleep (Balkin et al., 2002). In fact, any transition from an unconscious to a conscious state involves a gradual "ramping up" of executive capacities. This transition period is characterized by a state of less than optimal mental and motor functioning usually referred to as sleep inertia. Sleep inertia typically resolves within the first 5 to 20 minutes after awakening. During this time, executive capacities gradually improve to levels typical of the person's normal wakeful state (Balkin, et al.). The role of executive capacities during this period of sleep inertia can be characterized as a nonconsciously mediated process of "turning on" the various neural circuits needed to enable greater self-control by higher tier executive capacities.

For some people like Caroline, sleep inertia symptoms can persist for hours, causing many problems with effectiveness of daily functioning. Problems also can result when, under the influence of sleep inertia symptoms, a person who starts to enter the wakeful state returns to sleep rather than engaging in mental or physical activity that would eventually lead to the dissipation of the sleep inertia symptoms. While executive control activity at this lowest tier typically is mediated nonconsciously in the form of a gradual return to wakefulness, some forms of habituated executive cueing can be activated consciously to assist with the transition to a full waking state, or to reduce the effects of prolonged sleep inertia.

Self-Regulation

The self-regulation tier is comprised of a large number of executive functions that are responsible for cueing and directing functioning within the all-inclusive domains of sensation and perception, emotion, cognition, and action. Whether we are consciously aware of it or not, these self-regulation capacities form the basis of the executive function operations that get us through our day-to-day routines. Consciously or nonconsciously, one or more of these self-regulation functions are involved in all that we perceive, feel, think, and do nearly every waking moment of every day. The proposed model of executive functions explicitly identifies 23 self-regulation capacities that are used to varying degrees and in varying combinations to direct and cue our sensing, thinking, feeling, and acting. Table 3.1 provides a brief description of each of the 23 self-regulation executive functions. Module 3 of the CD provides a handout that expands these definitions and offers examples of problem behaviors reflecting difficulties with each self-regulation capacity.

Not only are the 23 self-regulation executive functions distinct from one another, they are not uniform in their degree

Table 3.1   Brief Definitions of the 23 Self-Regulation Executive Function Capacities

Perceive

The Perceive function cues the use of sensory and perception processes to take information in from the external environment or "inner awareness" to tune into perceptions, emotions, thoughts, or actions as they are occurring.

Initiate

The Initiate function cues the initial engagement of perceiving, feeling, thinking, or acting.

Modulate/Effort

The Modulate function cues the regulation of the amount and intensity of mental energy invested in perceiving, feeling, thinking, and acting.

Gauge

The Gauge function cues identification of the demands (perceptual, emotional, mental, physical) of a task or situation and cues the activation of the perceptions, emotions, thoughts, or actions needed to effectively engage the task or situation.

Focus/Select

The Focus/Select function cues the direction of attention to the most relevant specifics (perceptions, emotions, thoughts, and/or actions) of a given environment, situation, or content while downgrading or ignoring the less relevant elements.

Sustain

The Sustain function cues sustained engagement of the processes involved in perceiving, feeling, thinking, or acting.

Stop/Interrupt

The Stop/Interrupt function cues the sudden, immediate discontinuation of perceiving, feeling, thinking, or acting.

Inhibit

The Inhibit function cues resistance to, or suppression of, urges to perceive, feel, think, or act on first impulse.

Flexible/Shift

The Flexible/Shift function cues a change of focus or alteration of perceptions, emotions, thoughts, or actions in reaction to what is occurring in the internal or external environments.

Hold

The Hold function cues activation of the necessary cognitive processes required to maintain initially registered information and continues cueing these processes until the information is manipulated, stored, or acted on as desired.

Manipulate

The Manipulate function cues the use of working memory or other cognitive processes for the manipulation of perceptions, feelings, thoughts, or actions that are being held in mind or being accessed in the environment.

Table 3.1 (continued)   Brief Definitions of the 23 Self-Regulation Executive Function Capacities

Organize

The Organize function cues the use of routines for sorting, sequencing, or otherwise arranging perceptions, feelings, thoughts, and/or actions, to enhance or improve the efficiency of experience, learning, or performance.

Foresee/Plan (Short Term)

The Foresee/Plan function cues the anticipation of conditions or events in the very near future, such as the consequences of one's own actions, or cues the engagement of the capacities required to identify a series of perceptions, feelings, thoughts, and/or actions, and the likely or desired outcome that would result from carrying them out in the very near future.

Generate

The Generate function cues the realization that a novel solution is required for a current problem, and cues the activation of the resources needed to carry out the required novel problem solving.

Associate

The Associate function cues the realization that associations need to be made between the current problem situation and past problem situations and cues the activation of the resources needed to carry out the required associative problem-solving routines.

Balance

The Balance function cues the regulation of the trade-off between opposing processes or states (e.g., pattern vs detail; speed vs accuracy; humor versus seriousness) to enhance or improve experiencing, learning, or performing.

Store

The Store function cues the movement of information about perceptions, feelings, thoughts, and actions from the mental processing environment of the present moment into "storage" for possible retrieval at a later time.

Retrieve

The Retrieve function cues the activation of cognitive processes responsible for finding and retrieving previously stored information about perceptions, feelings, thoughts, and actions. The more specific the demands or constraints placed on the retrieval task, the greater the requirements for precision of retrieval cues.

Pace

The Pace function cues the awareness of, and the regulation of, the rate at which perception, emotion, cognition, and action are experienced or performed.

Time

The Time function cues the monitoring of the passage of time (e.g., cueing the engagement of the mental functions that enable a person to have an internal sense of how long they have been working) or cues the use of time estimation routines (e.g., cueing the engagement of mental functions that enable a person to have an internal sense of how long something will take to complete, or how much time is still left in a specific period of time).

Table 3.1 (continued) Brief Definitions of the 23 Self-Regulation
Executive Function Capacities

Execute

The Execute function cues the orchestrating of the proper syntax of a series of
perceptions, feelings, thoughts, and/or actions, especially in cases where automated
routines are being accessed or are initially being developed.

Monitor

The Monitor function cues the activation of appropriate routines for checking the
accuracy of perceptions, emotions, thoughts, or actions.

Correct

The Correct function cues the use of appropriate routines for correcting errors of
perception, emotion, thought, or action based on feedback from internal or external
sources.

of control capacity; a person's effectiveness with each one can
vary greatly. For example, a person might be very effective at
using the focus/select cue to direct attention, but be very ineffective in their use of the sustain cue when it would be advan-
tageous to maintain attention for an extended period of time.

Self-Regulation and Domains of Functioning

Note that in Figure 3.1 there are four separate boxes representing the functioning domains of sensation/perception, emotion,
cognition, and action. The model makes clear that self-regulation functions cue and direct how we perceive, feel, think,
and act. The delineation of domains is meant to highlight the
fact that self-regulation, in the context of these four separate
domains of functioning, is not cued and directed in perfect
unison. Instead, executive control of these domains (and of
subdomains within these domains) is dissociable—that is,
each domain (and subdomain) has its own set of executive
controls. In addition, the effectiveness of executive capacities
might not be equivalent across the four domains or within the
subdomains of each domain. For example, as shown in Figure 3.2, while the self-regulation executive function called
Monitor cues mental processes for checking and keeping track
of what is happening at a specific point in time, separate cueing processes occur for monitoring sensations and perceptions,
for monitoring feelings, for monitoring thought processes, and
for monitoring actions. Consequently, a person's capacities to

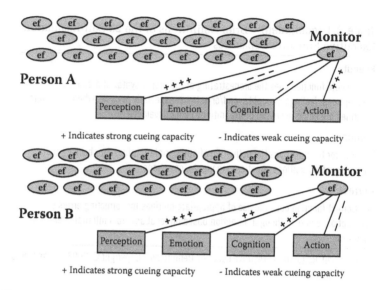

Figure 3.2   Examples of Variations in Cueing Capacity Strength for the Monitor Self-Regulation Executive Function Across the Four Domains of Functioning.

effectively cue the engagement of cognitive processes used for monitoring can vary greatly across the four domains. A person might be very good at cueing the monitoring of initial sensations, poor at cueing the monitoring of feelings and thoughts, but good at cueing the monitoring of actions. Another person might be good at monitoring sensations, feelings, and thoughts, but very poor at monitoring actions.

Table 3.2 shows the specific self-regulation functions within specific domains of functioning that are thought to be associated with the problem behaviors of the six children described in Chapters 1 and 2. Note that the behavior problems exhibited by each child reflect difficulties with one or more self-regulation capacities, and that the number and type of self-regulation difficulties and the affected domains of functioning vary greatly among these six individuals.

Justin's academic struggles reflect difficulties with the use of 14 of the 23 self-regulation cues within the Cognition domain and difficulties with 12 of the 23 self-regulation cues within the Action domain. In contrast, Justin exhibits difficulties with 3 of the 23 self-regulations cues within the Perception domain and no difficulties with self-regulation cueing within the Emotion domain. Similar to Justin, Morgan's academic difficulties appear to be associated with underutilization of many

Table 3.2 Self-Regulation Executive Function Difficulties Identified for the Six Case Study Subjects

Justin	Self-Regulation	Domain
Takes a long time to get into gear to do things.	Initiate	Action
Difficulty "sizing up" the demands of a task; often thinking that assigned tasks are much easier than they really turn out to be; often believing that he did well on a task when in actuality he did very poorly.	Gauge	Perception Cognition Action
Difficulty applying the proper amount of effort to thinking about, or doing, school-related tasks and often thinking that the amount of effort expended was sufficient when in actuality it was much less than needed.	Modulate	Cognition Action
Almost always has difficulty stopping an activity of very high interest and "shifting gears" to respond to a request from his parents to engage school-related tasks.	Interrupt/Stop Shift/Flexible	Action
Has a lot of trouble "getting organized" for school. This includes difficulty organizing his notebooks; difficulty organizing his thoughts about school projects, especially writing assignments; difficulty organizing an approach to studying for tests; and difficulty keeping track of school materials such as books, notebooks, announcements, pencils, etc.	Organize	Cognition Action
Tends to rely on his memory of what is said in class rather than taking notes or reviewing material before tests, only to realize while taking the test that his recollection of what was said in class was not very organized and not detailed enough to enable him to make subtle distinctions when answering multiple choice items or to provide an adequate amount of detail when answering essay questions.	Gauge Hold Manipulate Store Execute	Cognition
Very poor with both short- and long-term planning for school tasks. He often starts in on tasks without having everything he needs to get the job done. As a result, he spends a lot of time interrupting work to locate needed materials one at a time. He often fails to bring home books or materials from school that are needed to complete homework assignments.	Foresee/Plan	Cognition

Table 3.2 (continued)   Self-Regulation Executive Function
Difficulties Identified for the Six Case Study Subjects

Justin	Self-Regulation	Domain
Justin is perceived as a very smart boy, but despite his intellectual capacity, he often has difficulty self-generating good solutions to school-related problems. Efficient solutions to problems don't seem to occur to him and he often spends a long time doing things "the long way" or not doing them at all.	Generate Associate	Cognition
Tends to miss or skip over details that are important for accurate completion of homework assignments, projects, and tests. These types of detail errors are especially apparent in Justin's work with math problems.	Balance	Cognition Action
Sense of time is very poor when working on academic tasks. He frequently underestimates how long things will take to do and is very poor at knowing how long he has been working on a task.	Time	Cognition Action
Seems to have one gear for working on academic tasks—a slow one. Even when encouraged or prompted, he seems unable to speed up his work pace.	Pace	Cognition Action
Often makes what are usually called "careless" errors on homework assignments and tests, as these errors occur with relatively simple material. Sometimes Justin notices the errors that he makes, but then does not always follow through with correcting the errors he finds.	Monitor Correct	Perception Cognition Action
Demonstrates the ability to do many academic tasks well, but he can be surprisingly inept in his efforts to complete a task in situations where he is called on to perform these tasks without advance warning.	Execute	Action
Kevin		
Frequently misperceives the actions and statements of other children.	Perceive	Perception
Quickly takes offense from comments or actions that are not necessarily antagonistic, and tends to overreact to these perceived slights.	Inhibit	Perception Emotion Action

Table 3.2 (continued) Self-Regulation Executive Function
Difficulties Identified for the Six Case Study Subjects

Kevin	Self-Regulation	Domain
Once angry, seems unable to control temper; things escalate when other children respond to statements.	Modulate	Emotion Action
Once an argument has occurred, can't stop thinking about it and can ruin the entire day.	Stop/Interrupt	Emotion Cognition
Recalls comments or insults made by classmates during an argument, but very poor at listening to classmates in normal conversation, often quickly forgetting what is said; finds it hard to follow longer conversations.	Sustain Hold Manipulate Store	Perception Cognition Emotion
Even with emotionally charged events, often doesn't remember the details of who said what to whom the next day.	Store Retrieve	Perception Emotion Cognition
Has very specific ideas of how to perceive, think about, feel about, and do things and usually will not consider alternatives to his own ways.	Shift/Flexible	Perception Emotion Cognition Action
In discussions focused on positive problem solving, Kevin demonstrates very little ability to articulate workable solutions for his behavior problems.	Generate Associate	Cognitive Action
When discussing social interactions, overfocuses on specific words used by other children and misses what their voice intonation and body posture communicate.	Perceive Balance	Perception Emotion
Has difficulty acknowledging as well as monitoring own emotional reactions as well as those of others.	Perceive Monitor	Emotion
Seems unaware of how his actions affect others and does not seem to be able to anticipate the consequences resulting from his emotional outbursts.	Foresee/Plan	Emotion Cognition Action
Refuses to say he's sorry to classmates even when he knows he was wrong.	Correct Execute	Emotion Action
Caroline		
Difficulty initiating tasks, even those that she finds pleasurable, unless she is cued by others as to how and when to begin.	Initiate	Action

Table 3.2 (continued)   Self-Regulation Executive Function Difficulties Identified for the Six Case Study Subjects

Caroline	Self-Regulation	Domain
Difficulty sustaining effort and attention, frequently starting, but not finishing, many tasks.	Sustain	Cognition Action
Difficulty in estimating the time frame of getting things done, tending to either over or underestimate the amount of time needed to complete tasks.	Time	Cognition Action
Difficulty coming up with a plan for completing a self-care activity, showing difficulty in breaking the activity into a sequence of smaller actions.	Foresee/Plan	Cognition Action
Difficulty in organizing belongings, often spending much time trying to locate things at the last minute.	Organize	Cognition
Demonstrates little ability to self-monitor and evaluate the effectiveness of her interactions with others and as a result usually does not make an effort to clarify or correct social miscues.	Monitor Correct	Perception Emotion Cognition Action
Because of her sense of being "adrift" in such interactions, she is often unable to engage interpersonal skills that she has used effectively in the past.	Retrieve Execute	Cognition Action
Often seems to be in a fog, during which time her emotional and cognitive functioning seems to be "occurring in slow motion."	Pace	Perception Emotion Cognition Action
In spite of pharmacological intervention, continues to demonstrate difficulties with tuning in to and regulating her emotions, especially as they pertain to her own internal states and behavior, often becoming very upset with herself for not being able to make things be the way she would like them to be, and is usually unaware of how negative her emotions and thoughts have become.	Perceive Modulate	Perception Emotion Cognition
Brett		
Seems oblivious to any possible dangers that the environment might pose.	Perceive	Perception

Table 3.2 (continued)   Self-Regulation Executive Function
Difficulties Identified for the Six Case Study Subjects

Brett	Self-Regulation	Domain
Shows very little restraint and often "acts without thinking."	Inhibit	Action
Once something is begun, seems to be unable to stop or alter actions when requested or commanded to do so.	Interrupt/Stop Shift/Flexible	Action
Seems to delight in seeking out those aspects of his surroundings that pose the greatest risk. Everyday seems to be a high speed adventure; he seems to have one gear—overdrive.	Modulate	Action
Nothing seems to hold Brett's interest for very long.	Sustain	Perception Action
When involved in an activity, his actions reflect no planning or foresight about the possible consequences of the things he does.	Foresee/Plan	Cognition Action
Shows little ability to pick up on details in the environment that would suggest the best way to initiate or complete actions or that would cue him in to possible risks.	Perceive Focus/Select	Perception
Timing of motor acts is somewhat off.	Time	Action
Fails to "pay attention to," or make necessary corrections to, motor routines. These difficulties result in many "accidents" like bumping into other children, knocking glasses off of tables, and breaking less sturdy toys.	Monitor Correct	Action

self-regulation cues within the domains of Cognition (10 of 23) and Action (11 of 23), a few in the domain of Perception (4 of 23), and none in the domain of Emotion.

Kevin's self-regulation cueing difficulties appear to be concentrated in the Emotion domain (15 of 23), but these problems are accompanied by difficulties with self-regulation cues within the domains of Perception (9), Cognition (9), and Action (7).

Although Caroline's problems are relatively severe (Perception (3), Emotion (4), Cognition (9), Action (8)), overall she exhibits difficulties with fewer different self-regulation capacities than either Justin or Kevin. Alex's situation is similar to Caroline's, as he exhibits difficulties with self-regulation cues within the domain of Perception (3), Emotion (5), Cognition (7), and Action (7). Brett, whose specific self-regulation difficulties are very severe, exhibits difficulties with the fewest different self-regulation capacities across the four domains (Perception (3), Cognition (1), Action (8)) with his difficulties being concentrated primarily within the Action domain.

Self-Realization and Self-Determination

The third tier of the executive function model in Figure 3.1 is comprised of self-control processes that extend beyond basic self-regulation, termed *self-realization* and *self-determination.*

Self-Realization

Being able to direct and cue the use of self-regulation executive capacities does not require a person to be consciously aware of what they are doing or how they are doing it. It is possible for a person to function on a day-to-day basis and never really engage in any act of self-realization beyond a vague registration of the fact that moment to moment functioning is occurring. Engagement of specific neural circuits involving specific portions of the frontal lobes is necessary for a person to take stock of their sensations, emotions, thoughts, and actions and be aware of the self-regulation capacities they may or may not be effectively utilizing in a nonconscious manner and reflect on these in a manner that produces an awareness of self. Activation of these neural circuits produces a deeper realization of self that initiates the emergence of self-awareness. The more organized and sustained the use of these neural pathways becomes, the greater the development of a sense of self. Without a sense of self as it is being defined here, it is difficult, if not impossible, for a person to develop any meaningful sense of others; without realizing yourself as a "self," it is not possible to realize others as "selves." Persons diagnosed with Autism and Asperger's are typically very deficient in the executive capacities related to the development of self-awareness, and consequently very deficient in the development of awareness of the selves of others. These executive deficiencies of self-realization manifested in persons diagnosed with Autism and Asperger's typically have been researched and applied in practice under the rubric of theory of mind (Atwood, 2007; Klin, Volkmar, & Sparrow, 2000).

Engagement of self-awareness functions for prolonged periods of time supports the emergence of self-analysis executive capacities. Self-analysis involves sustained and enhanced reflection on perceptions, emotions, thoughts, and actions in a manner that yields judgments about one's functioning in these domains. Over time, these reflections and judgments lead to a more refined and detailed idea of self, that is, a sense of "who I am" as defined by "what and how well I perceive, feel, think, and do." Added to this can be the capacity for becoming aware of how others react to "what I perceive, feel, think and do," and consideration of this information can provide multiple dimensions to the process of defining "who I am." Through greater exertion of executive control at this tier, self-analysis can be used to develop a sense of personal strengths and weaknesses and lead to reflection on how a person's specific constellation of abilities and skills can be applied effectively to enhance daily functioning.

It is important to note that increased self-awareness and self-analysis can inform and enhance the use of self-regulation capacities, but they are not required for the use of self-regulation capacities. Conversely, development of a sense of self and an awareness of what a person can, and cannot, do can be greatly enhanced by the effective use of self-regulation executive functions, but is not necessarily dependent on the effective development of any or all of the 23 specified self-regulation executive functions. A person can be very deficient in one or more self-regulation executive function and be painfully self-aware of these deficiencies. On the other hand, some self-regulation deficiencies can make it extremely difficult to develop self-awareness or to engage in self-reflection. For example, a person who is exceptionally poor at inhibiting impulsive perceiving, feeling, thinking, or acting, and who cannot sustain attention to perceptions, feelings, thoughts, or actions for more than a few seconds will find it extremely difficult to engage in any prolonged form of self-reflection or self-analysis.

As will be discussed in Chapter 4, self-awareness, like all other executive capacities, follows a chronological age developmental trajectory. While all six of the children in the case studies have developed at least a rudimentary degree of self-awareness, these capacities are not as well-developed as is typical for same-age peers. Perhaps the most self-aware of these six individuals is Justin, who, many times, is painfully aware of, and frustrated by, his limitations in dealing with school work. Justin has begun to take stock of his own strengths and weaknesses and is showing the potential to use this information to begin to understand how to work around some of his difficulties. Even though she is only in elementary school, Morgan is beginning to develop a useful understanding of her learning difficulties. Morgan's awareness of the specific impact that her reading disability had on her school work enabled her to develop a very positive self-image in other areas.

Although Alex is considered an adult by virtue of his chronological age, his level of self-awareness is less developed than that of Justin. Alex is often surprisingly unaware of the extent to which his perceptions, emotions, thoughts, and actions are compromised by his self-regulation difficulties. Alex's lack of awareness makes it difficult to have a meaningful discussion with him about how to change his perceptions, feelings, thoughts, and actions so that he can begin to move toward becoming a contributing member of society. Although Kevin has developed a sense of self, his capacity to extend the concept of self to the consideration of the selves of others is greatly limited as he has little insight into the motives, needs, and desires of others, even those closest to him. Despite her age, Caroline, like Alex, is not as far along as Justin or Morgan in developing the kind of self-awareness that would enable her to engage in productive self-analysis of her perceptions, emotions, thoughts, and actions. While as the youngest Brett predictably is the least developed in self-awareness and seems oblivious to the consequences of his own actions and the effects of them on others, when not in motion (which is very infrequently) he does demonstrate an age-appropriate awareness of, and sensitivity to, his own internal states and the internal states of others.

Self-Determination

Just as being able to direct and cue the use of self-regulation functions does not require the capacity for self-realization, use of self-regulation functions also does not require any self-determined goal or self-desired outcome. Consequently, it is possible for a person to function on a day-to-day basis and never really engage in any act of self-determination beyond ephemeral inner urges or fleeting external demands encountered in immediate moments. To act in a self-determined manner requires the use of specific neural circuits involving portions of the frontal lobes that enable goal setting and long-term planning (Luria, 1980). Engagement of these circuits makes it possible for a person to develop foresight and to formulate plans that extend beyond the brief time span of the short-term-oriented Plan function identified as a self-regulation capacity listed in Table 3.1 and described in Table 3.2.

Executive capacity for self-determination also enables evaluation of the adequacy of self-regulation efforts—and the perceptions, emotions, cognitions, and actions they direct—in moving toward or achieving self-selected goals or carrying out self-selected plans. The development of long-term goals signals an appreciation of the potential benefits of foregoing immediate, lesser rewards to work toward greater rewards to be derived at a much later point in time. The self-determination executive capacities that generate, maintain, monitor, and revise long-term goals and plans often are in competition with desires and urges that are focused on much shorter time frames. The better developed a person's self-determination capacity, the more effectively it can be called into play, and the more likely it is that a person will suppress desires for immediate gratification in order to achieve long-term goals.

As was the case with self-realization capacities, while self-determination functions can greatly influence how self-regulation functions are used to direct day-to-day perceptions, feelings, thoughts, and actions, they are not required for the use of self-regulation capacities. It is certainly possible for a person to live his or her entire life with no personal goals or plans, following instead the goals and plans set out by others, and doing so with great success through the effective application of lower-tier self-regulation executive capacities. Conversely, efforts to engage self-determination functions can be greatly enhanced by the effective use of these lower-tier self-regulation executive functions. It is not necessary, however, to have developed all 23 self-regulation functions to a high degree in order to successfully execute a self-determined plan or achieve a self-determined goal. The better developed a person's self-determination capacities the more capable they are at finding ways to make the most of the many, or the few, self-regulation functions they might possess. When self-determination capacities are beginning to emerge, or are relatively less well-developed, concomitant self-regulation deficiencies are more likely to loom large as obstacles to carrying out plans or achieving goals, many of which may be ill-advised or poorly formulated to begin with. Even in the case of exceptional self-determination capacities however, it is possible that the number and extent of self-regulation deficits are so great as to make it highly unlikely that the person will ever achieve any of the goals he envisions or carry out any of the plans that he is capable of devising unless the self-regulation functions of others are enlisted to aid in the process.

Among the six individuals in the case studies, Justin and Morgan are the only ones who are demonstrating self-determination capacities. Justin is exhibiting an age-appropriate level of vocational maturity, expressing interest in career areas that are in line with his personal likes and dislikes. Although only in elementary school, Morgan has taken a very active role in self-selecting extracurricular activities that appeal to her and appear to hold great promise for future development into potential areas of career interest. She has clear goals in terms of social standing and these goals direct her use of self-regulation executive cues to plan and organize social events. Although Caroline and Alex are older than Justin and Morgan, they have not really demonstrated any signs of becoming self-directed, even for brief periods of time. Kevin also has shown little in the way of self-determination, but this is less unusual given that he is only in elementary school. Although some adults believe Brett to be very self-determined, the self-directed behaviors that create this impression are focused on immediate gratification of needs and desires and serve no real purpose beyond the present moment except to create more constraints on Brett's ability to satisfy his immediate desires.

Self-Generation

The previous tiers have addressed how we exert control over the perceptions, feelings, thoughts, and actions of daily life. While they encompass our experience of both the physical and mental realms, they are focused primarily on a person's approach to navigating through day-to-day existence. At some point in life however, a person might begin to pose questions about the nature of the physical and mental realms that seem to be taken for granted by most people. Questions such as: Why am I here? Where, or what is "here"? Why do I exist? What is existence? Is there a grand scheme of things? If there is, what is my place in the grand scheme? If there isn't, then how and why am I able to pose these questions? Does life have a purpose? If it does, what is my life's purpose? If it doesn't, then why should I act in a principled manner toward others? These questions are clearly of a metaphysical nature and go beyond those aspects of physical and mental existence that most people deal with on a daily basis. Some persons pose these questions, either to others or to themselves, and spend varying amounts of time and energy seeking answers to them. Other persons never even pose these questions, investing no time or energy in their pursuit. The propensity to pose these questions represents the next tier of executive control identified in this model as self-generation. When effectively engaged, this executive capacity initiates inquiries into the nature of existence; the purpose of life and the ultimate source(s) of what is experienced as reality; contemplation of concepts such as spirit and soul; the nature of the relationship of mind to body; and speculation that considers the possibility of existence of a God, "Mind" or a form of consciousness existing beyond the physical plane. Pursuit of the answers to these questions often leads to spiritual paths and/or the development of a personal philosophy of life and/or generation of a set of principles that can be used to guide thoughts, feelings, and actions. On a collective level, engagement of this executive capacity cues and directs efforts to grapple with the most difficult aspects of codes of ethical behavior, systems of justice, and communal existence. While some might question the appropriateness of including self-generation, as defined here, in a model of executive capacity, there are some compelling reasons for doing so. First, research in the neurosciences has clearly indicated that the ability to pose these questions and to grapple with ethical dilemmas is associated with neural circuits heavily dependent on areas of the frontal lobes (Greene, Nystrom, Engell, Darley & Cohen, 2004; Greene, Sommerville, Nystrom, Darley, & Cohen, 2001; Newberg, D'Aquili & Rause, 2001). Second, the posing of these questions can have a tremendous impact on how a person engages all of the lower tier executive capacities, as it can serve as an ultimate source of intentional direction for many, or all, aspects of the person's life (Frankl, 1984; Wilber, 1995; 1997; 2000).

Consistent with the functioning of the other tiers of self-control, self-generation capacities can emerge independent of the other executive capacities, and can be engaged with varying degrees of effectiveness regardless of the state of development of the other executive capacities. A person might spend a great deal of time and effort developing a highly refined philosophy of life intended to guide all aspects of the person's existence, but be unable to effectively direct daily functioning in a manner that enables the realization of long-term goals or consistent behavior patterns associated with such a philosophy. In a similar vein, a person might be extremely invested in understanding the meaning of life or determining ethical principles for guiding human behavior but lack self-awareness of personal strengths and weaknesses related to self-regulation and emotional functioning. Once again, it is important to keep in mind that self-generation functions need not be engaged in order to make effective use of the lower tiers of executive capacity. A person might direct his or her life in a coherent and meaningful manner with great personal insight and success in achieving personal goals through well-developed self-regulation functions, and yet never spend a single moment questioning the meaning of it all, i.e., never activating neural circuits that are involved with engaging self-generation capacities. While some persons never ask themselves the questions that emanate from the engagement of self-generation capacities, some others spend most of their waking moments engaging this capacity in a spiritual quest or a personal search for the meaning of life in general, and their lives in particular.

As self-generation capacities are typically not engaged for extended periods of time at ages such as those of our six case study children, it is not surprising that none of these six individuals have gone beyond simple childhood curiosity about the deeper matters of the meaning of life. Although both Justin and Morgan attend church services every week and pray for help with school work, neither one really has started to explore deeper issues of the meaning of life. A year ago, Caroline had what she refers to as a "spiritual experience" that she has only spoken about with a few select individuals. Unable to create a context for understanding what she was experiencing during that time, the event has not really had a lasting influence on her. Although Alex has the intellectual capacity to pose and debate questions about the meaning of life, he has shown very little interest in doing so. Alex's intellectual discussions and personal reading tend to be very concretely oriented and center on sports and, to a lesser degree, business. As very literal beings, both Kevin and Brett have a very rigid conception of God as an all-powerful being who sits in judgment of their every thought and act. Although Kevin and Brett hold this belief about God and can state it readily, thoughts about God and judgment tend not to enter their minds during waking hours, whether they are behaving very well or very poorly.

Trans-Self Integration

Whether or not a person has chosen to pose questions about the meaning or purpose of life and existence, they might seek out activities and states of consciousness that lead to a realization that in some ways, the concept of an autonomous self is merely an illusion—a state created by our physical brains. These individuals are often determined to see past the illusion of self to get a glimpse of what seems to lie beyond. These efforts to experience "ultimate truth" or the "reality beyond reality" often lead to what the mystic traditions of the world refer to as unity consciousness.

As is the case with self-generation some might question the appropriateness of including trans-self integration, as defined here, in a model of executive capacity. Also as in the case of self-generation, there are the same equally compelling reasons for doing so. First, research in the neurosciences has clearly indicated that the ability to experience the phenomenological state of egolessness or unity consciousness is directly linked to neural circuits heavily dependent on areas of the frontal lobes (Benson, Malhotra, Goldman, Jacobs & Hopkins, 1990; Newberg & D'Aquili, 2001; Herzog, Lele, Kuwert, Langen, et. al., 1990; Newberg, Alavi, Baime, Mozley, D'Aquili, 1997; Newberg et al.). Second, the experiencing of a trans-self integral experience can have a tremendous impact on how a person engages all of the executive capacities at lower tiers, as it can serve as an ultimate source of intentional direction for many, or possibly all, aspects of the person's life (Wilber, 1979; 2006).

When dealing with children and young adults, the likelihood of encountering an individual who has advanced their frontal lobe activation to this degree is quite low. Not surprisingly, none of the six children portrayed in the case studies have demonstrated any tendencies toward generating thoughts of a trans-self integrative nature.

Arenas of Involvement for Executive Functions

Understanding how executive function engagement can vary widely across the four domains helps to see how a person might have difficulty with executive control in only one of the domains while functioning very capably in the other three, whereas another person might have regulation difficulties in two, three, or even all four of the domains. While the concept of domains of functioning helps to clarify the nature of many executive control difficulties, it does not explain all of the variation that is observed in the daily use of self-regulation executive functions and the use of executive functions at all subsequent tiers. The concept of arenas of involvement, introduced briefly at the end of Chapter 2, offers an additional critical dimension for greater understanding of the full range of variability of engagement of self-regulation capacities. Executive control can vary greatly depending on whether the person is attempting to control one's own internal states (*intrapersonal arena*), interactions with others (*interpersonal arena*), interactions with the environment around them (*environment arena*), or engagement with the tools of the culturally derived symbol systems used to process and share information (*symbol system arena*). Elaboration of the nature of executive function involvement in each arena is provided below.

The Intrapersonal Arena

The intrapersonal arena refers to a person's involvement with him or herself, that is, a person's perceptions, feelings, thoughts, and actions in relation to her or himself. In terms of executive functions, this arena is where control processes are turned inward to cue and regulate self-referencing perceptions, feelings, thoughts, and actions. The overall result of effective engagement of intrapersonal executive functions is the enabling of the capacity to control one's own perceptions, feelings, thoughts, and actions in relation to the self, that is, self-control and self-discipline. Effective use of executive functions in the intrapersonal arena enables a person to avoid addictions and other self-destructive habits and behavior patterns, set and maintain goals for oneself, and drive purposeful, positive behavior.

The Interpersonal Arena

The interpersonal arena refers to a person's involvement with others, that is, a person's perceptions, feelings, thoughts, and actions in relation to other persons. In terms of executive functions, this arena is where control processes are turned outward to cue and regulate a person's perceptions, feelings, thoughts, and actions in relation to the perceptions, feelings, thoughts, and actions of other persons. The overall result of the effective engagement of interpersonal executive functions is the ability to interact appropriately with others as circumstances dictate, the ability to appreciate and deal with the perspectives of others; the ability to generate a theory of mind that enables a person to understand, infer, and predict the motivations, needs, and desires of others; and the ability to find ways to balance the needs of the self with the needs of the community.

The Environment Arena

The environment arena refers to a person's involvement with the natural and man-made elements of the world, that is, a person's perceptions, feelings, thoughts, and actions in relation to their surroundings. In terms of executive functions, this arena is where control processes are directed outward to cue and regulate a person's perceptions, feelings, thoughts, and actions in relation to the environment. The overall result of the effective engagement of executive functions in relation to environmental surroundings is the ability to carry out daily functioning in a manner that utilizes natural and man-made resources appropriately resulting in the desired outcomes. Executive control in this arena enables a person to avoid "accidents" by anticipating the impact and consequences of one's own actions in, and on, the physical environment.

The Symbol System Arena

The symbol system arena refers to the realm of culturally-driven human designed symbol systems used to refine communication and enhance thought processing capacities. These include the use of language, mathematics, and other systems of logic and associated information media such as words, numbers, figures, diagrams, schematics, computer programming codes, and the like. A person's sensations, perceptions, feelings, thoughts, and actions in relation to these information systems are the focus of this domain of functioning. In terms of executive functions, this arena is where control processes are directed toward cueing and regulating a person's perceptions, feelings, thoughts, and actions relating to the processing of information transmitted through symbol systems. The overall result of the effective engagement of executive functions in relation to symbol systems is the ability to effectively direct self-expression through reading, writing, and speaking one or more languages, to direct work with the conceptual bases of mathematics, science, and other formal systems of thought and knowledge, to direct the use of symbol system communication tools such as computers, and to enhance learning and performance in all of these areas. Although executive function difficulties are not synonymous with the concept of learning disabilities, many individuals with learning disabilities also experience executive control difficulties in the symbol system arena that greatly exacerbate their learning problems.

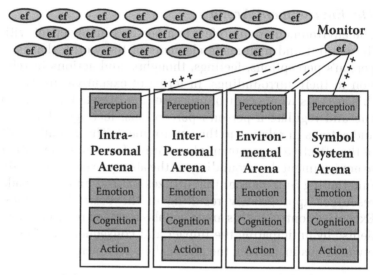

+ Indicates strong cueing capacity   - Indicates weak cueing capacity

Figure 3.3 Examples of Variations in Cueing Capacity Strength for the Monitor Self-Regulation Executive Function for the Perception Domain of Functioning Within the Four Areas of Involvement.

As is the case with domains of functioning, arenas of involvement are dissociable, meaning that a person with executive control difficulties in one or more of the arenas can alternately be demonstrating very effective control in one or more of the other arenas. The dissociable nature of the self-regulation capacities also can be evidenced within a single arena of involvement and for a single domain of functioning as well. For example, a person might effectively engage many self-regulation capacities within the cognition domain within the Interpersonal Arena while being very poor with the use of other self-regulation capacities within the cognitive domain within that same arena. Figure 3.3 demonstrates the full dissociable nature of executive functions, illustrating a possible combination of executive function strengths and weaknesses for a single self-regulation function (Monitor) within a single domain of functioning (Perception) across the four arenas of involvement. Table 3.3 uses the descriptions of the case study student's difficulties with the Modulate, Foresee/Plan, Monitor, and Correct cues to illustrate how self-regulation problems can manifest differently across the four arenas. (While this table does not explore all the self-regulation difficulties of the case studies, the reader can get an idea of how those executive

Table 3.3 Case Study Self-Regulation Difficulties Compared
Across Arenas of Involvement

Modulate

Justin has difficulty applying the proper amount of effort to thinking about, or doing, school-related tasks and often thinking that the amount of effort expended was sufficient when in actuality it was much less than needed.	Modulate	Cognition Action	Symbol System
Once angry, Kevin seems unable to control temper; things escalate when other children respond to statements.	Modulate	Emotion Action	Interpersonal
In spite of pharmacological intervention, Caroline continues to demonstrate difficulties in regulating her emotions, especially as they pertain to her own internal states and behavior, often becoming very upset with herself for not being able to make things be the way she would like them to be.	Modulate	Emotion	Intrapersonal
Brett seems to delight in seeking out those aspects of his surroundings that pose the greatest risk. Everyday for Brett seems to be a high speed adventure; he seems to have one gear—overdrive.	Modulate	Action	Environment

Foresee/Plan

Justin is very poor with both short- and long-term planning for school tasks. He often starts in on tasks without having everything he needs to get the job done. As a result, he spends a lot of time interrupting work to locate needed materials one at a time. He often fails to bring home books or materials from school that are needed to complete homework assignments.	Foresee/Plan	Cognition	Symbol System

Table 3.3 (continued)   Case Study Self-Regulation Difficulties
Compared Across Arenas of Involvement

Kevin seems unaware of how his actions affect others and does not seem to be able to anticipate the consequences resulting from his emotional outbursts.	Foresee/Plan	Emotion Cognition Action	Interpersonal
Caroline has difficulty coming up with a plan for completing a self-care activity, showing difficulty in breaking the activity into a sequence of smaller actions.	Foresee/Plan	Cognition Action	Intrapersonal
When Brett becomes involved in an activity, his actions reflect no planning or foresight about the possible consequences of the things he does.	Foresee/Plan	Cognition Action	Environment
Alex demonstrates very little in the way of anticipating how activities or plans will unfold over time and shows little capacity for preplanning to deal with alternate outcomes.	Foresee/Plan	Perception Emotion Cognition Action	Intrapersonal

Monitor

Justin often makes what are usually called "careless" errors on homework assignments and tests, as these errors occur with relatively simple material.	Monitor	Perception Cognition Action	Symbol System
Kevin has difficulty monitoring his own emotional reactions as well as those of others.	Monitor	Emotion	Intrapersonal Interpersonal
Caroline demonstrates little ability to self-monitor and evaluate the effectiveness of her interactions with others.	Monitor	Perception Emotion Cognition Action	Intrapersonal
Brett fails to "pay attention to" motor routines.	Monitor	Action	Environment
Alana often hands in incomplete work and often does not check her work for errors.	Monitor	Cognition Action	Symbol System

Table 3.3 (continued) Case Study Self-Regulation Difficulties
Compared Across Arenas of Involvement

Correct

Sometimes Justin notices the errors that he makes, but then does not always follow through with correcting the errors he finds.	Correct	Perception Cognition Action	Symbol System
Kevin refuses to say he's sorry to classmates even when he knows he was wrong.	Correct Execute	Emotion Action	Interpersonal
Caroline usually does not make an effort to clarify or correct social miscues.	Correct	Perception Emotion Cognition Action	Intrapersonal
Brett does not make necessary corrections to motor routines. These difficulties result in many "accidents" like bumping into other children, knocking glasses off of tables, and breaking less sturdy toys.	Correct	Action	Environment

capacities, or lack thereof, impact functioning in these multiple arenas.) The accompanying Module 4 of the CD provides a document that details each self-regulation executive function by domain of functioning within each arena of involvement.

SUMMARY

This chapter provided an overview of a comprehensive model of executive functions that can be used to guide case conceptualizations, assessment, and intervention planning. We propose that executive functioning difficulties impact an individual's control of perceptions, cognitions, emotions, and actions in multiple arenas: intrapersonal, interpersonal, symbol system, and environment. While clinicians are most likely to deal with children, like those in our case studies, who experience self-regulation executive difficulties, control process deficits at the levels of self-activation and the upper tiers of self-realization and self-determination, self-generation, and even trans-self generation can have an impact on functioning. Given the dissociable nature of these difficulties within the multiple domains and arenas, the reader can see that there needs to be explicit and thorough review of an individual's executive capacities: Saying that an individual experiences executive functioning difficulties is not particularly helpful in developing a conceptual understanding or plan of action. Understanding and use of this model, then, dictates the multidimensional assessment process delineated in Chapters 5 and 6 as well as the direct and comprehensive intervention approaches discussed in later chapters.

4

Executive Function Development and Related Issues

To this point, we have profiled six children and offered a detailed model for understanding the multifaceted nature of executive functions. This chapter will provide further understanding of executive functions through discussion of important topics such as the progression of executive function development, its impact on academic and interpersonal learning, its relationship to the diagnosis of mental health problems, and its involvement in brain-behavior relationships.

EXECUTIVE FUNCTION DEVELOPMENT

Although the six children in our case studies are all different ages, we have used the same general framework of self-regulation capacities to discuss their executive function difficulties. Such view might raise questions about the development of executive function capacities over time. In fact, parents and professionals alike often pose questions about development when discussing executive functions. These questions include: When does executive control begin to emerge? Are there specific stages of executive function development that all children follow? Do all executive function capacities develop together at the same rate?

Popular media conceptions of self-regulation often give the impression that executive functions begin to become accessible to children during the adolescent years. Much attention has been given to adolescent brain development, emergence of decision-making capacities during the adolescent years, and the idea that adolescent brains are not "fully developed." Those familiar with Piaget's developmental stages might think of executive functions as representing a mode of *formal operational* thought associated with adolescent development of abstract reasoning capacities. However, one must be cautious not to obscure the distinction between executive functions and intelligence or reasoning. Although Piaget's stage of *formal operational* thought often describes noticeable shifts in cognitive capacities representing increases in both reasoning abilities and executive functions, it is important to avoid thinking of executive functions as synonymous with either abstract reasoning ability or *formal operational* thought.

Executive function capacities actually begin to develop in early infancy (Eliot, 1999; Posner & Rothbart, 2007), and aspects of executive control continue to develop possibly throughout a person's life. However, large developmental shifts in executive control are noticeable during the adolescent years. In her book, *What's Going on in There?*, Eliot (1999) provides a comprehensive description of early brain development. In her discussion of developing neural structures, the emergence of executive capacities is apparent. For example, Eliot describes aspects of early visual processing development as follows:

> Finally, between three and six months, infants become able to anticipate, as opposed to merely follow, the position of a steadily moving object. Careful measurements have shown that during this period, the eyes begin to focus slightly ahead of where the object is moving. This anticipatory tracking is a function of special eye-movement control regions in the frontal cortex, and it is a major landmark in cognitive development, because it suggests the baby is actually *choosing* where to look. (p. 212)

As highlighted by Eliot, between the ages of 3 and 6 months, areas of the frontal lobes become sufficiently myelinated to enable the child to exert control over the perceptual process of seeing. Eliot's description of the developmental sequence can be considered as the emergence of the self-regulation cue, *Perceive*, as it is applied to visual processing. Rather than reacting in a stimulus bound manner, the young brain can now cue specific neural components of the visual system to choose how and what to look at. In order for the child to utilize this new capacity effectively, other newly emerging self-regulation functions also are engaged, including the *Focus/Select* and the *Sustain* cues. Posner and Rothbart (2007) also point out the essential role of frontal lobe development in early childhood:

It has long been believed that the development of the frontal cortex allows the child to move away from being bound to external stimuli. The development of frontal control mechanisms allows children to demonstrate voluntary control of actions and to delay gratification. The child's ability to resist control from current input gives rise to our feeling that toddlers, unlike infants, have a mind of their own. (p. 79)

The Holarchical Model of Executive Function presented in Chapter 3 provides an effective framework for characterizing executive function development. The arrangement of executive capacities in tiers has meaning developmentally and neuropsychologically. The tier structure is not meant to represent a static nor a traditional hierarchical progression of neuropsychological development. Strict hierarchical models typically represent a distinct progression of development where one level must be completed before advancement to the next level is possible. Traditionally, all movement progresses in a single direction from a lower tier to the next higher tier.

In contrast to the hierarchical model, a developmental holarchy is a dynamic model that places no such rigid constraints on the processes of movement across tiers. In a holarchical arrangement, a person can progress from a lower tier to a higher tier without mastering all of the capacities represented at the lower tier. In addition, development at a lower tier can continue to progress after a person has moved on to the development of capacities at one or more higher tiers. Most importantly, a person can develop highly refined capabilities at higher tiers while still demonstrating substantial deficiencies in functioning at one or more lower tiers. The holarchical structure provides a framework for characterization of the development of executive functions over time. However, each executive function capacity within the model can be thought of as separate and relatively self-contained developmental line, as depicted in Figure 4.1. Regardless of which framework is used, practitioners should keep in mind most individuals develop at least some executive capacities at the self-regulation and self-realization tiers. Yet, it is less common for development to occur at the self-generation and trans-self integration tiers, regardless of age.

As shown in Figure 4.1, large developmental shifts are noticeable around adolescence, as the self-realization capacities involving self-awareness and self-determination increase

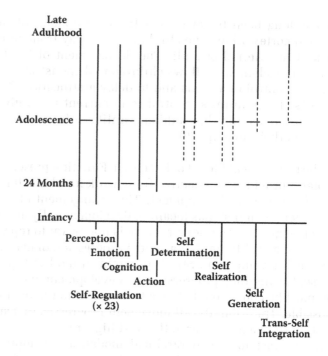

Figure 4.1   Executive Function Development: Lines and Levels.

in many children. The cultural transition of the educational system in the United States from the smaller, teacher-directed environments of elementary schools to the larger, self-directed environments of middle or junior high schools coincides with noticeable increases in brain development that enable greater executive control, especially at the tiers beyond self-regulation. The confluence of educational transition and specific aspects of frontal lobe development centered in the adolescent years provides a natural focal point, which leads to the erroneous assumption that executive capacities in general are only beginning to emerge during adolescence. On the contrary, the lower tier self-regulation executive functions have been developing since early childhood.

The development of any executive control capacity is a slow, gradual process over time. Although each executive capacity follows a general timeline that is similar across all individuals, the developmental trajectories of specific individuals can vary greatly. The developmental trajectory of any executive capacity over time is observable. Using the self-regulation

capacity of Inhibit as an example, 4-year-olds are more proficient at cueing the Inhibit function than 2-year-olds. Likewise, 14-year-olds are more proficient than 4-year-olds and
24-year-olds are more proficient than 14-year-olds. With each
passing year, the magnitude of difference in the capacity to
inhibit becomes less obvious. The difference in capacity to
inhibit between a 2-year-old and a 4-year-old is large and more
easily recognizable than the difference between a 22-year-old
and a 24-year old or even that between a 24-year-old and a
44-year-old.

Although most individuals show growth in executive
capacities over time, the developmental trajectory (i.e., the rate
of growth over time) of each executive function capacity is
variable from person to person. At the same age, different individuals can vary considerably in their level of development
of any specific executive capacity. Using the Inhibit cue as an
example, some 2-year-olds are relatively proficient at cueing
the Inhibit function across many different situations, while
other 2-year-olds are nearly incapable of doing so in any situation. In developmental continuum terms, some 2-year-olds are
able to demonstrate Inhibit cueing as effectively as the average
4-year-old, yet other 2-year-olds may have a capacity for use of
the Inhibit cue that more closely resembles that of the average
1-year-old. Such inter-individual variation is observable at all
ages for all executive capacities.

Intra-individual variation is an equally important consideration in the development of executive functions. For a specific child, development of each executive control capacity
does not necessarily progress at the same rate. For example,
within the self-regulation tier, one self-regulation capacity can
be more or less developed than any other at any given point
in time. Even when one or more of these capacities are well
developed in a child, this does not guarantee that all self-
regulation functions will be equally developed for that child
(recall Figures 3.2 and 3.3). In fact, for the same child, he or
she may demonstrate one or more self-regulation capacities
that are below the age-expected level.

The rate of executive function development can change
from time to time in a given child. For instance, a child who
is developing at a slow rate in one or more capacities might
suddenly experience a rapid growth spurt in which significant
increases can be observed. This rapid growth period might be
followed by a leveling off at a relatively typical rate or even the
originally slower rate.

The wide variation in development of executive capacities is understandable and consistent with the wide variations in children's physical development that are visibly obvious to the casual observer. Consider a typical group of 13-year-old students encountered in an eighth grade classroom. Within this group, many students will be of similar general appearance. However, some students appear more similar to an elementary school-age child in both size and physical characteristics while others have the physical appearance that resembles that of a high school senior. This phenomenon of developmental variability is also present in terms of these students' abilities to use specific executive capacities, such as the Inhibit cue. Although some students will progress in development at a typical rate, others will fluctuate in their acquisition of these capacities. We must recognize the dissociable nature of mental and physical development—that is, those eighth grade students exhibiting the most advanced physical development are not necessarily the same students who are demonstrating advanced executive function capacities. In some situations, a 13-year-old who most closely resembles a younger elementary-age child in appearance might exhibit self-regulation capacities that are mature for his or her age. Yet, the more physically mature student might only demonstrate the use of various self-regulation capacities comparable to those of a much younger child.

The fact that the variation in executive function development is not physically apparent and not easy to observe seems to create a number of barriers to the appreciation of the significant impact of developmental variation within school settings and on instructional processes. Students the same age but at varying stages of physical development are not expected to perform comparably in gym class (e.g., 80 pound boys are not expected to wrestle 120 pound boys) in order to earn a passing grade. This acknowledgment of the need to accommodate for physical differences in development when judging the adequacy of performance, however, is not matched with an acknowledgment of the need to accommodate for brain development differences in terms of executive functioning. All students are expected to perform comparably in terms of executive function-dependent capacities labeled as responsibility, self-organization, self-direction, self-discipline, and the like, in order to earn passing grades in most academic classes. Equally detrimental is the incongruent belief that physical development is out of the direct control of the individual child, while

Table 4.1   Cultural/Educational Transitions Imposed on Children's Developing Brains in the United States

From	To	Typical Age
Home	Preschool	2-4
Preschool	Kindergarten	5
Kindergarten	First Grade	6
Elementary School	Middle School or Junior High School	11/12
Middle School or Junior High School	Senior High School	14/15
Senior High School	College or Work	18

brain development, especially in the form of executive function capacities, is thought to be well within the control of the child. In addition, many parents and educators attribute natural maturational variation in brain development to the child's willingness and desire to demonstrate these capacities in the more demanding environments of the middle, junior high, and senior high schools. Often in school settings, and even in many homes, there are very rigid expectations that executive function development be at a specific level for all same-age children. The negative consequences applied to a child not performing up to the expected standards can be severe, unreasonable, and often uncompromising in nature. Appreciation of the natural variations in maturation of brain functions is crucial for ensuring appropriate educational experiences for those children who are demonstrating nothing more than natural maturational delays in the development of executive function capacities.

As the example of executive function development in adolescent students illustrates, the developmental progression of executive capacities does not necessarily coincide neatly with the cultural/educational transition points imposed on most children living in the United States. Table 4.1 provides an overview of these transition points. While each of these important transitions assumes a developmental level of executive control that will be required for success in the new setting, nearly all of these transitions are highly restrictive in the chronological age range during which transitions must occur. In some cases, the children making these transitions are not developmentally ready to handle challenges of the more demanding newer environment, and are at-risk of failing to adapt quickly enough to the newly imposed conditions for no other reason than a lack of maturity of the necessary executive capacities. Given that the developmental rate can change over time, a student might demonstrate a consistent lack of readiness for all educational transitions, or experience a delay in readiness for some transition situations while making an effective change in others.

To illustrate the developmental variation of executive functions, let's revisit the case of Brett, who demonstrated many characteristics of AD/HD. Barkley (2000), who views AD/HD as an executive function-based clinical syndrome, estimates a general pattern of delay of approximately 30% of chronological age in the development of executive capacities such as the Inhibit, Time, and Sustain cues. Applying this guideline to a child such as Brett, we can see that when making the transition from kindergarten to first grade at 6 years of age, Brett would be demonstrating executive control similar to that of the average 4-year-old. At 12 years of age, when the transition to junior high school is occurring, Brett will likely be demonstrating executive control similar to that of an 8-year-old child. As Brett approaches the legal driving age of 16 years of age, many of the executive capacities critical to good driving skills will have only reached maturation levels consistent to those of an 11-year-old child. The implications for these types of developmental delays can have a tremendous impact on the child and his or her social, academic, home, and vocational functioning.

INTERNAL COMMAND VERSUS EXTERNAL DEMAND

An important aspect of executive function development that is critical for understanding variations in everyday functioning relates to the locus of intentionality for executive control. Executive control can stem from a person's own internal desires, drives, aspirations, plans, and proclivities, namely by *internal command*. On the other hand, if summoned by sources outside of the person, executive control is being initially cued by *external demand*. Executive control that arises from internal command utilizes specific neural networks routed through portions of the frontal lobes as well as other specific areas of the brain. These networks are distinct from, but not necessarily completely independent of, the neural networks of the frontal lobes and additional areas that must be activated when a person attempts to engage executive control in response to an external demand (Barkley, 2005; Freeman, 2000). Executive control by internal command is generally much easier to engage because it flows naturally from the persons' own internal states. Summoning executive control in situations of external demand, however, requires much more mental effort and much greater control capacity. In the case of internal control, a person is directing functioning in concert with internal desires and motivational states that are already in place. In the case of externally demanded executive control, the person must first disengage from any ongoing internally commanded executive routines that are directing current processing of perceptions, feelings, thoughts, and actions. Following the interruption of these ongoing processes, the person must take stock of the situation and determine the executive control capacities needed to effectively direct and react to the external demand. Finally, the person must activate the necessary executive control processes and associated mental capacities required to comply with the demand. All of these steps can be carried out either through conscious or nonconscious direction, but as is the case with most of our mental functioning, reactions to externally demanded executive control typically are carried out nonconsciously.

Many parents and teachers of children who demonstrate executive function difficulties are often baffled by the seeming paradox of the child who functions so effectively when engrossed in activities of their own choosing, yet who seems woefully inept when requested to perform the simplest of household chores or classroom assignments. The examples could fill a book themselves, such as the child who can play guitar for hours on end but is unable to focus on a work project for more than a few seconds, the socially capable child who becomes anxious to the point of physical sickness when required to present a talk to classmates, or the meticulous builder of models whose school work products look like they were assembled in the dark. Parents and teachers who view these disparities often cannot help but think that the child's "sudden" incapacities are a matter of conscious choice—a convenient sham to avoid the hard work and effort that is being required of them. In actuality, most of these observed inadequacies are not a matter of conscious choice, and instead, are the result of undeveloped, underutilized, or ineffective executive control capacities.

The easiest analogy for understanding these difficulties is the situation of gifted athletes who fail to perform effectively in competition. These individuals spend a great deal of time training and preparing for competition and their dedication to their sport is unquestionable, as is reflected in the endless hours of time taken to perfect their skills. In practice, their performance is often flawless; yet, at some of the most crucial times in competition, these individuals' skills fail them. How could they not have seen that one? How could they have allowed that feeling of self-doubt to creep in at a time like that? What could they have been thinking? How could they have mishandled that one? How does this happen? Do dedicated athletes all simply choose to fail? Was it simply that they did not want it bad enough? Do they all lack the desire to win? Were they not serious enough about their pursuit of excellence? After all, you have seen them do that perfectly a thousand times before. How is it that when the demand was the highest, their performance was the lowest? In situations such as these, it is much easier to see that even the most capable of individuals can have difficulty directing and controlling perceptions, feelings, thoughts, and actions under conditions of external demand. If handling external demands can be difficult even for those who have attempted to perfect executive control of specific perceptions, feelings, thoughts, and actions, it should not be hard to imagine what it must be like for a child with executive difficulties faced with sudden external demands and the expectations for immediate compliance that often accompany them.

As parents and teachers, we often fail to appreciate the plight of the child who has not mastered the fine art of instant obedience and flawless execution. We want it done right now! Didn't I just tell you what to do? Why are you still here? Haven't you gotten started yet? You call this clean? Hasn't anyone taught you how to do this right? How many times am I going to have to tell you this? It is extremely important for parents and teachers to realize that responding to external demands is a skill set that develops over time and usually requires much input from others in the way of modeling, teaching, and assisted practice. Patience, a nonjudgmental attitude, and a realization of the work and effort required on the part of all involved can go a long way in helping children to develop greater on-demand control of their faculties. And even under the best of conditions, consistent production might not be realized. Conversely, attributing a child's lack of compliance with external demands to negative personal traits such as laziness, apathy, a sense of entitlement, a desire to undermine authority and the like will only serve to alienate the child, diminish any personal sense of connection, and often further reduce the likelihood of compliance with the demands.

EXECUTIVE FUNCTIONS AND CLINICAL DIAGNOSES

In the previous section, AD/HD was referred to as a disorder involving executive function deficits. This reference is likely to raise questions in reader's minds regarding the labels that might be associated with executive function deficits or developmental delays. Do such deficits or delays constitute a distinct disorder? Does such a disorder have a name? While it would seem practical to have a specific diagnostic category with a name such as Executive Dysfunction Syndrome or the like, the diagnostic puzzle related to executive functions cannot be put together quite that simply.

The connection between AD/HD and executive function difficulties is probably the most obvious. The *Diagnostic and Statistical Manual of Mental Disorders, Fourth Edition, Text Revision* (DSM-IV-TR; American Psychiatric Association, 1997) definition of AD/HD includes reference to difficulties with both inhibition and attention. Additionally, the DSM-IV-TR definition of AD/HD clearly reflects behavioral problems involving difficulties with the self-regulation cues of Inhibit, Focus/Select, and Sustain. Consistent with the behavioral evidence, brain function studies of children and adults with and without AD/HD have identified the specific neural circuits affected by AD/HD that pass through regions of the frontal lobes, as well as other areas of the brain (Bunge, Ochsner, Desmond, Glover, & Gabrieli, 2001; Daw, Niv, & Dayan, 2005; Denckla & Reiss, 1997; Hill et al., 2003; MacMaster et al., 2003; Voeller, 2001; Zang et al., 2007). Although individuals accurately diagnosed with AD/HD often demonstrate difficulties with the Inhibit, Focus/Select, and/or Sustain cues, many of these individuals also demonstrate other self-regulation difficulties (Barkley, 2006; Biederman et al., 2006; Pennington & Ozonoff, 1996; Seidman, Biederman, Faraone, Weber & Ouellette, 1997). Barkley (1997, 2006) suggests that most individuals diagnosed with AD/HD also experience difficulties with the Time and Foresee/Plan cues. Moreover, individuals diagnosed with AD/HD are likely to demonstrate some degree of self-realization difficulties involving delayed development of self-awareness, self-analysis, long-term goal setting, and long-term foresight/planning.

The obvious connection between AD/HD and executive function difficulties has led some professionals to think of all individuals with executive difficulties as having AD/HD. This is clearly not the case. As discussed here, the ADHD diagnosis encompasses a core set of self-regulation difficulties, as well as possible deficits in Foresee/Plan and Time cues, and other executive difficulties. Although individuals with AD/HD display multiple executive function deficiencies, the specific difficulties displayed beyond the common core, and the total number and severity of deficiencies demonstrated, will vary from individual to individual and by age. This is one of the reasons why professional consensus on all aspects of AD/HD has been, and remains, difficult to achieve. Although there is a well-established link between AD/HD and a core set of executive function difficulties (Barkley, 1997, 2006; Seidman et al., 1997), there are many individuals who do not have problems with Inhibit, Focus/Select, and Sustain cues, but who have many difficulties with other executive capacities within one or more of the tiers, and therefore do not meet the diagnostic criteria for AD/HD.

Terms such as executive dysfunction and dysexecutive syndrome (Wilson et al., 1996) are sometimes used to refer to individuals with executive difficulties, though these terms currently do not relate to any specific diagnostic schema that is widely agreed upon. For example, the most recent version of the DSM (DSM-IV-TR) offers no diagnostic category of Executive Dysfunction or Dysexecutive Function Syndrome; however, such a diagnostic category likely is being considered for inclusion in future editions of the DSM.

Although there could be some merit in the development of a separate diagnostic category or educational classification for executive function difficulties, the greatest challenge to such an approach is the fact that the diagnostic criteria of most clinical conditions encompass difficulties with one or more executive capacities. In many ways, the DSM-IV-TR can be thought of as a behavioral user's guide to all the things that can go wrong with the frontal lobes. A number of researchers and clinicians share this perspective (see Arnsten & Robbins, 2002; Goldberg, 2001; Lichter and Cummings, 2001; Miller & Cummings, 2006; Pennington, Bennetto, McAleer, & Roberts, 1996; Stuss & Knight, 2002), especially when frontal lobe functions are operationally defined as all executive capacities combined with working memory processes. For example, Arnsten and Robbins succinctly articulated this view by stating:

Deficits in PFC [prefrontal cortex, aka frontal lobe] function are evident in every neuropsychiatric disorder (indeed, the term "psychiatric problem" seems synonymous with PFC dysfunction). Abilities carried out by the PFC can also become impaired in so-called "normal" individuals under conditions of uncontrollable stress, fatigue, and with advancing age. (p. 51; text within [ ] added for clarification).

It is important not to interpret such statements (e.g., Arnsten & Robbins, 2002) as implying that executive function difficulties are the sole cause of all disorders and syndromes in DSM-IV-TR. Additionally, it cannot be inferred that frontal lobe dysfunction is only found in these disorders, as some individuals will present with executive difficulties in the absence of a specific diagnosis. What is clear, however, is that executive difficulties are associated in some way with all of these syndromes. For example, Generalized Anxiety Disorder (GAD) involves neural circuits routed through a number of subcortical structures classified as part of the limbic system, with the paths of these circuits also passing through the frontal lobes. While dysfunction of the neural circuit within the limbic system might be the root cause of a person's anxiety disorder, the disruption of the circuit within the subcortical region can impact the frontal lobes. This results in executive function difficulties while the person is in a state of anxiety. Therefore, some of the diagnostic criteria for GAD include difficulty *controlling* worry, difficulty concentrating, irritability, and sleep disturbance. All of these symptoms represent difficulties with the engagement of various executive function capacities, which are the outcome of experiencing anxiety.

In addition to the Holarchical Model of Executive Functions, the concepts of domains of functioning and arenas of involvement are critical to understanding the complex nature of association between executive function difficulties and clinical and educational diagnostic categories. For example, the behavioral difficulties experienced by children diagnosed with Oppositional Defiant Disorder (ODD) or Conduct Disorder (CD) clearly represent multiple self-regulation and self-realization deficits. Important distinguishing features are that the deficits are expressed in one arena of involvement—the interpersonal arena—and involve primarily the emotion and cognition domains of functioning. The control difficulties of children with accurate diagnoses of CD or ODD will be evident in the way these children cue perception, emotion, thought, and action when they are interacting with others. These difficulties are often accompanied by difficulties with self-analysis and self-awareness. The Autism Spectrum Disorders (ASDs) also include executive function deficiencies related to the *interpersonal arena*. However, while the executive function difficulties of those with ASDs also typically involve all four domains of perception, emotion, cognition, and action, the difficulties with self-analysis and self-awareness are much more severe and are accompanied by severe deficits in self-determination.

It is our perspective that simply including a new diagnostic category for executive function difficulties in future revisions of the DSM will not sufficiently address the central role that executive function difficulties play in most of the existing DSM diagnostic categories. The new edition of the DSM, therefore, would have greater clinical utility if it were to incorporate a new axis that could be used to identify specific executive function difficulties experienced by an individual along with the various clinical diagnoses that might be assigned. Following this line of reasoning, the pervasiveness of executive function difficulties of one type or another associated with most of the mental disorders experienced by children makes clear the need to carefully assess and specify the nature of the executive function difficulties of these children so that appropriate interventions can be identified and implemented.

EXECUTIVE FUNCTIONS AND SCHOOL

Children come to school to learn all the skills that will help them to become productive members of society. They learn to read, to write, and to do arithmetic, as well as to learn specific content about science, history, geography, health, physical exercise, music, and art. Moreover, they learn how to interact with others and grow as individuals. Teachers lead their students through classroom exercises to deliver important content that helps them to develop skills in all these areas. The executive demands of a learning situation can be, and often are, mediated by a teacher who cues students to engage the mental processes needed to learn effectively.

How do teachers know if children have learned and can apply what they have been taught? How do they know if children have absorbed and retained the content presented? In order for a teacher to know if school has been a "place of learning," the child must demonstrate in some way that learning has occurred. Such demonstration requires production on the student's part; responding to questions in class, taking teacher-made tests, handing in homework assignments, writing papers; generating portfolios; completing science lab reports; taking standardized tests; as well as planning, organizing, and completing long-term projects. To be judged an adequate learner, a child must produce specified amounts of work at specified levels of quality on any number of these tasks. The important word here is "produce." To be a good student, a child must produce what is required in the manner in which it is required. Such production involves knowledge and the engagement of various combinations of executive capacities at various times. Unlike the process of learning in the classroom, demonstration of the outcome of that learning usually is not mediated by a teacher, thereby leaving the executive cueing of most aspects of producing in the hands of the students themselves. For any student, performance of school tasks can be greatly affected by the nature of the executive demands that the teacher builds into tasks intended to demonstrate what students have learned. In many situations, the production demands of schools are aligned at least roughly with the capabilities of the average or above average students with regard to executive capacity development. On the other hand, however, there are some situations where there is a mismatch between production demands and the expected executive capacities, which can have a notable affect on outcomes for all students.

Students whose executive function development has kept pace with the culturally determined timetable for educational transitions are able to handle the production demands placed on them during formal schooling effectively. With little or no cueing from parents and teachers, these students effectively engage their developing executive capacities to self-direct their school production efforts. On the infrequent occasions when their executive capacities fail them, these students are able to make the necessary adjustments to quickly recover and return to their more characteristic levels of effective performing.

Students whose executive function development is lagging somewhat in one or more areas are much more likely to have difficulty consistently producing at levels that effectively demonstrate what they have learned, especially during the initial transition from one level of schooling to the next. When an educational transition occurs ahead of the development of adequate executive capacities, the student is underprepared for taking on the responsibilities of the new learning environment, and the result often is a lack of adequate production including failing grades. The lack of adequate production can be bewildering to the parents and the student alike, especially if the student's rate of development of executive functions up to that point had been progressing well within the average range compared to same-age peers. Whether a first-time occurrence or a chronic pattern, the results of a mismatch between a student's executive function development and the executive demands of a required educational transition can be very stressful and disconcerting for a student and his or her parents as well. As the student's development of executive functions progresses to the point where his capabilities now are more in line with the demands of the educational setting, the difficulties that were originally experienced begin to subside. Although adjustment to the new setting eventually occurs for these students when the difficulties they are experiencing are handled appropriately, the timeline for such adjustment can vary greatly from one student to the next.

Students with more extreme developmental delays or medical conditions resulting in severe executive function deficits frequently are unable to produce work that is judged adequate by established standards, although they have been able to acquire academic skills and learn new content. Martha Denckla (2007) has used the term "Producing Disabilities," rather than Learning Disabilities, to describe the condition of these students because their difficulties do not necessarily stem from problems with learning to communicate with language, read, quantify with number systems, or learn new information in a number of different ways. What these individuals have difficulty with is complying with the demands for production that demonstrates what they have learned. This includes issues such as recording their thoughts in writing, responding effectively to oral and/or written test questions, completing projects that are done within specified timelines and that contain all required elements or follow the required rubric, or remembering to do and/or hand in homework assignments or lab reports. The number and severity of the executive function delays or deficits of these students put them at great risk of persistent failure in school, due to the lack of production. The lack of specific classification of executive function difficulties typically leaves these students ineligible for identification to receive needed services.

EXECUTIVE FUNCTIONS AND BRAIN BEHAVIOR RELATIONSHIPS

Earlier in the book, we cautioned against thinking of executive functions as a unitary mental capacity, such as "the CEO of the brain." Instead, we illustrated how understanding the multifaceted nature of executive functions offers information that is more detailed for the purposes of accurate diagnosis and treatment of executive function-related problems. We have also stated that executive functions represent neuropsychological capacities typically associated with the prefrontal cortex of the brain, a region also referred to as the frontal lobes (Lichter & Cummings, 2001; Miller & Cummings, 2006; Krasnegor et al., 1997; Stuss & Knight, 2002). While it is important not to think of executive functions as the "CEO of the brain" representing a unitary directive capacity, it is equally important not to think of the frontal lobes of the brain as the "CEO's office" representing a single unitary location where executive function processing occurs. Just as the nature of executive control varies depending on the specific executive function or combination of executive functions involved, only specific areas of the frontal lobes, not the entire frontal lobe region, are activated when a specific executive function capacity is engaged (Lichter & Cummings, 2001; Mesulam, 2002). Additionally, because executive functions are only directive capacities, they are not activated in isolation. Therefore, any time part of the frontal lobes is activated, this activation occurs in concert with the activation of other parts of the brain (Picton, et. al., 2002; Frackowiak et. al., 1997; Taylor, 1998).

An effective way to think about brain activation during the processing of any sensation/perception, emotion, cognition, or action is to think of a complex neural circuit that involves activation of various neural structures in many different parts of the brain. While some executive functions might overlap to some degree in terms of portions of the frontal lobes that are activated when they are in use, each executive capacity has its own unique pathway through parts of the frontal lobes, as well as through other parts of the brain. If some form of directive control is involved in the mental processing, then part of this neural circuit will be routed through one or more areas of the frontal lobes (Frakowiak et al., 1997; Lichter & Cummings, 2001; Mesulam, 2002; Miller & Cummings, 2006; Stuss & Knight, 2002).

Although each specific executive function has its own circuit path through the frontal lobes, different regions of the frontal lobes have been identified with different general types of pathways. These divisions follow along the three dimensional axes of the brain in space—left-right, top-bottom, and front-back (Diamond et al., 1985; Eliot, 1999; Berninger & Richards, 2003).

Frontal lobe activation while an executive function is engaged can vary in terms of left and right hemisphere involvement. For example, left hemisphere involvement is more prominent when executive functions are regulating positive emotional engagement while right hemisphere involvement is more prominent when executive functions are regulating negative emotional engagement (Mayberg, 2001; Springer & Deutsch, 2001). The anterior region of the frontal lobes is more involved with regulating thoughts, and the posterior region is more involved with regulating sensations and actions (Lichter & Cummings, 2001). The lower regions of the frontal lobes are more involved with regulation of emotions, and the upper regions are more involved with regulation of perception and cognition (Lichter & Cummings, 2001; Miller & Cummings, 2006).

In the past few decades, a large number of research studies have explored the various roles of frontal lobe functions in mental processing and behavior (Bar-On, Tranel, Denburg, & Bechara, 2003; Bunge et al., 2001; Frakowiak et al., 1997; Johnson et al., 2002; Lichter & Cummings, 2001; Mesulam, 2002; Miller & Cummings, 2006; Posner & Raichle, 1994; Posner & Rothbart, 2007; Stuss & Knight, 2002). Table 4.2 provides a list of specific areas of the frontal lobes associated with various aspects of sensation/perception, emotion, cognition, and action (that is, the areas of the frontal lobes that are activated when specific types of processing are occurring). When discussing brain function associated with executive functions there are two important concepts to keep in mind: (1) the specific sub-areas of the frontal lobes activated during control processing depend on the specific executive functions being engaged, and (2) when a frontal lobe area representing executive function processing is activated, additional non-frontal lobe areas of the brain are also being activated. These key con-

Table 4.2   Probable Brain Structures Involved in the Use of
Executive Function Capacities

Executive Function Capacity	Implicated Brain Structures	References
Self-Activation	Reticular activating system, epithalamus, caudate nucleus, anterior cingulate, dorsolateral cortex	Balkin et al. (2002); Stuss et al. (2000); Lichter and Cummings (2001)
Self-Regulation		
Perceive	Prefrontal cortex, ventromedial prefrontal, paracingulate	Grafman (2002); Johnson et al., (2002); Picton, Alain, & McIntosh (2002)
Initiate	Orbitofrontal cortex, anterior cingulate; dorsolateral prefrontal cortex; superior medial	Baxter, Clark, Iqbal, & Ackermann (2001); Stuss et al. (2000); Ratey (2002); Lichter & Cummings (2001)
Focus/Select	Anterior cingulate; dorsolateral prefrontal cortex	Lichter & Cummings (2001)
Gauge	Anterior cingulate, dorsolateral prefrontal cortex	Bunge, Ochsner, Desmond, Glover, & Gabrieli (2001); Lichter & Cummings (2001)
Modulate	Cingulate gyrus, orbitofrontal cortex, basal ganglia	Vaitl et al. (2005); Mesulam (2002)
Interrupt/Stop	Orbital prefrontal cortex, anterior cingulate, amygdale; right inferior frontal gyrus	Howard (2001); Picton et al. (2007); Rolls (2002)
Flexible/Shift	Left inferior frontal gyrus; rostrodorsal prefrontal cortex, left parietal; orbitofrontal cortex, dorsolateral prefrontal cortex, anterior cingulate	Hirshorn & Thompson-Schill (2006); Nagahama et al. (2001); Nagahama et al. (2005); Picton, Alain, & McIntosh (2002); Rolls (2002); Stuss et al. (2002)
Inhibit	Middle and interior frontal gyrus, orbitofrontal cortex, caudate nucleus, basal ganglia, striatum; left superior frontal cortex	Baxter, Clark, Iqbal, & Ackermann (2001); Picton et al. (2007)
Sustain	Dorsolateral prefrontal cortex, orbitofrontal cortex, thalamus, anterior cingulate	Stuss et al. (2000); Lichter & Cummings (2001)
Hold	Dorsolateral prefrontal cortex, anterior cingulate gyrus, left frontal cortex, anterior insula, frontal gyrus, cerebellum, hippocampus	Goldman-Rakic & Leung (2002); Bunge et al. (2001); Salmon, Heindel, & Hamilton (2001)

Table 4.2 (continued)   Probable Brain Structures Involved in the Use of Executive Function Capacities

Executive Function Capacity	Implicated Brain Structures	References
Manipulate	Dorsolateral prefrontal cortex	Lichter & Cummings (2001)
Organize	Dorsolateral prefrontal cortex	Lichter & Cummings (2001)
Store	Left prefrontal cortex, basal ganglia	Lichter & Cummings (2001)
Retrieve	Hippocampus, dorsolateral prefrontal cortex, ventrolateral prefrontal cortex	Lichter & Cummings (2001); Petrides & Pandya (2002)
Foresight/Plan	Dorsolateral prefrontal cortex, orbitofrontal cortex, striatum, hippocampus, cerebellum	Diamond (2002); Dagher, Owen, Boecker, & Brooks (2001); Lichter & Cummings (2001)
Generate	Left inferior frontal gyrus, bilateral frontal cortex and superior parietal lobes; dorsolateral prefrontal cortex; anterior cingulate	Baldo, Shimamura, Delis, Kramer, & Kaplan (2001); Goel and Dolan (2004); Picton, Alain, & McIntosh (2002)
Associate	Left dorsolateral prefrontal cortex	Goel & Dolan (2004)
Balance	Cerebellar-frontal pathway, anterior cingulate	Lichter & Cummings (2001)
Time	Orbitofrontal cortex	Berlin, Rolls, & Kischka (2004); Lichter & Cummings (2001)
Pace	Basal ganglia, dorsolateral prefrontal cortex; anterior cingulate	Diamond (2002)
Execute	Dorsolateral prefrontal cortex, interior parietal, striatum,basal ganglia	Lichter & Cummings (2001)
Monitor	Dorsolateral prefrontal cortex, anterior cingulate; right lateral prefrontal cortex	Lichter & Cummings (2001); Picton, Alain, & McIntosh (2002); Picton et al. (2007); Stuss et al. (2000)
Correct	Dorsolateral prefrontal cortex, orbitofrontal cortex	Rolls (2002)
Self-Realization		
Self-Awareness	Posterior cingulate or paracingulate sulcus, anterior medial and ventromedial prefrontal cortex, parietal region, left and right basal temporal regions, left orbitofrontal cortex, frontal gyrus, limbic and insula regions	Morin (2004); Bar-on, Tranel, Denburg, & Bechara (2003); Berthoz et al. (2002); Johnson et al. (2002); Stuss et al. (2002)

Table 4.2 (continued)   Probable Brain Structures Involved in the Use of Executive Function Capacities

Executive Function Capacity	Implicated Brain Structures	References
Self-Determination	Orbitofrontal cortex, ventromedialprefrontal cortex	Vaitl et al. (2005)
Self-Generation	Medial frontal gyrus, posterior cingulate, angular gyrus, dorsolateral prefrontal cortex, anterior cingulate	Greene, Nystrom, Engell, Darley, & Cohen (2004); Greene, Sommerville, Nystrom, Darley, & Cohen (2001)
Trans-Generation	Prefrontal cortex, anterior cingulate, reticular and middle thalamic region, basal ganglia, dorsolateral prefrontal cortex	Cahn & Polich (2006); Newberg, Alavi, Blaine, Mozley, & D'Aquili (1997); Newberg et al. (2001); Newberg, D'Aquili, & Rause (2001); Vaitl et al. (2005)

Brain Structures/Systems for Broad Executive Functions	
Implicated Frontal Structures/Systems	Broad Executive Functions
Dorsolateral prefrontal circuit	The managing functions: holding, manipulating, planning, executing, organizing and shifting
Orbital prefrontal circuit	Regulation of emotions and behaviors: Initiating, timing, sustaining, modulating, and inhibiting
Anterior cingulate circuitry	Monitoring, gauging, inhibiting, and shifting

In identifying the probable brain structures for these executive functions, it is important to understand several points: First, the literature is only beginning to identify these locations as the understanding of what comprises executive skills is emerging. Secondly, there is some suggestion in the literature that the areas of involvement and arenas of activity may determine what part of the prefrontal cortex is activated. For example, while set-shifting for symbolic material may involve the dorsolateral prefrontal cortex, being able to shift behavioral set may activate the orbitofrontal cortex. These do not appear to be discrete brain-based behaviors. Most importantly, it is necessary to understand that many cortical and subcortical areas of the brain are involved in the employment of executive functions. The looping circuitry from the frontal cortex is the most common and direct pathway for this brain activity (Lichter & Cummings, 2001).

cepts are critical for a greater understanding of issues related to diagnosis and treatment of executive function problems as discussed later in this book.

Although we have a great deal of knowledge about the relationship between frontal lobe regions and executive control processes, we continue to have much to learn. In the theoretical model presented earlier, the distinctions made among many aspects of executive capacity push beyond the current knowledge of specific brain-behavior relationships researched to date. For example, the concept of *arenas of involvement* makes a clear distinction between self-regulation cueing capacities as they are utilized in intrapersonal, interpersonal, environment, and symbol system contexts. This theoretical distinction is based on empirical observations of the dissociable nature of self-regulation functions across the four arenas. Using the self-regulation of inhibition as a specific example, it is apparent that some persons who are unable to inhibit their impulses to engage in addicting behaviors (intrapersonal arena) do not have difficulty inhibiting certain aspects of mental processing and action in interpersonal situations (e.g., inhibiting the impulse to tell their boss exactly what they think of them), in environmental situations (e.g., they do not experience road rage), or when working with symbol systems (e.g., the experience no negative emotional reactions to reading, writing, doing math calculations, or using a computer). An important question for neuroscience research would be to understand the differences in neural circuit activation patterns in the frontal lobes and other areas of the brain responsible for producing this observable dissociation of self-regulation capacities across the four arenas. Does this dissociability represent four separate, highly distinct neural circuits passing through the frontal region? Or, does it start with one major circuit initially, which branches fourfold at some point within the frontal lobes?

Research in the neurosciences has clearly provided many important insights into the functioning of various brain structures and has provided the scientific basis for understanding many aspects of the relationship of the pre-frontal cortex to human behavior. There is much more to be learned however, in terms of the specific nature of the neural mechanisms that are involved when executive control is engaged, and there is little question that advances in neuroscience research will lead to modifications of theoretical conceptions and clinical practices. (For the most up-to-date summaries of research in this area, see websites such as www.neurotransmitter.net.)

CASE VIGNETTES REVISITED

The information offered in this chapter can be used to expand our understanding of the situations of the children in our six case vignettes. Although no attempt is made here to identify the specific regions of the frontal lobes that are being under or over-utilized in the case of each child, it should be apparent that each of these children is experiencing difficulties with some aspect of executive functions.

Justin

Justin is in the throes of that developmental stage in which the media has provided so much attention. However, unlike many of his peers, Justin is still waiting for that "explosion" of frontal lobe growth that will enable him to keep abreast of his peers in terms of planning, organization, and many other directive capacities that would make his life in junior high school much easier than it is now. The culturally imposed transition to an educational environment that demands greater self-regulation has not gone well for Justin, and the lack of adequate production in school is what has gotten the attention of his parents and teachers. Although it is apparent to his parents and teachers that Justin tries his best to comply with external demands, his good intentions often do not result in the kind of performance that is expected of him given his intellectual capacity. Justin is one of those children for whom there is no adequate diagnostic category to help educators or mental health professionals appreciate the nature of his difficulties.

Kevin

Kevin appears to be lagging behind his elementary school-age peers in the development of executive capacities that could help him to regulate his perceptions, feelings, thoughts, and actions in relation to others more effectively. It is possible, however, that these capacities are adequately developed relative to Kevin's age, though they are not being utilized properly due to a lack of specific education in the effective use of these capacities when dealing with others. For Kevin, compliance with external demands is only a problem when he is emotionally distraught, which unfortunately is a sizeable portion of most every day. If Kevin's problems persist, it is very likely that he will end up with a diagnosis of CD or ODD and he may meet the criteria under IDEA for an emotional disturbance.

Caroline

Caroline clearly represents the case of a child whose executive function capacities have been compromised by her symptoms of depression. Her subsequent diagnosis and treatment by a psychiatrist for depression was not surprising to her parents. What is still baffling her parents, however, is the lack of adequate development of a number of executive function capacities that would enable her to function more effectively when she is not feeling depressed, such as her failure to initiate homework and social engagements and difficulties in organizing her belongings or daily routine. While many of Caroline's executive difficulties can be viewed as a result of her depression (e.g., a sense of being "adrift," seeming to be in a fog), some of them are likely due to other factors, such as slow development or underutilization of existing capacities.

Brett

Brett, with his difficulties in perceiving his environment, inhibiting responses, and sustaining attention, certainly displays many characteristics that are typically associated with the diagnosis of AD/HD. The only consistent thing about Brett's actions is his lack of compliance with external demands. Brett's parents cannot recall the last time he heeded any command of theirs without multiple promptings or physical assistance. While there is likely to be a developmental progression relative to improvement in behavioral control, his current functioning is significantly below what would be expected for a 5-year-old. Without an effective plan for managing Brett's behavior, the likelihood of poor academic production in school is great.

Morgan

Morgan also is exhibiting many characteristics that are typically associated with AD/HD. The existence of significant learning disabilities in reading and written expression, however, is complicating the picture at this time. Morgan's parents are having a hard time figuring out whether the AD/HD-like behavior is simply the result of attempts to avoid reading and writing activities that Morgan perceives as too difficult, or whether her AD/HD symptoms are making it difficult for her to concentrate on and perform these academic tasks. Whatever the case, Morgan's development of many executive capacities appears to be lagging behind that of her same-grade peers. Although Morgan is generally quite good at responding to external demands for executive control, she is surprisingly deficient when these demands involve reading or writing activities, another reason why her parents suspect that she might be using these behaviors simply to avoid hard work that she prefers not to do despite her professed desire to succeed in these areas.

Alex

Alex represents a total enigma to his parents. How can an individual as talented as Alex choose to do nothing with his life? In Alex's case, his lag in the development of many executive functions is so obvious to all that it is a real source of embarrassment for his parents. They cannot help but view Alex's difficulties as an indictment of them and their parenting practices, and are still trying to figure out where they went wrong. At times, Alex's inability to "get his act together" even when he desires to do so, and the obvious pain and suffering that he endures as a result, leave no doubt in their minds that something is wrong here. But at other times, the extreme disparity between what Alex can do "when the spirit moves him" as opposed to what he does when they make a request of him leaves them wondering if Alex is not just a big-time con artist in the making. Without some form of structured intervention, it is hard to know where Alex's frontal lobes are going to lead him. Alex's parents fear that it might not be a good place, though they have no idea how to help steer him in a different and positive direction.

CONCLUSION

In this chapter, we have reviewed various issues related to executive function, including the importance of understanding the developmental progression. The six vignettes reflect common cases seen in schools, and they highlight the unique developmental and diagnostic considerations that can have an impact on assessment and intervention. Clinicians interested in helping children with executive function difficulties and their parents should realize the importance of the concept and the developmental progression of executive functions. With a sound understanding of the possible nature of specific executive difficulties experienced by children, such as those in these cases, clinicians will be better able to offer a conceptualization that will help guide intervention plans to produce positive outcomes.

Part 2

ASSESSMENT AND INTERVENTION

5

Assessment of Executive Function Capacities
Methods, Techniques, and Interpretation

THE STATE OF THE ART IN ASSESSMENT
OF EXECUTIVE FUNCTIONS

Although the assessment of executive functions is not yet a standard practice for many psychologists who evaluate children, the likelihood that this will change in the near future is great. Michael Posner has devoted much of his career as a neuroscientist to understanding the specific workings of the human frontal lobes (Posner & Cohen, 1984; Posner & Petersen, 1990; Posner & Raichle, 1994; Posner & Rothbart, 1991, 1998, 2000). Over the years, Posner has chosen to use the terms *attention* and *self-regulation* as the overarching concepts in his studies of frontal lobe functions. Most recently, Posner and Rothbart (2007) describe the mental capacities he refers to as attention in the following way:

> Everywhere in cognitive neuroscience, specific brain networks seem to underlie performance. However, some of those networks have the important property of being able to modify the activity in other networks. For example, much in this volume rests on discoveries made in cognition and cognitive neuroscience under the topic of attention. From a psychological view, attention includes changes from sleepiness to high alertness, from focused orienting to a single object to unfocused awareness of the general scene, from responsiveness to external events to responses driven by the achievement of a particular goal. . . . attention also involves regulation of the activity of

other networks, thus improving the prospects of acquiring an unlimited number of skills. Attentional networks
interact with other brain systems to establish priorities in
perception and action. This ability to regulate brain function makes attention relevant to all domains of learning
. . . . attention serves as a different kind of formal discipline that can influence the efficiency of operations of a
wide range of cognitive and emotional networks. (p. 16)

Based on information presented in previous chapters, readers may have noticed that Posner's remarks are describing a
broader set of neural mental mechanisms than those typically
associated with the narrow term *attention*. The mental capacities that he describes are in fact what we have been referring to
as *executive functions*. Posner's comments serve to underscore
the importance and relevance of executive function assessment in any attempt to gain a comprehensive understanding
of the mental capacities of a child.

Although not yet fully part of mainstream practice,
executive function assessments have been developed and
used for many decades. These measures have traditionally
been applied in clinical neuropsychology settings, most frequently with adult clients. In recent decades, a number of
well-standardized assessments of executive function for use
with children have been developed. A major obstacle to the
effective assessment of executive function capacities is the
fact that standard practices have focused almost exclusively
on the role of executive functions in cueing and directing
perception, cognition, and action only within the symbol
system arena. Traditional measures of executive functions,
such as the Wisconsin Card Sorting Test (WCST; Heaton et al.,
1993), the Rey Complex Figure (RCF; Meyers & Meyers, 1995),
the NEPSY (Korkman, Kirk, & Kemp, 1998, 2007), the Delis-
Kaplan Executive Functions Scale (D-KEFS; Delis, Kaplan,
& Kramer, 2001), the Behavioral Assessment of Dysexecutive Syndrome in Children (BADS-C; Wilson et al., 1996) all
fit into this restricted category. Although each of these has
merit and embodies a unique approach to assessing specific
executive capacities, we must recognize that they are limited
to evaluation within the context of the symbol system arena.
In addition, the specific formats and contents chosen as the
vehicles for assessment are relatively narrow in scope. As a
result, these tests often do not address the application of executive capacities directly to academic skill development. The

bias toward engagement within the symbol system arena is understandable as assessment in this arena fits the direct formal methods of individually administered, standardized, norm-referenced measures that dominate assessment practices in clinics and schools. While understandable, this bias greatly restricts the scope of executive function assessment and consequently limits the clinical utility of the assessment process.

The expectation that symbol system executive function measures are appropriate for effective identification of executive function strengths and weaknesses in all situations has produced somewhat misleading findings in the research literature. Although research has consistently shown abnormal patterns of frontal lobe neural activation in conduct disordered children (Avila, Cuenca, Felix, & Pacet, 2004; Baving, Laucht, & Schmidt, 2000; Blake & Grafman, 2004; Clark, Prior, & Kinsella, 2000; Demekis, 2003; Oosterlaan, Scheres, & Sergeant, 2005), psychometrically oriented research studies have failed to consistently identify specific test performance deficits (Demekis, 2003; Oosterlaan, Scheres, & Sergeant, 2005; Avila, Cuenca, Felix, & Pacet, 2004). The reason for the lack of consistent findings in these studies is that they have used symbol system assessments to identify executive function deficits in children and adults whose primary executive function problems were not manifested necessarily in their engagement with symbol systems, but rather in their functioning in the interpersonal and intrapersonal arenas. Consistent with the theoretical model presented in Chapter 3, there is no reason to expect that all individuals with self-regulation executive difficulties in the interpersonal arena will also manifest such difficulties in the intrapersonal, symbol system, or the environment arenas. A lack of such expectancy, however, does not preclude the possibility that a person might exhibit executive function difficulties in one or more of the other three arenas along with interpersonal arena deficits. In fact, some of the subjects in these research studies exhibited deficits in the symbol system arena along with the initially observed intrapersonal deficits that were associated with the identification of their conduct disorder (Avila, Cuenca, Felix, & Pacet, 2004).

In addition to their narrow focus, symbol system measures of executive function must be used with great caution to avoid overgeneralization of assessment results. As discussed earlier, we must heed Denckla's (1996) warning not to turn executive functions into a neuropsychological version of thinking of executive capacity as a unitary trait. Because the concept of executive functions embodies a wide array of processes that are brought into play in various combinations to direct mental processes across multiple arenas of involvement, it is not possible to construct a single measure that will provide an accurate estimate of all of a person's executive function capacities. Even a large multi-subtest battery will not be able to capture all of the facets of executive control that might need to be considered during an assessment. Likewise, combining the scores from the multiple subtests of a large battery into a single *executive function composite* score frames a narrow view of executive capacity, similar to that of *g*. When formal direct measures of executive functions are viewed for what they are (i.e., specific measures of self-regulation executive functions within the symbol system arena), their validity and utility is enhanced because clinicians have a clear appreciation of what such tests can, and cannot, tell us about a child's executive control capacities. When these measures are believed to assess more than specific self-regulation capacities (i.e., generalized indicators of the capacity to use executive functions across all arenas of involvement), their validity and utility are greatly reduced because clinicians are engaged in obscuring, rather than clarifying, the nature of the child's executive function capacities and how they are, or are not, used in day-to-day functioning.

A comprehensive framework that goes beyond the narrow focus of direct formal measures and addresses the multifaceted perspective that is needed to effectively assess a child's use, or disuse, of executive function capacities will be discussed throughout the remainder of this chapter. As discussed in Chapter 4, executive function difficulties are associated with most, if not all, mental health disorders and many learning difficulties. Although executive function difficulties are quite ubiquitous, this chapter is not intended to present a comprehensive model of psychological assessment and diagnosis of all the childhood disorders in which executive function difficulties play a role. Rather, we will focus on how to identify the specific nature of the executive function difficulties a particular child might be experiencing, regardless of whether or not a specific diagnosis applies.

ESTABLISHING A GENERAL FRAMEWORK
FOR ASSESSING EXECUTIVE FUNCTIONS

The general philosophy guiding the discussion of assessment in this book is that the purpose of assessment is not to determine whether a diagnostic label of executive dysfunction should be assigned to a child. Rather, assessment should clearly identify problems and concerns, specify existing strengths and weaknesses, and lead to specific interventions that draw on strengths while addressing specific problems and concerns. To achieve this goal, each assessment is structured to answer the following four questions from the perspective of executive function capacities:

1. What executive functions does the child use effectively (What are the EF strengths)?
2. What executive functions does the child have difficulty using (What are the EF weaknesses and/or challenges)?
3. What needs to be done to help the child overcome the executive function difficulties that contribute to the problems and concerns that led to the referral?
4. Who can do what needs to be done in terms of executive function interventions to help the child overcome the problems and concerns?

Discussing assessment of executive functions in this manner is consistent with the previously offered theoretical perspective. In Chapter 3, the purpose for the elaboration of 23 distinct self-regulation executive functions was to define self-regulation in enough detail to enable the development of educational plans that can help children obtain greater access to these important self-regulation capacities.

Demonstration of executive function capacities can vary greatly depending not only on the specific capacities required, but also on arenas of involvement, domains of functioning, and the status of additional contextual factors. Table 5.1 shows all of the specific dimensions that an assessment of executive functions could address. Because of the multiple factors that can contribute to variability in the demonstration of executive functions, a multidimensional, multi-method approach is necessary to accurately characterize how a child is currently using, or not using, executive function capacities. In all cases, the assessment methods employed should attempt to determine the effectiveness of executive functions for the

Table 5.1   Executive Function Assessment Dimensions

Executive Function Levels and Capacities	
Self-Activation • Perceive • Focus/select • Initiate • Gauge • Modulate • Inhibit • Sustain • Interrupt/stop • Flexible/shift • Hold • Manipulate • Organize • Foresee/plan • Generate • Associate • Balance • Store • Retrieve • Pace • Time • Monitor • Execute • Correct	*Self-Realization* • Self-awareness • Self-analysis *Self-Determination* • Goal generation • Long-term foresight and planning *Self-Generation* *Trans-Self Integration*
Arenas of Involvement	
Intrapersonal • Executive control in relation to self *Interpersonal* • Executive control in relation to others	*Environment* • Executive control in relation to one's surroundings *Symbol System* • Executive control in relation to culturally determined modes of communication
Domains of Functioning	
Perception • Executive control of modes of input including perception of external (sensory) and internal (representational) stimuli	*Cognition* • Executive control of thoughts and thought processes

Table 5.1 (continued)   Executive Function Assessment Dimensions

Domains of Functioning	
Emotion • Executive control of feelings and emotional processes	*Action* • Executive control of modes of output including behavior in the external world and storage and retrieval of internal representations

Contextual Factors	
Mental Stance • Consciously directed vs. nonconsciously convected *Locus of Intention* • Internally commanded vs. externally demanded *Maturation* • Chronological age and degree of neural development *Biological Constraints* • Medical conditions ranging from common allergies to low incidence conditions such as colossal agenesis *Generalization* • Setting specific vs. setting nonspecific	*Energy* • Executive control stamina fluctuations *Temporality* • Temporal nature of any observed stamina fluctuations *Multi-Cueing Capacity* • Simultaneous vs. sequential ordering of multiple EF capacities, multitasking, and EF "syntax" *Task Constraints* • Constraints on how information is processed when performing a task

Information Processing Capacities	
Basic Processing • Attention • Phonological processing • Orthographic processing • Oral-motor processing • Visual-motor processing • Grapho-motor processing • Sequencing • Estimating • Fluency • Processing speed	*Abilities* • Language • Visuospatial • Reasoning • Quantification • Idea generation • Gross and fine motor *Additional Capacities* • Building lexicons • Accessing lexicons • Creating strategies • Accessing strategies

Table 5.1 (continued) Executive Function Assessment Dimensions

Time Frames of Reference (Memory Capacities)	
Immediate • Initial registration *Extended Immediate* • Active working memory	*Remote and Recent Past* • Retrieval from long-term store (access of lexicons)

Areas of Academic Skill	
Reading • Sight word reading • Phonics and decoding skills • Reading rate • Comprehension • Building a vocabulary lexicon • Building genre knowledge lexicons *Written Expression* • Text formation and transcription • Text production automaticity • Spelling/text generation • Text editing and revising • Building a spelling/grammar lexicon • Building a punctuation/capitalization • Lexicon • Building genre writing style lexicons	*Mathematics* • Computation skills • Basic fact automaticity • Problem solving • Applications • Building mathematics concepts lexicons • Building procedural knowledge lexicons • Building mathematics fact lexicons

cueing and directing of perceiving, feeling, thinking, and act-ing in relation to self (intrapersonal), others (interpersonal), the world (environmental), and the cultural tools of communi-cation (symbol system). In many cases, it will be necessary to elaborate on the role of contextual factors such as:

• The extent to which executive capacities are, or are not, being engaged consciously to regulate functioning (Men-tal Stance)
• Whether engagement varies depending on self-motivated cueing (Internally Commanded Locus of Intention) or cueing by others or by external circumstances (Exter-nally Demanded Locus of Intention)

- The age of the child and the expected degree of development of neural processes that support the use of executive control capacities (Maturity)
- Whether executive control problems are situation specific or occur across a wide range of settings (Generalization of Control)
- Possible patterns of fluctuation in executive control stamina (Energy)
- Whether such fluctuations are cyclical and/or time-related (Temporality)
- The extent to which the child can utilize more than one executive capacity at one time (Multi-Cueing Capacity).

In some cases where the integrity of one or more underlying mental processes is in question and/or academic achievement is being affected, assessment methods also will need to address the child's facility with specific information processing capacities (i.e., subdomains such as attention, reasoning, language, visuospatial). These information processing components are directed by executive functions during task performance and they can have an impact on specific academic skills and achievement. The blueprint for the specific areas that need to be considered when attempting to answer the four questions of the assessment process includes the seven dimensions provided in Table 5.1.

Different approaches and methods can be applied during the assessment of executive function processes. Assessment of executive functions can be engaged using direct or indirect approaches, using either formal or informal methods. Direct assessment methods involve collection of information through direct interaction with, or observation of, the child or his or her work products. Indirect assessment methods involve the collection of information using methods that do not involve direct contact with the child, such as self-report measures, or involve sources other than the child, such as parents, teachers, and school records. Formal assessment methods involve the use of norm-referenced or criterion-referenced measures that compare the child's performance or ratings of the child's behavior to predetermined standards, whereas informal assessment methods involve the use of interviews, records reviews, and observation and interpretation methods that do not employ predetermined comparison standards. Table 5.2 provides a summary of these four assessment methods.

Table 5.2 Approaches and Methods for the Assessment of Executive Functions

Assessment Approach	Assessment Method	
	Informal	Formal
Indirect	Interviews of parents and teachers Review of school records Process-oriented interpretation of parent and teacher ratings and self-reports	Parent behavior ratings Teacher behavior ratings Self-report ratings
Direct	Child interview Systematic and nonsystematic behavioral observations Process-oriented Interpretation of Standardized test Administration and Classroom work samples	Individually administered standardized tests

Indirect Informal Methods

Indirect informal methods offer the greatest degree of flexibility in assessment as they are able to address the full multifaceted constellation of executive function components and their interactions as described in this book. The primary method in this category involves the use of interview techniques with informants other than the child. Typically, these sources are the child's parents and teachers, although other persons who are very familiar with the child's behavior could be included as sources of information. In terms of content coverage, these techniques are limited only by the clinician's knowledge of executive functions and skill in conducting interviews. A second type of indirect informal method is records review. The clinician can peruse information gathered to document the child's educational and social history to identify situations where executive function difficulties would be highly probable based on descriptions of the child's behavior and related outcomes.

Effective indirect informal assessment is a skill that requires time and practice along with sufficient breadth and depth of knowledge of executive functions. In addition, although parents and teachers generally are considered to be reliable sources of information about a child's functioning, the results of a single interview with a single informant can produce a skewed accounting of the child's capacities. Clinicians who use this technique should collect information from as many informants as possible, preferably in the context of more than a single interview session. Clinicians are not advised to use this technique as the sole source of information about a child's executive function capacities. Information gathered from additional sources provides valuable and necessary perspective for characterizing as accurately as possible what a child can and cannot do in the way of executive function capacities.

Conducting Informal Interviews with Parents and Teachers

Clinicians are advised to start the assessment process by interviewing the child's parents or caregivers. This is critical in that it establishes the necessary rapport with the persons most directly involved with the child and most likely to be capable of providing a clear picture of the child's executive function use across multiple settings. Parents typically have the greatest store of historical information. Many parents have keen powers of observation in matters involving their children. Their personal investments of love, caring, and time put many parents in a position of having the greatest amount of information about the child. As the persons responsible for the well-being of the child and with the special connection that can be formed only between parent and child, parents can play a unique and central role in helping a clinician understand how a child perceives the world, what they feel and think about, and how they express themselves in their daily actions.

We recommend that the interview process start with one or more open-ended questions that enable the parents to selectively focus on issues and concerns that are foremost in their minds. This also enables the clinician to listen to the parents to obtain a sense of their general language usage and communication styles, the contexts that shape their opinions and understanding of their child, and the ways in which they selectively talk about the child's mental processes, feelings, and behavior across the various arenas of involvement.

During this open-ended interview, the clinician should keep notes about specific executive function capacities, domains of functioning, arenas of involvement, information processing capacities, academic skills, and contextual factors referenced in the parents' comments. At this stage, questions should focus on clarifying the parents' statements to best understand the information they offer in the context of executive capacity involvement. Depending on the skill of the interviewer and the communication abilities of the parents, the open-ended interview process typically lasts from 15 minutes to an hour. Although some parents might require more than an hour to offer their perspective, interviewers need to use their clinical judgment to ensure that the parents remain on topic. This includes redirecting discussion when an inordinate amount of time is being spent on minute details or when disagreements of perspective arise between parents, and moving through the interview process in a timely and meaningful way.

It is possible for an experienced interviewer to conduct the entire interview in the open-ended format, utilizing follow-up questions to ensure adequate coverage of the various executive function dimensions and contextual factors. Clinicians who are less experienced might not have the needed expertise to conduct an effective unstructured interview process, and they may obtain better information through a process that is more structured. Additionally, although parents and caregivers have a wealth of information about the child available to them and a willingness to share that information in order to help their child, not all parents are skilled at communicating in a manner that provides the most relevant information clearly and succinctly. Many parents will require some degree of structure provided by the clinician in order to get to the information that would be of greatest value in the assessment process.

For clinicians needing assistance with selecting questions during the more structured stage of the interview, the Executive Function Structured Interview Form (EFSI) located on the CD that accompanies this book can be printed and used as an aid in completing the interview process. The EFSI lists each of the executive function capacities by level from self-activation through self-realization including all 23 of the self-regulation functions. Space is provided on the form to note engagement based on domains of functioning and arenas of involvement. The interviewer can use this form to guide additional questioning to ensure that all relevant areas are addressed during the interview.

The informal interview of parents or caregivers should be followed by a similar interview of the child's teachers and/or other school staff who work closely with the child. Interviews with school staff should be conducted in a manner similar to that used with the child's parents. Upon completion of the interview process, the clinician is likely to have a very good understanding of the areas where additional information will need to be gathered using other methods in order to complete the assessment process.

Indirect Formal Methods

Indirect formal assessment does not involve direct interaction with the child, but rather includes methods such as parent and teacher ratings scales and child self-report measures. Information from these sources is collected using standardized measures and translated into quantitative scores. Scores obtained from specific types of raters (e.g., parents, teachers, child) are then compared to the scores obtained from a sample of raters with similar relationships to the children whom they rated. In some situations, separate norms are offered depending on the sex of the child (i.e., separate norms for boys and girls) and/or the sex of the parent doing the rating (i.e., separate norms for mother and father ratings). Presently, indirect formal methods specifically designed to rate the use of executive function capacities are limited to the parent and teacher rating scales and the child self-report scale of the Behavior Rating Inventory of Executive Functions series (BRIEF, Gioia, et al., 1996; BRIEF-Preschool Version, Gioia, et al., 1996; BRIEF-Self-Report Version, Guy, Isquith, & Gioia, 1996). These scales provide scores that reflect parent and teacher report and child self-report judgments of the frequency of a child's ineffective use of executive capacities based on personal recollections of behavior during the most recent six-month period.

The BRIEF offers norm-referenced documentation of parent, teacher, and self-appraisals of executive function deficits as they manifest within a number of subdomains derived primarily from factor analysis of item response data without the use of a specific, overarching theoretical model to guide the process of subdomain identification. This approach to scale development produced measures that address many important aspects of executive control, but do so in a very unsystematic manner, at least from the perspective of the model presented in this book. All of the BRIEF forms are structured on fewer than the 23 self-regulation functions posited in the model presented in this book. In addition, the descriptive language of each item is relatively general making it very difficult to identify a single, specific executive function cue likely to be involved in directing the described behavior. As a result, behaviors representing many of the 23 distinct self-regulation capacities are lumped together within a single subdomain or spread across several subdomains. In some cases, the name of the subdomain scale obscures the nature of the specific executive functions that the items actually are assessing. For example, the items of the subdomain named Working Memory represent behaviors that could be associated not just with the Hold and Manipulate cues that are necessary for engaging working memory, but also with no less than eight additional self-regulation capacities, including Perceive, Focus/Select, Modulate, Sustain, Organize, Execute, Monitor, and Correct.

Despite the limitations of the BRIEF inventories, they can be an important clinical tool for gathering objective, norm-referenced evidence of executive function difficulties. This type of evidence can be crucial to obtaining educational support in many situations where assistance is needed in a school setting. The McCloskey Executive Functions Scales (MEFS, 2007), a set of norm-referenced rating scales currently in development will enable clinicians to more effectively identify specific executive function strengths and weaknesses within the context of the comprehensive model of executive functions introduced earlier in Chapter 3.

Direct Formal Methods

Direct formal methods are perhaps the most familiar to psychologists and educators working in the schools as they represent all forms of standardized, individually administered tests. As such, direct formal assessments involve direct interaction with the child following a pre-established set of procedures that dictate most aspects of the interaction with the child. A primary benefit of the use of direct formal measures is that they are norm-referenced. These tests involve collection of information through standardized procedures, that is, all children assessed with these methods receive the same instructions for task performance and their work products are judged using the same set of standards for performance. The results of a child's performance are translated into quantitative scores, and the child's obtained scores are compared to the performance of a sample of peers of similar age who were assessed during the development of the test. Norm-referenced tests, therefore, enable clinicians to compare a child's performance of tasks requiring the use of executive function capacities to the performance of a reference sample of same-age peers.

The growing awareness of executive functions and their role in learning and behavior has led to the publication of several executive function assessments in the last decade (e.g.,

NEPSY, 1997; 2007; D-KEFS, 2001; BADS-C, 2003) intended for use with school-age populations. This new generation of measures joined a core of well-established tests (e.g., WCST, 1993; RCFT, 1995) that have traditionally been used by neuropsychologists in the evaluation of patients suffering brain damage or strokes. The fact that formal direct measures of executive function were used almost exclusively by neuropsychologists in previous decades does not mean that only neuropsychologists are qualified to use such measures to accurately characterize children's executive function capacities. In fact, it is important that all psychologists who assess children on a regular basis, especially school psychologists, understand the central role that executive functions play in children's learning and production and become adept at assessing how various executive functions are shaping a child's learning and production. In developing the competencies needed to effectively characterize a child's executive capacities as they are applied in school and at home, however, it is important for all clinicians, regardless of specific backgrounds, to appreciate the constraints inherent in the use of direct formal measures of executive functions.

As noted earlier in this chapter, formal direct assessments of executive functions using individually administered norm-referenced tests are limited in scope and usefulness because of their exclusive reliance on symbol system content to assess various executive function capacities. This includes self-regulation in executive control related to various aspects of task completion, explicitly those involving perception, cognition, and action. Although limited in their applicability for understanding a child's executive capacities in additional arenas of involvement, these tests are still very effective in helping to understand a child's executive function capacities when directing perception, cognition, and action in the symbol system arena. Such information plays a vital role in assessment since learning how to effectively use the symbol systems of our culture to learn and achieve is the major daily focus of schooling activities. These tests, therefore, are most appropriately utilized in school settings to help understand a child's learning and academic production, as long as their limitations are acknowledged and interpretation remains focused on those purposes for which the test results can be validly interpreted and applied. In acknowledging the limitations of direct formal measures, clinicians will need to supplement the use of these instruments when concerns related to executive capacities extend into the intrapersonal, interpersonal, and environment arenas, or the levels above and below self-regulation.

Use of norm-referenced tests can greatly enhance the clinician's understanding of how a child uses executive functions to direct the use of the various information processing capacities and academic skills that are listed in Table 5.1. Direct formal measures also provide the basis for the application of informal direct assessment procedures, as described later in this chapter.

WHAT DO FORMAL TESTS OF EXECUTIVE FUNCTION TEST?

When reviewing the content of formal tests of executive functions, it becomes clear that these measures employ a wide array of tasks for the purpose of assessing executive capacities. Given the extremely heterogeneous nature of the content of these tests, a clinician might get the impression that assessment of executive functions is structured in a manner similar to that of batteries of general intelligence. That is, although the specific subtests of each battery might vary substantially, a composite score obtained from each of these tests would be roughly equivalent depending on the extent to which each of the tests is an adequate measure of executive functions in general. It should be apparent that this logic suggests the existence of a general *ef* factor, similar to that of the concept of the *g* factor favored by general intelligence theorists. Recall that several times through this book we have cautioned readers against turning executive functions into the neuropsychological equivalent of the intelligence theorists' *g*. Test authors have made a concerted effort to counter the appearance and use of a general *ef* factor primarily by avoiding the development of composite score tables.

Even with the consensus disavowal of a general *ef* factor, clinicians are still faced with the fact that each of these tests includes one or more tasks that vary greatly in terms of their general format, specific content, and task complexity. If these tasks are not simply intended to be variations on a major theme with their only purpose being that of contributing to a general, global measure of executive capacity, what then, is the purpose of having so many different types of tasks for assessing executive function capacity? The logical conclusion would be that the tasks assess various specific, unique dimensions of executive control within a broad, multidimensional conception of executive functions. Unfortunately, this logical conclusion is not supported by the facts. Although most test manuals acknowledge the complex nature of executive functions and provide a basic rationale for the multiple measures of executive functions offered in the test battery, none of them espouses an overarching model of executive capacities on which the selection and inclusion of specific tasks is based. Additionally, these tests do not clearly specify the nature of the relationship of each of the executive function tasks to academic learning and production. This lack of an overarching structure based on a common theoretical model tied to specific assessment needs creates significant challenges for clinicians who are attempting to adequately assess the executive function capacities of school age children. A clinician presented with a difficult case might ask themselves, "Should I use the tasks of the NEPSY Attention/Executive Functions Domain or selected tasks from the D-KEFS?" "Will these two sets of measures provide me with the same results leading to the same conclusions?" "Would it be better to use the D-KEFS Tower Test in this situation or the NEPSY Tower Subtest?" "Does the D-KEFS Sorting Test measure the same executive functions as the Wisconsin Card Sorting Test?" "Does it matter whether or not these tests measure the same or different executive functions?" These are certainly legitimate questions that merit thoughtful consideration. Traditional measures of executive function, however, provide little in the way of answers for those who pose such questions.

We believe that these questions are important and critical to the competent selection and interpretation of tests of executive function. Table 5.3 provides an example of the type of analyses that we believe necessary in order to organize clinical thinking about the assessment of executive functions. This table lists a number of factors that should be considered when attempting to determine the clinical utility of an executive function measure. Consideration of these factors is part of a theoretically based rational analysis, referred to here as a Process-Oriented Rational Task Analysis, in an attempt to identify specific self-regulation executive function cues that are most likely to be utilized in the successful performance of the task. The theoretical basis for the rational analyses of tasks derives from the operational definitions of the 23 self-

Table 5.3 (continued)   Process-Oriented Rational Task Analyses of
Various Cognitive Measures

Task	D-KEFS Card Sorting Free Sorting Condition	Wisconsin Card Sorting
Description/ Directions	The child is asked to sort six multi-concept cards into two groups of three cards in as many different ways as possible No feedback about the accuracy of sorts is provided	The child views four response cards and is shown an individual item card and asked to match the item card to one of the response cards The child is not told how the cards are supposed to match, but is given feedback about the accuracy of the match they choose for each item Correct match concepts shift but the child is not told this
Time constraints	240 seconds of cumulative sorting time	None
Time frames of reference	Immediate Extended immediate (working memory)	Immediate Extended immediate (working memory)
Materials	Two sets of six picture cards	Four response choice cards Set of 64 item trial cards
Input format	Visual and kinesthetic	Visual and kinesthetic
Information processing demands	Attention processing Orthographic processing Language ability Visuospatial ability Reasoning ability	Attention processing Visuospatial ability Language ability (optional) Reasoning ability
Output format	Manual motor	Manual motor
Task-specific executive function demands	Perceive Gauge Flexible/shift Hold Manipulate Generate/associate	Gauge Inhibit Flexible/shift Hold Manipulate Generate/associate Correct
Contextual constraints on executive functioning	240 seconds of cumulative sorting time	No time limits imposed on responding No directions are provided for how to arrive at a correct response

Table 5.3 (continued) Process-Oriented Rational Task Analyses of Various Cognitive Measures

Task	WISC III WAIS IV Vocabulary	KAII Definition
Description/Directions	Child explains the meaning of words presented by the examiner	Child provides the word that fits a set of clues; one clue is a phrase related to the meaning of the word, the other clue is a visual that shows some of the letters of the word in their proper location
Time frames of reference	Immediate Long-term	Immediate Long-term
Materials	None	Each item printed on an individual easel page
Input format	Auditory verbal	Visual verbal and auditory verbal
Information processing demands	Language ability Accessing lexicons	Orthographic processing Sequencing Language ability Accessing lexicons
Output format	Oral-motor verbal	Oral-motor verbal
Task-specific executive function demands	Retrieve	Retrieve
Contextual constraints on executive functioning	No time limit imposed on responses Unrestrained free recall with prompting for additional input	30-second response time limit per item Constrained, specifically directed recall with no prompting for additional input

regulation executive functions specified in the McCloskey Model of Executive Functions presented in Chapter 3.

Table 5.3 summarizes the results of the process-oriented rational analyses. From these analyses, it can be seen that the D-KEFS Tower Test and the NEPSY Tower Subtest use similar materials, similar formats for administration of the task, and similar content for task items. All of these common factors lead to the likely use of a common set of self-regulation executive function cues during task performance. It is important to note, however, that critical differences in the contextual constraints of these two similar tasks result in some important differences in additional executive function cues needed for task completion and task performance. These differences can lead to significant differences in levels of performance by the same person on these two seemingly similar tasks, an outcome that has been observed in clinical assessments.

PRINCIPLES OF FORMAL EXECUTIVE FUNCTION ASSESSMENT

The results of the process-oriented rational task analyses of the executive function demands of various measures reported in Table 5.3 illustrate four important principles necessary for understanding how to interpret the role of self-regulation executive functions in the performance of any type of direct formal assessment task.

1. *All tasks identified as measures of executive function also measure other information processing capacities.* Self-regulation executive functions cannot be assessed "in a vacuum." Because these executive functions are directive processes that guide the use of other information processing capacities and academic skills, executive functions can only be assessed in tandem with these capacities and skills. Specific measures of executive functions always involve the assessment, to some degree, of one or more information processing capacities (and in some cases, academic skills) in addition to the executive functions the test is intended to assess. In order to make valid inferences about the role of executive functions in regulating perception, thought, and action, the contributions to task performance by these information processing capacities and academic skills need to be minimized, controlled for, or otherwise acknowledged in some way when interpreting test results.

2. *All tasks identified as measures of information processing capacity (i.e., process or ability measures) and/or academic skills also measure executive functions.* Just as executive capacities cannot be assessed without directing one or more other aspects of mental processing, conscious mental processing of the type assessed by direct formal measures cannot occur without some degree of executive control to guide perception, thought, and action. Many well-developed standardized tests that were not intended as direct measures of executive

functions, however, minimize the need for self-directed executive control by providing explicit directions for how to perceive, think about, and respond to test items. Recall our example of test directions that minimize executive control demands presented in Chapter 2. With such directions in place, the need for the child to engage directive cues is minimized, often to the point where even a child with self-regulation deficits can perform well. Even the best set of task directions, however, cannot completely eliminate the need for the respondent to use some basic self-regulation cues in order to engage, process, and respond to test items. This fact is evident in the performance of some children who, due to severe executive deficits caused by focal brain damage, are unable to perform even the simplest of cognitive tasks not intended as measures of executive functions. Realizing the ubiquitous nature of executive function involvement in assessment tasks, clinicians are in a position to evaluate the extent to which the need for executive function involvement limits, or enhances, performance of tasks primarily intended to assess information processing capacities and/or academic skills.

3. *All tasks are measures of multiple executive functions; no measure assesses the use of only one self-regulation executive function capacity.* Performance of any assessment task, no matter how simple, requires the use of multiple executive functions engaged either simultaneously (in parallel) or in ordered sequences. Considering the nature of the 23 self-regulation functions, it is apparent that even the simplest of assessment tasks designed to assess information processing capacities, such as repeating digits or copying symbols, require the use of several executive control cues. Unless the directions of a test specifically direct the examiner to cue the child on every item, the Perceive cue will need to be used to ensure that test stimuli are adequately perceived. In the absence of near-continuous prompting, the child will need to use the Focus/Select cue, and likely the Sustain cue, to regulate attention capacities while engaged with a task. At the other end of the continuum, highly complex tests specifically designed to assess executive functions intentionally require a child to engage the use of multiple self-regulation capacities in order to succeed with the task. Realization of the multifaceted nature of

the self-regulation demands of assessment tasks is necessary in order to effectively interpret executive function involvement in task performance.

4. *The amount and nature of executive function involvement in an assessment task* will vary greatly depending on the format, content, and complexity of the task. Direct formal tests currently in use offer an array of tasks that, intentionally or unintentionally, assess the use of executive functions. It is important for clinicians to realize that the majority of these tasks are in no way equivalent. These tasks vary widely in terms of the content and formats used for assessment. For example, the NEPSY Tower Subtest requires the child to view a picture representing the final position of three colored balls on a three-peg stand. The child is provided with a three peg stand that has the three colored balls placed in positions that do not match the picture. The child must rearrange the balls on the pegs to match the arrangement in the picture, but constraints are placed on how the child can move the balls and how many moves can be made (e.g., "Make yours look like the picture in five moves."). In contrast to the NEPSY Tower Subtest, the Delis-Kaplan Color-Word Interference-Inhibition Subtest requires the child to view a page with the words representing the names of the colors red, green, and blue printed in rows across the page in random order. Each color name word is printed in colored ink, but the color of the ink does not match the color name word. For example, the color name word "red" is printed in blue ink or green ink, but never in red ink. The child is instructed to name, as quickly as possible, the color of the ink each word is printed in rather than read the word. It does not require complex analyses to realize that although both of these tasks are considered measures of executive function, they are very different in terms of task format, content, information processes utilized, level of complexity, and the number and type of self-regulation capacities required for successful performance.

Understanding these basic principles is necessary for developing a competent approach to selecting executive function assessment instruments and interpreting assessment results. From these principles and the analyses in Table 5.3 that illustrate them, it should be apparent that standard scores from individual measures of executive function may or may not be good indicators of some aspects of self-regulation executive control depending on the extent to which test performance is impacted by deficits in information processing capacities or academic skills also being measured by these tasks. That is, low scores on one or more individual subtests or tasks thought to assess executive functions do not necessarily confirm the presence of self-regulation deficits nor do they indicate that deficiencies in self-regulation will be observed in the daily performance of symbol system activities.

It should also be apparent from these principles and the results of the process-oriented task analyses that many tests designed to assess information processing capacities or academic skills also involve the assessment of self-regulation executive functions. With an adequate interpretive framework, it is possible to assess and interpret the contribution of executive functions to task performance on these tests as well. That is, low scores on tasks not specifically designed to assess executive functions might be strong indicators of the presence of self-regulation deficits and better indicators of when deficiencies in self-regulation are likely to be observed in the daily performance of symbol system activities.

INTERPRETATION OF FORMAL TESTS USING CASCADING PRODUCTION ANALYSIS

Two methods of test performance analysis referred to here as *Cascading Production Decrement Analysis* and *Cascading Production Increment Analysis* offer ways to expand interpretation of formal test performance beyond the overly narrow interpretation of single subtest scores in isolation or the overly general interpretation of composite scores formed by summing scores from multiple subtests. By looking at performance across more than one task at a time without aggregating scores, these techniques can lead to effective interpretation of the contribution of self-regulation executive functions to task performance either when using measures primarily intended to assess executive functions or when using measures primarily intended to assess other information processing capacities and/or academic skills.

The term *cascading production* refers to a stepwise change in the effectiveness of task performance that occurs as the result of alterations in task demands, as illustrated in Figure 5.1.

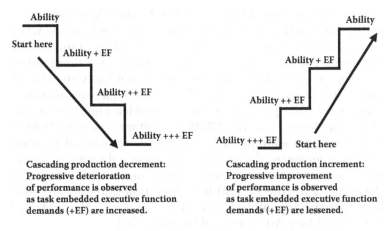

Cascading production decrement:
Progressive deterioration
of performance is observed
as task embedded executive function
demands (+EF) are increased.

Cascading production increment:
Progressive improvement
of performance is observed
as task embedded executive function
demands (+EF) are lessened.

Figure 5.1   Cascading Production Decrements and Increments.

Cascading production is most likely to emerge when alterations of task demands involve either an increase or decrease in the need for self-regulation for effective performance. When self-regulation demands are increased and performance decreases, a Cascading Production Decrement has occurred. When self-regulation demands are decreased and performance increases, a Cascading Production Increment has occurred.

Cascading Production Decrements

When the effectiveness of a child's performance decreases due to increases in the need for the use of self-regulation cues, this is referred to as a Cascading Production Decrement. Cascading Production Decrements are easy to orchestrate when using direct formal assessment methods. Many standardized executive function measures are purposefully designed to increase self-regulation demands across similarly structured, successive tasks, or subtasks. These task sequences intentionally provide the opportunity to observe at least one measurable stepwise decrement. The NEPSY Auditory Attention Subtest is an excellent example of a task that is structured to allow for the emergence of a Production Cascade Decrement resulting from an increase in self-regulation executive function demands. The NEPSY Auditory Attention Subtest is divided into two specific subtasks: Part A Auditory Attention and Part B Auditory Attention and Response Set.

When the effectiveness of a child's performance decreases due to increases in the need for the use of self-regulation cues, this is referred to as a Cascading Production Decrement. Cascading production decrements are easy to orchestrate when using direct formal assessment methods. Many standardized executive function measures are purposefully designed to increase self-regulation demands across similarly structured, successive tasks, or sub-tasks. These task sequences intentionally provide the opportunity to observe at least one measurable step-wise decrement. The NEPSY Auditory Attention Subtest is an excellent example of a task that is structured to allow for the emergence of a production cascade decrement resulting from an increase in self-regulation executive function demands. The NEPSY Auditory Attention Subtest is divided into two specific subtasks—Part A Auditory Attention, and Part B Auditory Attention and Response Set.

The NEPSY Auditory Attention and Response Set Part A involves the child listening to an audiotape of spoken words and every time the word RED is spoken on the audiotape, pointing to the red circle on an easel page that shows a red, blue, yellow, and black circle. The tape plays for approximately three minutes, during which time 180 words are presented. Part A requires the direction of focused, sustained attention to the audiotape, the direction of quick motor responses on auditory cue, and direction of response inhibition when other color words (yellow, black, blue) or command words (e.g., point, now) are spoken. Part B represents a substantial increase in executive demands. For this task, the child listens to an audiotape of spoken words and must follow three rules to guide the pointing to circles on the easel page. These three rules include: point to the YELLOW circle when you hear the word RED; point to the RED circle when you hear the word YELLOW; point to the BLUE circle when you hear the word BLUE. The use of three rules in Part B greatly increases the executive demands for multitasking with the inclusion of the Hold and Manipulate cues to direct the holding and manipulating of the multiple rules, directing the matching of the auditory stimulus with the rules, and directing motor movement toward the correct response choice.

In addition to tasks that build in conditions conducive to eliciting production decrements, stepwise decrements can be revealed across different independent tasks. This can be accomplished by comparing performance on a standardized measure of information processing capacities that minimizes self-regulation demands with performance on a task that measures similar capacities, but that also is designed to measure the use of executive functions to regulate the use of these capacities. A good example of this technique is the comparison of performance on matrix reasoning tasks selected from a traditional intelligence or cognitive assessment battery with performance on the WCST (more specifically, the WCST Percent of Conceptual Level Responses standard score).

For example, although specific self-regulation executive functions are required to complete each WISC IV Matrix Reasoning item, the directions provided by the examiner help to greatly reduce the need for a child to self-engage these executive functions. When a child performs relatively well with Matrix Reasoning (i.e., the obtained score is above the age-norm or equal to or better than scores obtained on measures that assess similar reasoning capacity but require less executive involvement), the assessment of executive control of reasoning can proceed forward with tasks such as the WCST and/or the D-KEFS Card Sorting task. In these situations, the contrast between a high Matrix Reasoning score and a significantly lower WCST Conceptual Level Responses score would constitute a cascading production decrement.

If the child performs relatively poorly with Matrix Reasoning (i.e., the obtained score is below the age-norm of 15 less than the scores obtained on measures that assess similar reasoning capacity but require less executive involvement), the assessment should use one of the other tasks involving reasoning to establish the baseline for reasoning capacity. In such a case, it could be reasonably hypothesized that the lower Matrix Reasoning subtest performance is the result of an increase in executive function demands and therefore could be considered the first step down in a production cascade decrement involving the self-regulation of reasoning with nonverbal material.

With careful selection of assessment tasks, cascading performance decrement analyses can be conducted to reveal the effects of altering self-regulation demands with tasks involving one or more of all of the information processing capacities and/or most of the academic skills listed in Table 5.1. Some of the tasks and task combinations particularly well-suited for eliciting cascading performance decrements and the results of analyses with these tasks are presented in Table 5.4.

When conducting cascading performance decrement analyses such as those illustrated in Table 5.4, we recommend, as a rule of thumb, looking for score decreases of a magnitude of at least one standard deviation or more (e.g., 3 scaled score points for a mean 10, standard deviation 3 metric; 15 standard

Table 5.4 Examples of Ability or Process Production Decrement Cascades

EF Decrement Involving Verbal Expression and Reasoning with Verbal Information

Ability Measures
  WISC-IV Similarities Scaled Score 14 (91st percentile)
  WISC-IV Comprehension Scaled Score 14 (91st percentile)
    Ability + Increased Executive Functions Measures
      D-KEFS 20 Questions Test Initial Abstraction Scaled Score 7 (16th percentile)
      D-KEFS 20 Questions Test Total Achievement Scaled Score 4 (2nd percentile)

EF Decrement Involving Verbal Fluency

Process Measure
  NEPSY Semantic Fluency Scale Score 13 (84th percentile)
    Process + Executive Function Measure
      NEPSY Phonemic Fluency

EF Decrement Involving Auditory Attention

Process Measure
  NEPSY Auditory Attention Scaled Score 12 (75th percentile)
    Process + Executive Function Measure
      NEPSY Auditory Response Set Scaled Score 8 (25th percentile)

EF Decrement Involving Retrieval of Verbal Information and Verbal Expression

Ability Measures
  K-SEALS Expressive Skills Standard Score 108 (70th percentile)
  WPPSI-III Receptive Vocabulary Scaled Score 11 (63rd percentile)
  NEPSY Verbal Fluency Scaled Score 10 (50th percentile)
  WPPSI-III Information Scaled Score 9 (37th percentile)
  WPPSI-III Picture Naming Scaled Score 9 (37th percentile)
    Ability + Executive Function Measures
      WPPSI-III Vocabulary Scaled Score 4 (2nd percentile)

EF Decrement Involving Auditory Attention/Auditory Processsing

Process Measure
  NEPSY Comprehension of Instructions Scaled Score 12 (75th percentile)
    Process + Executive Function Measure
      WPPSI-III Word Reasoning Scaled Score 9 (37th percentile)
        Process ++ Executive Function Measure
          NEPSY Repetition of Nonsense Words Scaled Score 4 (2nd percentile)
            Process +++ Executive Function Measure
              NEPSY Auditory Attention Scaled Score 1 (<1st percentile)
              NEPSY Auditory Response Set Scaled Score 1 (<1st percentile)

Table 5.4 (continued)   Examples of Ability or Process Production
Decrement Cascades

EF Decrement Involving Visual Discrimination Ability with Graphomotor Production

Process Measure
  WPPSI-III Symbol Search Scaled Score 8 (25th percentile)
    Process + Executive Function Measure
      WPPSI-III Coding Scaled Score 4 (2nd percentile)

EF Decrement Involving Reasoning with Visually Presented Information

Ability Measures
  KAIT Logical Steps Scaled Score 16 (98th percentile)
  WISC-IV Matrix Reasoning Scaled Score 14 (91st percentile)
    Ability + Increased Executive Functions Measure
      WISC-IV Picture Concepts Scaled Score 11 (63rd percentile)
        Ability+ + Increased Executive Functions Measures
          WCST Conceptual Level Responses Standard Score 97 (42nd percentile)

EF Decrement Involving Reasoning with Visually Presented Information with Manual Manipulation

Ability Measures
  KAIT Logical Steps Scaled Score 16 (98th percentile)
  WISC-IV Matrix Reasoning Scaled Score 14 (91st percentile)
    Ability + Increased Executive Functions Measure
      WISC-IV Block Design Scaled Score 7 (16th percentile)

EF Decrement Involving Retrieval of Verbal Information from Long-Term Storage

Retrieval from Storage Capacity Measure
  WISC-IV Vocabulary Scaled Score 12 (75th percentile)
    Capacity + Increased Executive Functions Measure
      KAIT Definitions Scaled Score 6 (9th percentile)

EF Decrement Involving Holding and Manipulation of Verbal Information with Graphomotor Production

Hold and Manipulate Capacity Measure
  KAIT Auditory Comprehension Scaled Score 12, (75th percentile)
    Capacity + Increased Executive Functions Measure
      PAL Note Taking A 3rd Decile (21st–30th percentile range)

EF Decrement Involving Retrieval of Verbal Information with Graphomotor Production

Retrieval from Storage Capacity Measure
  KAIT Auditory Comprehension Scaled Score 12, (75th percentile)
    Capacity + Increased Executive Functions Measure
      PAL Note Taking B 3rd Decile (21st–30th percentile range)

Table 5.4 (continued) Examples of Ability or Process Production Decrement Cascades

EF Decrement Involving Verbal Fluency

Process Measure
D-KEFS Category Fluency Scaled Score 13 (84th percentile)
   Process + Increased Executive Function Measure
   D-KEFS Letter Fluency Scaled Score 8 (25th percentile)

EF Decrement Involving Visuomotor Processing Speed

Process Measure
WISC-IV Symbol Search Scaled Score 11 (63rd percentile)
   Process + Increased Executive Functions Measure
   WISC-IV Coding Scaled Score 7 (16th percentile)

score points for a mean 100, standard deviation 15 metric) to ensure that the observed change in performance level is a reliable indicator of a cascading production decrement. In some instances where a pattern of diminishing performance has been clearly documented using multiple methods, however, score differences somewhat less than a full standard deviation in magnitude can justifiably be interpreted as supporting the presence of a production decrement.

Cascading Production Increments

Cascading production increments are less common and more difficult to orchestrate using direct formal assessments. Direct formal assessments of executive function or other information processing capacities typically are not purposefully constructed in a manner that progressively reduces executive demands across a sequence of similar tasks. Perhaps the best examples of sets of tasks designed to allow for a cascading production increment is the combination of the WISC-IV Coding Subtest and the WISC-IV Coding Copy Subtest, as well as the WISC-IV Cancellation Random and Cancellation Structured tasks.

For the WISC-IV Coding Subtest, the child is provided an 8 x 11 page with a code key at the top that matches each of the numbers 1 through 9 with an abstract symbol. Below the code key are several rows of double boxes. For each double box, the top box contains a number and the bottom box is empty. The child is instructed to use the code key as a guide and to copy into the lower boxes the symbols that match the numbers in the upper boxes. After a short practice with five code pairs, the child is instructed to work on this task until told to stop (task time is a total of two minutes). The multitasking aspect of this subtest requires the use of a number of self-regulation cues including the Gauge, Initiate, Focus/Select, Sustain, Execute, and Pace cues, and the Generate, Associate, Hold, and Manipulate cues if, for example, rather than using the strategy demonstrated (for each item, look at the symbol in the top box, look at the key to find the match, copy the number that matches the symbol into the empty box, repeat for each symbol) the child generates an alternate strategy of his or her own by holding the symbol-number associations in working memory rather than continually looking back at the box, and the Monitor and Correct cues if the child chooses to monitor performance for accuracy and correct any errors.

For the Coding Copy Subtest, the child is given a page with rows of double boxes. Each of the top boxes contains one of the symbols from the Coding Subtest while the bottom boxes are empty. The child is instructed to copy, as quickly as possible into each bottom box, the symbol that appears in the top box. This significant reduction in task demands, while not really reducing the number of self-regulation cues required for effective performance (the Gauge, Initiate, Focus/Select, Sustain, Execute, and Pace cues are still needed), does eliminate the complex multitasking aspect of the use of these cues that was present in the Coding Subtest. For a number of children who have difficulty coordinating the use of a number of executive function cues at one time, this reduction in the multitasking demands enables them to greatly improve task performance, thereby demonstrating the cascading increment effect.

The Cancellation Subtest is made up of two separate visual search tasks—Cancellation Random and Cancellation Structured. For the Cancellation Random task the child is presented with an 11 x 17 page full of pictures of animals and other objects randomly placed and spaced on the page and instructed to locate and draw a line through as many animal pictures as possible while working quickly (task time is a total of 45 seconds). For the Cancellation Structured task, the child is presented with another 11 x 17 page full of pictures of animals and other objects and instructed to find and cross out as many animal pictures as possible, though this time the pictures are arranged neatly in rows across the page.

For the Cancellation Random task, no specific search strategy is modeled, nor is the child instructed to conduct an organized search. As a result, the child is free to use, or not use, executive function cues such as the Gauge, Generate, Associate,

Table 5.5   Examples of Ability or Process Production Increment Cascades

EF Increment Involving Visual Processing Speed
    Process—Executive Function Demands
    WISC-IV Cancellation Structured Scaled Score 11 (63rd percentile)
Process + Executive Function Measure
WISC-IV Cancellation Random Scaled Score 5 (5th percentile)

EF Increment Involving Graphomotor Production
    Process Measure
    WISC-IV Coding Copy Scaled Score 14 (91st percentile)
Process + Executive Function Measure
WISC-IV Coding Scaled Score 8 (25th percentile)

Organize, Foresee/Plan to guide the search among the random objects, along with the cues of Initiate, Focus/Select, Sustain, Pace, and possibly Time. For the Cancellation Random task, the efficiency of performance is dependent on the executive function cues the child chooses to use, or not use, to direct performance. For the Cancellation Structured task, the organization of the stimuli into even rows across the page serves to reduce the need to self-direct use of the Generate, Associate, Organize, and/or Foresee/Plan cues as the visual layout provides a strong cue for the use of a row by row search routine. This reduction in complexity of the visual array enables many children who have difficulty with the use the Generate, Associate, Organize, and Foresee/Plan cues with visual nonverbal tasks to increase their performance as they are able to find a significantly greater number of animal pictures in the same time period when the structure is present, thereby demonstrating the cascading increment effect. Table 5.5 provides examples of ability or process production increment cascades.

Although few formal tests provide the structure for cascading increment analysis, the technique can be applied effectively through the use of informal direct assessment methods. These include the use of modifications of administration procedures to provide the conditions for possible emergence of the desired stepwise improvement in performance resulting from a reduction in executive demands. Additionally, a clinician who is well-trained in understanding how task structure can affect a child's perception of the need for self-regulation can make a strong case for the presence of a cascading production increment in cases where the increased executive function demands of a task act as a clear cue to the child for increased

Table 5.6   Examples of Paradoxical Production Increment
Cascades

Memory Performance Increment Due to Increased Cueing for Modulation of Effort

Capacity with Increased Cueing for Effort Modulation
  WISC-IV Digit Span Backward Scaled Score 11 (63rd percentile)
    Memory Capacity Measure
      WISC-IV Digit Span Forward Scaled Score 5 (5th percentile)

Oral Motor Production Increment Due to Increased Cueing for Modulation of Effort

Oral Motor Processing with Increased Cueing for Effort Modulation
  D-KEFS CWI Word Reading Scaled Score 10 (50th percentile)
    Oral Motor Processing Measure
      D-KEFS CWI Color Naming Scaled Score 7 (16th percentile)

Oral Motor Production Increment Due to Increased Cueing for Modulation of Effort

Oral Motor Processing with Increased Cueing for Effort Modulation
  D-KEFS CWI Inhibition Switching Scaled Score 11 (63rd percentile)
    Oral Motor Processing Measure
      D-KEFS CWI Inhibition Scaled Score 7 (16th percentile)

Retrieval of Verbal Information from Long-Term Storage Increment Due to Increased Cueing for Modulation of Effort

Retrieval with Increased Cueing for Effort Modulation
  KAIT Double Meanings Scaled Score 9 (37th percentile)
    Retrieval Capacity Measure
      KAIT Definitions Scaled Score 6 (9th percentile)

self-regulation. This type of cascading production increment
produces the apparent paradoxical results often obtained in
clinical settings where a child actually increases task performance as tasks become more complex. These types of paradoxical cascading production increments are illustrated in
Table 5.6.

CAUTIONS RELATED TO INTERPRETATION
OF EXECUTIVE FUNCTION DEFICITS
USING FORMAL TESTS

Direct Formal Methods

The discussion of formal direct assessment methods provided
here should make it clear that while these methods can pro-

vide valuable information, they cannot stand alone as comprehensive measures of executive function capacity. Clinicians should not view the administration of a few subtests from an assessment battery as an adequate means of addressing the area of executive functions in an assessment. The limited focus of formal direct measures on the symbol system arena makes it necessary to supplement direct formal testing with additional information gathering methods.

In terms of interpretation of direct formal test results, it should be clear that the identification of poor performance on a single subtest, or even on several subtests, cannot be taken as a clear indication of executive function difficulties that merit consideration. Expanding the assessment of executive functions to include measures that are not typically thought of as executive function assessments and using more sophisticated analysis techniques such as looking for evidence of cascading production decrements and increments are ways to increase the validity and effectiveness of direct formal testing. Without the use of a more expansive approach to direct formal testing, clinicians risk missing important information that would enable them to characterize more accurately a child's performance in terms of executive function capacities. It is also important to note that little has been said in this section regarding the connection between performance on executive function measures and learning and production in school. This topic is a complex one that merits individual attention; it will be dealt with briefly in a later section of this chapter and in detail in Chapter 6.

Direct Informal Methods

Direct informal methods involve evaluation of direct interactions with the child or evaluation of the direct products of the child's engagement in work or play activities. These methods include evaluation of the results of both structured and unstructured observations of a child's behavior in various settings, including observation of the child's behavior when performing the tasks of a direct formal assessment; evaluation of the results of clinical interviews conducted with the child; and review of the products of work or play that were generated by the child at school, in the home, or in other settings. When used for the purpose of assessing executive functions, these techniques focus on those specific aspects of a child's behavior, or products of the child's behavior, that are indicative of the use, or disuse, of executive function capacities. These approaches to assessment are considered informal either because they do not involve the translation of the child's performance into quantitative scores, they do not involve direct comparison of such scores to the performance of a standardization sample of same-age peers, and/or they use norm-referenced scores in ways that do not conform to standardized procedures.

Interviews with the Child

No matter the age of the child being assessed, it is always a good idea to try to get the child's perspective on his or her own perceptions, feelings, thoughts, and actions. Some children offer surprisingly clear assessments of their own executive function strengths and weaknesses and lucid insights into the reasons for difficulties they might be experiencing in school and/or at home. Children also offer their perceptions of the effects that the behavior of others has on their performance. In these situations, the clinician is provided a rich source of material that can become an integral part of the assessment process.

Conversely, clinicians might find that open-ended questions posed during an interview elicit little or no response from the child. Clinicians need to consider that the process of responding to interview questions can itself require the use of multiple self-regulation capacities. When faced with the external demand to self-regulate language production and generate new associations or retrieve from long-term storage information about their own functioning, many children are unable to comply effectively with such a request. In these instances, the clinician will need to provide the child with enough executive function cues to enable him to offer a greater amount of meaningful information (e.g., when the question, "Do you have any hobbies?" does not elicit a response, ask the child follow-up questions such as "What do you like to do after school? What kinds of things to you like to do outside when the weather is nice?" etc.).

Behavior Observations Across Multiple Settings

Observation of the child in the school environment can offer valuable information about executive function use. In the classroom, at lunch, on the playground during recess, in gym class or other special instructional periods—any of these situations may offer the clinician possible opportunities for observing the extent to which the child uses, or does not use, various executive capacities. While direct observation in these settings can at times provide valuable information that helps gain a greater understanding of the child's executive function capacities, this method is typically not considered a critical source of assessment information because of the degree of inference that must be applied to interpret observed behaviors. Observation for the use of executive capacities is a little different than typical behavioral observation in that the observer must be prepared to make judgments about the type of executive capacities required for effective functioning in various situations as well as the extent to which the child did, or did not, appear to utilize the needed executive capacities. Because the clinician has no direct access to the child's thoughts, it is often difficult to make inferences about what type of executive cues the child did, or did not attempt to engage.

Some observed situations are much easier to generate a valid interpretation for than others. For example, the inference that a child did not engage the Inhibit cue appears to be a valid interpretation in a situation where, after being accidentally bumped by a classmate, the child instantaneously reacts by punching the other child in the arm and shoving him away. In contrast, it is much more difficult to infer the lack of engagement of the Hold cue in a situation where a child appears to be listening intently to a lecture provided by a teacher, but is unable to provide any form of a response when asked a direct question about what the teacher had said. When incorporating data collected through direct observation, the clinician must keep in mind that the inferences attributed to the observed behavior will vary in degree of validity depending on the specific nature of the events observed. As always, the degree of familiarity of the observer with the self-regulation capacities will greatly affect the quality of the inferences drawn from the observed behavior.

 Clinicians conducting classroom observations may find the Executive Function Classroom Observation Checklist (EF-CO), provided on the CD accompanying this book, to be a useful tool. The EF-CO provides a format for interpreting the content of a classroom observation from the perspective of classroom executive function demands and the type of self-regulation capacities a student does or does not demonstrate to meet these demands.

PROCESS-ORIENTED ASSESSMENT

As the term is used here, *process-oriented assessment* is an approach to the analysis and interpretation of assessment data that involves careful observation of how the child performs the assessment task (McCloskey & Maerlender, 2005). It is important here to make a distinction between process assessment and a process-oriented approach to assessment. *Process assessment* refers to the use of tests to assess specific cognitive capacities that have been labeled as processes. Such assessments would include measures of phonological processing, visual processing, processing speed, and the like. In contrast, the *process-oriented approach to assessment* (simply referred to here as the *process approach*) refers to a clinician's use of a set of methods to observe and interpret performance on any measure of cognition, academic functioning, or behavior.

The process approach is predicated on the assumption that how the child performs the task is as important, and possibly more important, than the score that is used to quantitatively describe the outcome of the child's performance. The process approach also recognizes that incorrect responses are as important to interpretation as correct responses, and that the manner in which a child performs a task can provide insight into the mental processes that the child is most likely to be using in their attempt to complete the task. Therefore, by carefully observing how the child performs a task, in addition to the score obtained on the task, the clinician can generate hypotheses about the self-regulation functions that are, or are not, being used to perform tasks. Because the process approach involves observing what the child actually is doing during task performance, interpretation does not involve the application of a predetermined set of scoring rules, but rather involves description of how the score was obtained.

Application of the process approach begins with careful observations while the formal assessment is being administered, may continue with additional administration of the same or similar tasks after the completion of the formal assessment, and culminates with refined interpretation of the results of the formal assessment. The process approach can be employed effectively to help generate and test hypotheses about a child's use or disuse of executive function capacities. Process-oriented observation to obtain evidence of the use, or disuse, of executive function cues should be conducted throughout all formal assessment activities. This allows for the identification of patterns of executive function use or disuse across multiple tasks.

For example, a clinician using the process approach might observe that a child is not effectively using the Focus/Select cue while test items are being presented during a formal assessment task. During interpretation of the test results, the clinician uses the process assessment observation data to refine interpretation of the score earned for that task, realizing that the score really is not reflecting a level of performance of the cognitive capacities thought to be measured by the task, but more likely is reflecting a lack of adequate engagement of the Focus/Select cue. In such an instance, interpretation of the objective score results must be mediated by the process observations related to the presence of confounding executive function miscues. This example illustrates the fact that how a child performs a task can be as important, and possibly more important, than the actual score that is obtained on a direct formal measure. The importance of this process-oriented observation and its interpretation become more critical to characterizing the child's performance when similar difficulties with the Focus/Select cue are observed in the performance of other tasks and/or during classroom observations and/or are reported by parents or teachers using behavior rating scales.

The following example demonstrates how a child can enhance, or simply alter, performance of a task by self-regulating the use of executive function cues. Many cognitive assessments include a digit repetition, or digit span, task. These tasks require the child to listen to a series of digits, and repeat the series in the order in which it was stated to them. The task is composed of multiple items, successively increasing in the number of digits that are stated. The directions for these tasks instruct the examiner to present the digit series at the rate of one per second with no changes in intonation until after the final digit to signal the end of the series. The need to engage the Hold cue is implicit in the directions and the manner of administration of the task, and most children easily grasp this need. Far fewer children realize that the Manipulate cue can also be engaged in order to extend performance beyond what can be achieved through the passive holding of the digits in an initial registration buffer. A child's use of the Manipulate cue is readily apparent through process-oriented observation of the response that the child provides. One clear indicator of the use of the Manipulate cue is when the child delivers the response using a combination of intonation pattern and pauses, clearly reflecting the use of a chunking strategy to manipulate the digits into groups, allowing the child to repeat the digits in groups rather than simply trying to recall the digits one at a time. (That is, after listening to the series 9-2-7-8-1-4, a child who uses the Manipulate cue to engage working memory for effecting a chunking strategy might repeat the series as: 927 . . . 814, with a specific intonation pattern for each group of three digits.)

In the previous section on formal direct methods, the use of the WISC-IV Coding and Coding Copy and WISC-IV Cancellation Random and Structured tasks were discussed in relation to demonstrating incremental cascades in performance. In these discussions, how children performed these tasks was described. These descriptions were based on behaviors that could be observed using the process approach. For example, when a child performs the Coding Subtest, a clinician who closely observes performance can identify if a child chooses to alter performance strategy from the original instructions. Many children can be observed looking back at their own work to identify a symbol-number association rather than looking up at the code key. At some point during task performance, some children stop looking up at the code key or referring back to their own work and simply continue on with the task, demonstrating that they are holding the symbol-number associations in working memory. These alterations in performance strategy reflect the use of executive cues to redirect task performance in a manner that the child believes to be more effective and/or more efficient or simply better suited to their cognitive processing capacities or their learned ways of performing tasks.

In the case of the Cancellation tasks, the only way to determine if a child is using an organized search strategy while performing the Cancellation Random task is to closely observe the pattern produced by the child's movements of the pencil across the page while working. Likewise, although the Cancellation Structured task clearly provides strong visual cues for the use of a row by row search strategy, only the use of the process approach observation can confirm if, in fact, the child took advantage of the visual format cue. Some children completely ignore the structure of the visual array and proceed to engage in a random search that is as haphazard as the one they used for the Cancellation Random task.

Structured Methods for Employing the Process Approach

In some cases, specific methods can be applied to enhance process-oriented observation (McCloskey & Maerlender, 2005). A good example of these methods is the use of 30-second interval performance recording for the WISC-IV Symbol Search and Coding Subtests. The following examples from case reports serve to illustrate how this technique is employed and interpreted.

Symbol Search

Although Michael earned a Scaled Score of 11 (63rd percentile) on this subtest, the way in which Michael performed this task reveals much about how he did, and did not, apply his well-developed visual processing abilities. Michael's performance was task analyzed by recording the number of symbol items he was able to complete in each 30-second interval of the two-minute work period. This allowed the tracking of his productivity and the gauging of his ability to sustain attention and effort for the entire time period. Michael started work on this subtest in a relatively efficient manner. His visual discriminations were quick and accurate as he completed nine symbol items in the first 30 seconds of work. During the second 30 second period, Michael's production dropped to six symbols. This lower level of production was maintained for the next 30-second interval and then declined slightly again to five symbol items in the final 30-second period. Considering his faster and more efficient start with this task, it is hard to argue that Michael's average score was the result of "average" visual processing ability. If Michael had continued to work at his original pace of the first 30 seconds (which most 10-year-olds typically do), Michael would have completed 36 symbol items, and would have earned a Scaled Score of 16 (97th percentile). Although Michael initially engaged the task in an efficient and effective manner, he was unable to sustain his attention and effort consistently at this initial level for the entire two-minute period.

Coding

As was the case with the Symbol Search task, Michael was unable to maintain an adequate work pace for the entire two-minute period, but his pattern of performance across 30-second intervals was more unusual here. Michael's production during the first 30-second interval was relatively efficient as he completed 12 codings. These initial items made use of only 4–5 of the nine symbol-number pairs. During the second 30-second interval, Michael's output increased to 14 codings as he effectively adjusted to the inclusion of the additional code pairs in the task. As the predictability of the task increased during the third and fourth intervals, Michael's performance paradoxically deteriorated in a more pronounced manner than would be expected merely from slight fatigue effects experienced by many children doing this task. Michael completed only seven codings in the third interval and eight in the fourth interval. Michael's increase in efficiency followed by a substantial drop in efficiency resulted in an overall performance at the lower end of the average range (WISC-IV Coding Subtest Scaled Score 8, 25th percentile). If Michael had been able to maintain just the level of performance evidenced during the first half of the task, he would have earned a score at the higher end of the average range (Scaled Score 12, 75th percentile). Once again, although Michael began the task in a relatively efficient manner, he was unable to sustain his attention and effort consistently for the entire two-minute period.

Limitations of Informal Direct Methods

A limitation of observation techniques is that the observations are obtained in a naturalistic environment and there is no guarantee that the behavior observed during the observation period will elicit the use of executive functions of greatest interest, or offer a situation in which self-regulation difficulties might be observable. Process-oriented interpretation also can present challenges to the clinician. Clinicians must be adequately prepared to know what behaviors to look for during task performance and what specific executive capacity use or disuse can, or cannot, be inferred from the behavior. Also, it is possible that the clinician might over- or underinterpret the importance of observations in light of the fact that no specific norm-referenced basis is used to check the relative significance of the observations. While there is no question that the accuracy, consistency, and validity of clinician's process observations can be challenged, careful data collection methods and sound deductive reasoning can be used effectively to justify findings when the process-oriented approach is competently applied. Critics of the process approach seem to ignore the fact that formal direct assessment procedures face similar challenges, and that having a seemingly more objective source of data does not guarantee that direct formal measures are in fact more accurate, consistent, or valid in terms of the outcomes they produce or how these outcomes are interpreted.

SUMMARY

Consistent with the four questions format described in the introduction to this chapter, an assessment of a child's executive functions should provide a comprehensive picture of the extent to which a child does, or does not, use the various executive function capacities within the specific domains of functioning utilizing various information processing capacities across the various arenas of involvement while taking into account the specific contextual factors that can impact on effective use. As outlined in Table 5.2, a comprehensive assessment of executive functions therefore requires a multidimensional perspective that effectively employs all of the approaches and methods discussed earlier in this chapter. The general format proposed here moves from informal indirect to formal indirect to informal direct and finally formal direct with some elements of informal direct (such as the process approach) for analysis of formal direct assessment results. Assessment of the child's executive capacities in this manner would provide the information needed to help complete the four questions that form the framework for report writing (What executive functions can the child use effectively? What executive functions does the child have difficulty using? What needs to be done to help the child? Who can do what needs to be done to help the child?). Ideally, the outcome of the assessment should be one or more clear behavioral statements that can serve as the basis for making recommendations for appropriate intervention techniques and strategies.

6

Academic Skill Development and Assessment of Executive Functions

This chapter provides a general overview of self-regulation executive function involvement in academic skill production and discusses assessment methods to help with identifying executive function difficulties that can contribute to problems with academic skill production. The text presented here does not attempt to discuss in detail the research literature that explores the role of executive functions in academic skill performance. Readers interested in reviewing this literature base are encouraged to read the scholarly publications of Virginia Berninger and her colleagues, especially the relatively recent summary of that work provided in the book *Brain Literacy for Educators and Psychologists* (Berninger & Richards, 2002). The authors consider the Berninger and Richards text to be the best single source at this time for information about the role of executive functions in academic skill performance. Additional clinically-oriented information can be obtained from the book *School Neuropsychology* (Hale & Fiorello, 2004). Additional theoretical perspectives on the role of executive functions in the school setting can be obtained from the book *Attention, Memory, and Executive Functions* edited by Lyon and Krasnegor (1996) and the more recent volume *Executive Function in Education: From Theory to Practice* edited by Lynn Meltzer (2007).

EXECUTIVE FUNCTIONS AND CLASSROOM FUNCTIONING: LEARNING VERSUS PRODUCING

In Chapter 4, the distinction between classroom learning and classroom production was discussed briefly. Denckla's (1996) concept of producing disabilities was introduced to shed light on the problems that can arise in classroom functioning because of executive function difficulties. These producing disabilities stand in contrast with learning disabilities, where children experience difficulties learning and acquiring academic skills due to deficits in basic mental processes. The learning disability conception is best exemplified by the condition of developmental phonological dyslexia (Temple, 1997; Shaywitz, 2003), in which difficulties with processing subword sound units create problems in learning to decode words and develop grade-appropriate reading skills. It is critical to understand that while a child exhibiting developmental phonologic dyslexia may also demonstrate executive function difficulties, executive function difficulties per se are not a cause of the learning problems.

The difference between learning and producing disabilities, or more generally between learning and producing difficulties, is an important one because it helps one to understand many of the dynamics around the issue of educational support services that are, or are not, provided to children who are struggling in school. Although the focus of this book is on producing difficulties and not learning disabilities, it is certainly the case that a number of children demonstrate both learning problems due to processing deficits other than executive functions and production problems due to executive function difficulties. In fact, the clinical experiences of the authors suggest that children who have problems with both learning and producing are the most likely to be identified as learning disabled. Figure 6.1 illustrates the conceptual overlap between learning and producing difficulties. Students who would be placed in the center oval of the diagram are those who have both learning and producing difficulties. Typically, the lack of production is what initially draws teachers' attention to the difficulties of these students. When a closer look is taken, the learning difficulties are also revealed. The dual nature of the problems these students exhibit combined with assessment results indicating at least average reasoning abilities makes it easy for both teachers and parents to see the need for instructional modifications and/or specialized education settings so

assistance from school staff. School staff may be reticent in complying with parent requests at these later grades, especially if the student is earning passing grades. The problem here is that school staff does not see the inordinate amount of time and effort the student is placing into completing school work and the strain that this additional effort is placing on the child at home. In the best case scenario, the parents are able to convince school staff that some kind of assistance is needed.

Students who would be placed in the bottom portion of the diagram are those who do not have any learning difficulties per se, but whose developmental delays or deficits in one or more executive function capacities result in a lack of adequate production. Like the students with both learning and producing difficulties, the lack of adequate production of these students leads to scrutiny by teachers and parents.

In the case of some of these students, written expression production difficulties are noted, enabling them to be legally classified as learning disabled even though, had a thorough assessment been conducted, it would have been revealed that the written production deficiency was not due to a lack of understanding of how to write (i.e., not really due to a learning disability, but rather due to a producing disability). Although the labeling that occurs here is inaccurate, in some instances it at least provides an administrative means for helping the student to improve his or her writing skills. For other students in this group, assessment of their producing difficulties will lead to a classification of ADHD or ADD when specific executive function difficulties are documented, and interventions including a 504 accommodation plan will be established to help these students overcome their producing difficulties.

For a larger percentage of the students in the bottom portion of the diagram, however, when no specific learning difficulties are identified and ADHD is ruled out as the cause of their lack of production, they are frequently subjected to what amounts to character assassination. Rather than recognizing that the majority of the students in this group are being affected by developmental delays or severe deficits in executive functions, school staff and parents are much more likely to attribute these students' poor production to any number of negative traits or character deficiencies such as laziness, apathy, lack of willingness to take responsibility for their own actions, lack of motivation, overt hostility, or lack of respect for authority. While attributing the difficulties of these students to such nefarious origins might ease the conscience of some parents and teachers or enable them to shift responsibility for dealing with the situation completely onto the poorly developed brain of the child, they typically do not solve the problems that have been created by the lack of production and certainly do not provide any guidance to these students' developing brains as to how to solve their problems. Conversely, these attributions only serve to exacerbate the situation, often creating even more unwanted negative behavior, resulting in a larger rift between the child and authority figures. Without appropriate identification of the source of the difficulties of these children and assistance through interventions aimed at improving their executive capacities, this group faces the greatest risk of failing in school and being deprived of valuable educational experiences that would enable them to learn—perhaps not always in the immediate moment, but often at some point in the future—how to overcome their producing difficulties. The remainder of this chapter will focus on understanding the academic problems of students with producing difficulties, including those with combined learning and production difficulties, and ways to intervene on their behalf.

ASSESSMENT OF EXECUTIVE FUNCTION DIFFICULTIES INVOLVED IN ACADEMIC SKILL PROBLEMS

Executive function difficulties can have a wide variety of negative effects on production in all academic areas. In the elementary grades, these effects are most prominent in the impact they have on the demonstration of written expression, reading, and mathematics skills. In the upper grades, executive function difficulties with basic skill production often persist and are joined by difficulties with organization and planning and completion of projects and homework as well as inadequate regulation of the use of study skills and/or test-taking skills. In order to identify the impact of executive function difficulties on academic functioning, it is necessary to have a shared framework for conceptualization of the mental capacities involved in skill development in the areas of reading, writing, and mathematics. Figure 6.2 offers some basic definitions of various mental capacities that play roles in academic functioning. In each section that follows, a model will be provided that specifies the mental capacities used, and the

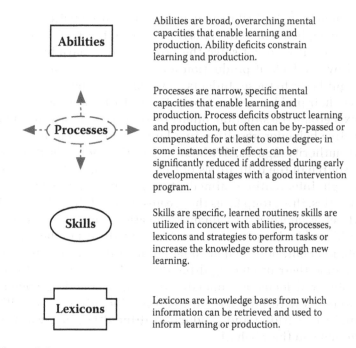

Abilities

Abilities are broad, overarching mental capacities that enable learning and production. Ability deficits constrain learning and production.

Processes

Processes are narrow, specific mental capacities that enable learning and production. Process deficits obstruct learning and production, but often can be by-passed or compensated for at least to some degree; in some instances their effects can be significantly reduced if addressed during early developmental stages with a good intervention program.

Skills

Skills are specific, learned routines; skills are utilized in concert with abilities, processes, lexicons and strategies to perform tasks or increase the knowledge store through new learning.

Lexicons

Lexicons are knowledge bases from which information can be retrieved and used to inform learning or production.

Figure 6.2   Definitions of Mental Capacities.

interrelationships among these capacities, when using the academic skill being discussed.

Each section that follows will offer methods for assessing the role of executive function in the specific academic area being discussed and insights into how to interpret results of such assessments. These sections will also offer additional insights into how integrating the concept of executive functions into assessment can alter the way clinicians view ideas about what various kinds of academic assessments are really measuring.

Self-Regulation Executive Functions and Reading

The diagram in Figure 6.3 shows the mental capacities involved in the reading process. The diagram represents a dynamic interaction of multiple capacities, first to develop and utilize specific skills, and second, to use these skills in an integrated manner to read fluently. (Fluent reading as used here refers to the full act of reading quickly and efficiently and extracting meaning from text as opposed to the subcomponents of speed and intonation achieved when reading orally.) Although a full

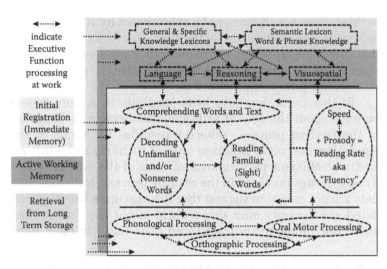

Figure 6.3   An Integrative Model Specifying Processes, Abilities, and Lexicons in Reading.

discussion of the reading process is beyond the scope of this book, it is important to recognize the number of separate mental processes required when reading.

In Figure 6.3, executive function involvement in the reading process is represented in two ways. First, note that each specific mental capacity is enclosed in a shape that denotes its function as either an ability, a process, a skill, or a lexicon, and that the contours of the shapes appear as dotted lines. The dotted lines enclosing these capacities indicate that executive function cues are required for the effective engagement of each of these components. In addition, there are arrows showing pathways between the various capacities. These arrows represent the coordinated multitasking of executive function cues required to integrate all of the components of the reading process. Thus, we see that self-regulation capacities apply specifically to the direction of specific cognitive processes, abilities, and lexicons, as well as the individual reading skills. Moreover, these capacities apply generally to the multitasking and coordination of executive function capacities to integrate the various processes, abilities, lexicons, and skills to produce fluent reading. Again, fluent reading is defined here as the ability to quickly and accurately recognize words as connected text, and comprehend both the meaning of the words and the connected text. It is therefore apparent that reading problems can result from, or be exacerbated by, disuse, or ineffective or inconsistent use, of the executive function capacities that direct all aspects of the reading process, specifically poor sight word recognition, poor word decoding, slowed reading rate, and/or poor comprehension.

To this point, we have been speaking in a more general manner about the role of self-regulation executive functions in the reading process. Table 6.1 specifies the kinds of self-regulation executive function cues most likely to be utilized to direct efficient performance of each of the various cognitive capacities involved in the reading process. Note that these lists are not meant to suggest that the executive function cues listed are the only ones that a child might use during these tasks, but rather to indicate those cues that are most likely

Table 6.1 Executive Function Self-Regulation Cues Used in Reading Production

Reading Skill Cues
Sight Word Recognition Cues   Focus/Select, Perceive, Inhibit, Retrieve, Monitor, Correct
Word Decoding Cues   Focus/Select, Perceive, Inhibit, Retrieve, Monitor, Correct
Reading Rate Cues   Pace, Retrieve, Sustain, Monitor, Correct, Balance

Reading Comprehension Cues
    Cues for Sight Word Recognition
        Focus/Select, Perceive, Inhibit, Retrieve, Monitor, Correct
    Cues for Word Decoding
        Focus/Select, Perceive, Inhibit, Retrieve, Monitor, Correct
    Cues for Reading Rate
        Pace, Retrieve, Balance
    Cues for Accessing and Coordinating the Use of Abilities and Lexicons
        Gauge, Modulate, Sustain, Flexible/Shift, Generate/Associate, Retrieve
    Cues for Activating Working Memory in the Extended Immediate Time Frame
        Initiate, Sustain, Hold, Manipulate
    Cues for Coordinating the Multitasking of All Cognitive Capacities and Tasks
        Sustain, Organize, Foresee/Plan, Balance, Flexible/Shift, Pace, Monitor, Correct
        Optional use: Time, Store

Note: The cues listed in this table represent those cues that are activated specifically for the direction of the reading skill listed. Additional self-regulation cues that are already engaged to some degree to enable a general state of active engagement with the classroom routine no matter what the task (i.e., Perceive, Focus/Select, Initiate, Modulate, Inhibit) are not listed unless the task requires an increase over the typical level of use of these capacities.

to be required for effective performance. Additional executive function cues may well be used by a child to assist in skill production depending on how they choose to approach any given task.

The skill of sight word recognition itself draws on several cognitive processes and lexicons that must be coordinated to effect instantaneous recognition of a word on the page. When engaged in sight word recognition, several executive function cues are needed:

- The Focus/Select cue for directing the reader to carefully focus attention on the word to be read
- The Perceive cue to ensure that all of the letters of the word are visually processed to achieve an accurate recognition match
- The Inhibit cue to suppress impulsive calling out of a possibly more frequently used "near match" word that shares orthographic features of the word to be read
- The Retrieve cue to access the appropriate lexicon to find a match between a stored word and the word on the page
- The Monitor cue to ensure that checking processes are engaged to confirm the match between the word on the page and the word retrieved from the word store lexicon
- The Correct cue to ensure that an attempt is made to correct a recognized error in the match between the word on the page and the word retrieved from the word store lexicon

In a similar fashion, overlapping and unique self-regulation executive functions are utilized to cue the use of multiple mental capacities for the effective application of word decoding skills when a word is not readily recognized as familiar to the reader. Children who have learned to recognize words or to apply decoding patterns, but who do not apply these skills with efficiency or consistency are not demonstrating learning difficulties, rather they are demonstrating producing difficulties. These difficulties are associated with the disuse, or ineffective or inconsistent use, of one or more of the executive function cues responsible for guiding the use of these reading skills.

The skill of fast, accurate word reading involves the use of orthographic oral motor processing speed guided by the executive function cues of Pace, Retrieve, Sustain, Monitor,

Correct, and Balance. An adequately developed capacity for multitasking these cues is necessary as they need to work in tandem to assure that the reader maintains (Sustain cue) a consistent rate of production at the maximum (Balance cue) speed attainable (Pace cue) while still maintaining perfect, or near perfect (Monitor cue) word recognition (Retrieve cue) and decoding (Retrieve cue) accuracy (Correct cue).

As illustrated in Table 6.1, reading comprehension is unquestionably the most complex of the reading skills. Use of this skill requires near continuous integration of:

1. All of the subordinate word reading skills (recognition, decoding, reading rate) and their executive function cueing needs
2. Additional cognitive capacities (reasoning, visuospatial, and language abilities; word knowledge and general knowledge lexicons) and the associated executive cues that guide their access and use
3. An additional set of executive functions responsible for cueing sustained extension of the immediate time frame (i.e., the need for active working memory engagement)
4. An additional set of executive functions responsible for coordination and multitasking needs created by the reader's attempt to derive meaning from written text

In situations where comprehension is immediately assessed, all of these capacities and the related executive function cues are joined by an additional set of cognitive capacities and executive function cues required for comprehending and responding to test questions.

Assessment of Self-Regulation Executive Functions Involved in Reading

Assessment of reading skills have most recently focused on measures of word reading (e.g., KTEA-II Letter and Word Recognition Subtest, WIAT-II Word Reading Subtest, WJ-III Letter/Word Identification Subtest), decoding skills (KTEA-II Nonsense Word Decoding Subtest, WIAT-II Pseudoword Decoding Subtest, WJ-III Word Attack Subtest), and measures of reading comprehension (e.g., KTEA-II Reading Comprehension Subtest, WIAT-II Reading Comprehension Subtest, WJ-III Passage Comprehension Subtest). In addition to these, measures of speed and automaticity with comprehension can be assessed using the WJ-III Reading Fluency Subtest and sight word efficiency (speed of accurate reading of a list of familiar words) and decoding efficiency (speed of accurate decoding of a list of nonsense words) can be assessed with the Test of Word Reading Efficiency (TOWRE; Torgesen & Wagner, 1999). Reading rate measures appear in many research-based measurement systems (still inaccurately referred to as curriculum-based measurements, e.g., see Salvia & Ysseldyke). Process measures of rapid automatic naming are available on the Process Assessment of the Learner (PAL; Berninger, 1998), and the Delis-Kaplan Executive Function System (D-KEFS; Delis, Kaplan, Kramer, 2001), while phonological processing measures appear on the Comprehensive Test of Phonological Processing (CTOPP; Wagner, Torgesen, & Rashotte, 1999), the WJ III (Woodcock, McGrew & Mather, 2001), the KTEA-II (Kaufman & Kaufman, 2005), the PAL (1998, 2007), and the NEPSY (1997, 2007).

Assessment for identifying the disuse or ineffective/inconsistent use of executive function cues in reading production can be accomplished most effectively with cascading production decrement analysis and application of the process-oriented approach to observing and interpreting task performance. To apply the cascading performance decrement analysis to reading assessment, the specific components being assessed by various reading achievement and process measures must be understood. Starting with rapid automatic naming, it is important to note that when children are given rapid naming tasks that focus on the repetition of a minimal set of extremely well-known orthographic stimuli (e.g., letters of the alphabet, a set of only eight familiar sight words, a set of numbers), use of the Focus/Select Pace, Retrieve, Monitor, Correct, and Balance cues is minimized but still necessary for efficient performance. Altering the manner in which the stimuli are processed increases the need for use of the Focus/Select Pace, Monitor, Correct, and Balance cues and adds additional executive function cues such as Perceive, Gauge, Modulate, and Inhibit to the mix. Examples of this would be interspersing numbers among words or providing a list of color name words that are printed in different ink colors (e.g., the word red printed in green ink; the word blue printed in red ink). Significant decreases in the child's performance on rapid naming tasks when these more complex forms of stimuli are introduced strongly point to executive function difficulties as the source of the poorer performances.

In a similar vein, altering the stimuli of rapid naming tasks to become more challenging in terms of word reading skills, such as lists of somewhat less familiar sight words or non-sense words, greatly increases the need for the engagement of the Pace, Retrieve, and Balance cues to guide either oral motor production or silent reading efficiency. This fact accounts for some children who, despite adequate performance on word recognition tasks and decoding tasks and on rapid naming tasks such as those on the PAL, demonstrate deficient perfor-mance on a sight word efficiency task such as that found in the TOWRE, and an even greater discrepancy between their adequate rapid naming performance and their deficient per-formance on decoding fluency tasks such as that found in the TOWRE. It is also important to note that process-oriented observation of the performance of these students on the word recognition and decoding tasks that yielded average scores typically reveals a poor quality of word reading and decoding efforts despite the average scores, as these children struggle to accurately read many of the words and nonsense words on these lists, sometimes requiring as much as 10–20 seconds or more to provide a correct response. Results of various cas-cading production decrement analyses conducted with rapid naming and word reading tasks are presented in Table 6.2.

Students who have difficulty using the Inhibit, Perceive, and Focus/Select cues when word reading demonstrate knowl-edge of word decoding rules yet frequently misapply them when reading words that have been accurately decoded in the past, or who demonstrate sight recognition of words but fre-quently misread them in sentences, often earn low scores on the PAL Receptive Coding Subtest. For individual items of the PAL Receptive Coding task, the student views a word for one second and then views another word and indicates whether the second word is identical to the first. Additional items fol-low this same pattern but show a word and then one or two letters and the student indicates whether the letter or letters appeared, and/or appeared in the same order in the word they initially viewed. Process-oriented observation and analysis of the errors these students make when reading words from lists typically reflects many whole word substitution errors that replace less familiar words with familiar words that share many of the same letters and letter configurations as the less familiar word, such as saying "photograph" for "phonograph," "ideal" for ideally," "useful" for "useless," "know" for "knew," or "bounce" for "bounties." Similar observation and analysis of nonsense word decoding efforts frequently reveals substi-tution of real words that share many of the same letters and

Table 6.2 Executive Function Cascading Production Decrement
Analysis Applied to Reading Skill Assessment

Oral-Motor Processing Decrements

Process Measures
    PAL RAN Letters 6th Decile (51st–60th percentile range)
    PAL RAN Words 5th Decile (41st–50th percentile range)
    PAL RAN Digits 6th Decile (51st–60th percentile range)
        Process + Executive Function Measure
            PAL RAN Words & Digits 3rd Decile (21st–30th percentile range)

Process Measures
    D-KEFS CWI Word Naming Scaled Score 11 (63rd percentile)
        Process + Executive Function Measure
            D-KEFS CWI Inhibition Scaled Score 8 (25th percentile)
            Process + + Executive Function Measure
                D-KEFS CWI Inhibition/Switching Scaled Score 5 (5th percentile)

Word Reading Skill Efficiency Decrement

Process Measures
    PAL RAN Words 5th Decile (41st–50th percentile)
    PAL RAN Letters 6th Decile (51st–60th percentile)
Skill Measure
    KTEA-II Letter & Word Recognition Standard Score 105 (63rd percentile)
        Skill + Executive Function
            TOWRE Sight Word Efficiency Standard Score 84 (14th percentile)

Decoding Skill Efficiency Decrement

Process Measures
    PAL RAN Words 5th Decile (41st–50th percentile)
    PAL RAN Letters 6th Decile (51st–60th percentile)
Skill Measure
    KTEA-II Nonsense Word Decoding Standard Score 100 (50th percentile)
        Skill + Executive Function
            TOWRE Phonemic Decoding Efficiency Standard Score 74 (4th percentile)

Table 6.2 (continued) Executive Function Cascading Production Decrement Analysis Applied to Reading Skill Assessment

Reading Comprehension Decrement
Process Measures
PAL RAN Words 5th Decile (41st–50th percentile)
PAL RAN Letters 6th Decile (51st – 60th percentile)
Ability to Reason with Verbal Information Measures
WISC-IV Similarities Scaled Score 12 (75th percentile)
WISC-IV Comprehension Scaled Score 13 (84th percentile)
Retrieval of Verbal Information from Lexicons Measures
WISC-IV Vocabulary Scaled Score 13 (84th percentile)
WISC-IV Information Scaled Score 12 (75th percentile)
Skill Measures
WIAT-II Word Reading Standard Score 109 (73rd percentile)
WIAT-II Pseudoword Decoding Standard Score 106 (66th percentile)
Skill + Executive Function Measure
WIAT-II Reading Comprehension Standard Score 86 (18th percentile)
Skill + + Executive Function Measure
WJ-III Passage Comprehension Standard Score 79 (8th percentile)

letter configurations as the nonsense words, such as saying "van" for "vum," "gasp" for "gusp," "sink" for "snirk," or "liquefy" for "lindify."

As was the case with rapid naming, word reading, and decoding skills, the contribution of executive function cues to the performance of reading comprehension tasks can be evaluated using cascading performance decrement analysis techniques as shown in Table 6.2. In a reading comprehension cascade, adequate performance is obtained on baseline measures of the cognitive processes underlying word reading and text comprehension as well as on measures of abilities and lexicons that may need to be accessed during reading comprehension. These effective performances are contrasted with poor performance on one or more measures of reading comprehension. A significant difference between baseline cognitive measures contributing to comprehension and measures specifically assessing reading comprehension strongly implicates disuse, or inefficient or inconsistent use, of executive function cues as the source of the poor performance.

Self-regulation involvement in reading comprehension tasks can also be assessed through application of the process-oriented approach to observing and interpreting task performance combined with clinical interviewing of the child. Clinicians can note the amount of time it takes the child to read paragraphs along with the behaviors exhibited when asked questions about what was read. When it can be confirmed that the child has the capacity to manipulate information in active working memory, frequent look-backs at text that was read very quickly suggest a lack of cueing for balance between speed of word reading and extracting meaning from text. Difficulties with cueing adequate resources for attention and effort can also be observed using the process approach.

The norm-referenced achievement tests typically used to assess students, reading skill levels are not well suited to identifying the kinds of executive function difficulties with reading that are likely to be the source of academic production difficulties in high school and college. As demands for reading for extended periods of time increase, some students who are able to score well on achievement tests are unable to keep up due to poor use of cues such as Time, Pace, Modulate, Sustain, Organize, and Plan. Students who are also affected by slow orthographic processing speed need to rely heavily on executive function cues to find ways to compensate for their inability to keep up with heavy reading loads. As text complexity increases, additional cues are needed to modulate effort, access the needed reasoning abilities, and coordinate efforts at studying content.

Interviewing older children about their reading habits and how they self-regulate their personal reading time can produce important information needed to supplement formal assessment efforts. Questions such as: "How long can you read before you have to get up and take a break?" "How often do you find yourself 'zoning out' while reading (i.e., you realize that while you are still reading words from the page, you are not really thinking about what you are reading)?" "How do you study what you read?" "If you want to remember something that you read, how do you do that?" Engaging in such dialogue, especially with adolescent readers, can produce many insights into the executive functions they do, and do not, use effectively when attempting to read for meaning.

When evaluating a child's reading comprehension skills, it is critical to take into account the constraints placed on performance by specific task demands. The concept of task constraints refers to the empirical fact that different test formats intended to assess the same processes, abilities, skills, and/or access of lexicons can produce significantly different results (McCloskey & Maerlender, 2005). In many of these situations, differences in format alter the requirements for executive function cues needed to direct effective performance. An excellent example of this is illustrated in the formats of the WIAT-II, KTEA-II, and WJ-III reading comprehension tasks. All of these tasks are intended as measures of reading comprehension, and all three require the child to read sentences and short passages and respond orally to questions about the meaning of what was read. Despite the highly similar requirements for the input of information in these tasks, the scores earned by a child who is administered all three can vary significantly. The primary source of this variation in performance involves the differences in the response demands of each task. The WIAT-II requires the child to respond orally to orally presented free recall questions about what was read. The examiner is allowed to repeat the question if the child asks for a repetition and cue the child to provide more information. For the KTEA-II, the questions are printed on an easel page along with multiple choice response options and the child is able to read the question as the examiner states it and then is able to read the response options, and if necessary, reread the question without asking for repetition before providing a response. For the WJ-III, the passage read by the child contains a blank where a word is missing from the passage. The child is required to provide the exact word, or a close variant, that would fill the blank to complete the passage in a meaningful way.

Although the kinds of self-regulation executive function cues needed to guide responding in these three situations are highly similar, there is great variation in how, and to what extent, directive capacities need to be engaged. The KTEA-II is the least demanding of the three in terms of the extent to which the Manipulate and Retrieve cue must be used, as response options are provided for the child, and these provide visual cues for the need to manipulate or retrieve certain information from the text. The real executive demands on the child with this format come in the way of directing the selection of a multiple choice option. Although this type of response format might appear to be much easier than the other two, some children experience great difficulty with the use of executive function cues to answer multiple choice questions. These children sometimes over utilize the Generate and/or Associate cues, and end up overanalyzing the question and the response options. For other children, the Generate and/or

Associate cues are underutilized and coupled with inadequate use of the Focus/Select and/or Inhibit cue result in impulsive selection of answers before all responses have been carefully considered. In addition to the examples described here, other miscue scenarios are possible; all leading to inadequate performance with the KTEA-II response format despite the child's adequate skill at comprehending what was read.

The WIAT-II response format is much more demanding than the KTEA-II in terms of the need to cue manipulation and retrieval of information from the text, and the need to use the Generate and/or Associate cues to structure free recall responses rather than evaluate multiple choice options. Additionally, self-regulation cues are needed to direct word retrieval processes for expressive language production needed to formulate a verbal response. Some children are very poor at using the Generate and/or Associate and Flexible/Shift cues to engage the cognitive capacities necessary to find the correct answer or interpret the text from the perspective of the question being asked. Some children underutilize the Execute cue to engage strategies they have learned for extracting meaning from text without the presence of specific cues, such as multiple choice options, for what information should be evaluated.

The WJ-III response format is very demanding in a very different way, as it requires the child to direct resources to the generation of a single word that would fit into a sentence grammatically, syntactically, and meaningfully in the context of the other sentences in the passage. This format requires the capacity to adapt (Flexible/Shift cue) to a very different testing format than what is typically encountered in reading comprehension assessment, and requires cueing of text manipulation (Manipulate cue), retrieval (Retrieve cue) of grammar, syntax, and meaning information, and deductive reasoning ability (Generate or Associate cues) in a manner that is quite different from the typical demands made on these processes in the more traditional response formats of free recall and multiple choice questions. Despite their comprehension of the text that was read, some children find this response format to be exceptionally difficult as they struggle to figure out (Gauge cue) what cognitive resources are required for effective performance, and/or have a hard time adapting (Flexible/Shift cue) to this unfamiliar response format.

From the process-oriented analyses of the response format demands of these three reading comprehension tasks, it is clear how variations in the capacity to access and use executive function self-regulation capacities can have a great impact on the quality of the responses obtained from a child. It should also be clear how these variations can impact scores, creating a situation where a child may obtain very different scores on each of these reading comprehension tasks. Children whose development of self-regulation executive function capacities needed for responding to all three of these response formats is appropriate for their age or grade level typically have no difficulty demonstrating a consistent level of performance across these three tasks and earning roughly equivalent scores on all three. Children whose executive function capacities are not as well-developed, on the other hand, are much more likely to show significant fluctuations in performance resulting in significant variability in the scores obtained from these three measures.

Learning and Producing Reading Disabilities

Returning to the issue of the contrast between learning and producing difficulties as discussed at the beginning of this chapter and depicted in Figure 6.1, our discussion here of executive function involvement in reading performance should help to clarify the difference between *reading learning disabilities* and *reading producing disabilities*. In the case of a child with a reading learning disability only (top region of Figure 6.1) such as developmental phonological dyslexia, deficits in phonological processing have made it difficult for this child to learn how to decode words effectively. The child's adequate executive function capacities have aided the child in effectively applying well-developed reasoning, language, and visuospatial abilities and word and knowledge lexicons to the performance of reading comprehension tasks and store a reasonable number of sight words. (This is possible because the reading comprehension tasks such as those on the WAIT-II, KTEA-II, and WJ-III are designed to measure the skills used to extract meaning from text rather than the skills of reading less familiar words that require decoding.) At the other end of the continuum (bottom region of Figure 6.1) is the child who does not display a reading disability but who does show evidence of a producing disability. Despite this child's effective performance with word reading tasks, process measures underlying reading skill development, and equally effective performance on tasks assessing the abilities and lexicons needed to support the text comprehension, this child struggles with the performance of reading comprehension measures. The pattern of this child's test results strongly implicates disuse, or inefficient or inconsistent use, of executive function cues as the source of the poor performance on reading comprehension measures. At the center of the continuum (center region of Figure 6.1 where the two conditions intersect) is the child with both learning and producing disabilities. This child demonstrates the poor performance on phonological processing measures and the associated word decoding deficiency, but also has had difficulty picking up an adequate sight word recognition store and also demonstrates a slow pace when reading. In addition, despite adequately developed abilities and word and general knowledge lexicons, this child struggles with the application of these to the comprehension of text, even when the passages to be read contain mostly high frequency words familiar to the child. Table 6.3 summarizes the contrasts in patterns of test results discussed here.

Self-Regulation Executive Functions and Written Expression

Written expression is the academic skill area most noticeably impacted by executive function difficulties due to the physical form of the final product. The diagram in Figure 6.4 shows the mental capacities involved in the writing process. As was the case with reading, the diagram represents a dynamic interaction of multiple capacities, first to develop and utilize specific skills, and second, to use these skills in an integrated manner to produce written text. Also similar to the diagram for reading, the dotted lines enclosing the cognitive capacities indicate that executive function cues are required to effectively engage each of these components, and the arrows showing pathways between the various capacities represent the coordinated multitasking of executive function cues required to integrate all of the components of the writing process. Similar to the case of reading, we see that self-regulation capacities (1) apply specifically to the direction of specific cognitive processes, abilities, and lexicons as well as the individual writing skills, and (2) apply generally to the multitasking and coordination of executive function capacities to integrate the various processes, abilities, lexicons, and skills to produce fluent writing. As was the case with reading, writing problems (specifically poor text formation, poor text production speed and automaticity, poor text generation, and/or poor text editing and revising), can result from, or be exacerbated by, disuse, or ineffective

Table 6.3 Reading Assessment Score Pattern Typical Differences by Learning and Producing Dimensions

Learning Difficulties Only (Developmental Phonological Dyslexia)	
Assessment Measure	**Score Range**
Ability Measures	Average to Above Average
Lexicon Measures	Average to Above Average
Reading Comprehension Skill Measures	Average to Above Average
Word Reading Skills	Low Average to Average
Decoding Skills	Below Average
Phonological Process Scores	Below Average
Oral-Motor Process Scores	Below Average to Average
Learning (Developmental Phonological Dyslexia) and Producing Difficulties	
Ability Measures	Average to Above Average
Lexicon Measures	Average to Above Average
Reading Comprehension Skill Measures	Below Average to Low Average
Word Reading Skills	Below Average to Low Average
Decoding Skills	Below Average
Phonological Process Scores	Below Average
Oral-Motor Process Scores	Below Average
Producing Difficulties Only	
Ability Measures	Average to Above Average
Lexicon Measures	Average to Above Average
Reading Comprehension Skill Measures	Below Average to Low Average
Word Reading Skills	Low Average to Average
Decoding Skills	Low Average to Average
Phonological Process Scores	Average to Above Average
Oral-Motor Process Scores	Average to Above Average

or inconsistent use, of the executive function capacities that direct all aspects of the writing process.

Table 6.4 specifies the kinds of self-regulation executive function cues most likely to be utilized to direct efficient performance of each of the various cognitive capacities involved in the writing process. As was the case with reading, even the basic skills involved in producing written text require the inte-

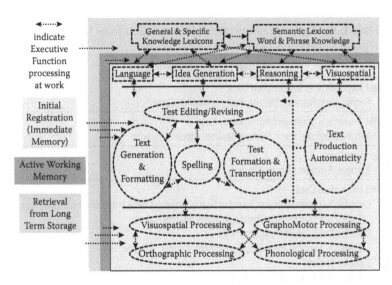

Figure 6.4 An Integrative Model Specifying Processes, Abilities, and Lexicons in Writing.

grated use of several self-regulation executive function cues. The writing of letters, referred to in Table 6.4 as text formation, is the gateway skill for developing fluent written communication skills. The focus of instruction in kindergarten and first grade, production of printed letters involves the acquisition, storage, and retrieval of a flexible visual-motor code. Luria (1973), a pioneer in the field of neuropsychology, used the term "kinetic melody" (p. 36) to describe the series of consecutive movements that take place in an activity such as letter formation. Executive function cues are needed to focus attention (Focus/Select cue) and direct the retrieval (Retrieve cue) and execution (Execute cue) of these learned kinetic melodies, and to provide self-generated feedback on the accuracy of graphomotor production (Monitor cue) and efforts to re-form poorly made letters (Correct cue). Once the kinetic melodies are practiced to the point of automaticity, further instruction in letter production involves the use of executive functions to cue the retrieval (Retrieve cue) and production (Execute cue) of letters with increasing speed (Pace cue) while maintaining accuracy in letter formation (Balance cue).

Fluent handwriting (referred to here as *text production*, that is, writing without a model, and applied in text transcription, that is, copying text) involves the use of graphomotor processing speed guided by the executive function cues of Pace,

Table 6.4   Executive Function Self-Regulation Cues Used in
Written Expression Production

Written Expression Skill Cues*
Text Formation and Transcription Cues   Focus/Select, Retrieve, Execute, Sustain, Monitor, Correct
Text Production Speed and Automaticity Cues   Retrieve, Execute, Pace, Sustain, Monitor, Correct, Balance
Spelling Cues   Retrieve, Execute, Monitor, Correct

Text Generation Cues
  Cues for Text Formation and Transcription (phased out once automaticity is achieved)
    Focus/Select, Retrieve, Execute, Sustain, Monitor, Correct
  Cues for Text Production Automaticity
    Retrieve, Execute, Pace, Sustain, Monitor, Correct, Balance
  Cues for Spelling
    Retrieve, Execute, Monitor, Correct
  Cues for Accessing and Coordinating the Use of Abilities and Lexicons to Generate Text
    Content
    Gauge, Sustain, Hold, Manipulate, Retrieve, Generate, Associate
    Optional use: Organize, Plan/Foresee, Balance, Monitor, Correct
  Cues for Activating Working Memory in the Extended Immediate Time Frame
    Initiate, Sustain, Hold, Manipulate
  Cues for Coordinating the Multitasking of All Cognitive Capacities and Tasks
    Gauge, Organize, Foresee/Plan, Balance, Flexible/Shift, Monitor, Correct
    Optional: Time, Pace
Additional Cues Needed for Reading Material
  Cues for Sight Word Recognition
    Focus/Select, Perceive, Inhibit, Retrieve, Monitor, Correct
  Cues for Word Decoding
    Focus/Select, Perceive, Inhibit, Retrieve, Monitor, Correct
  Cues for Reading Rate
    Pace, Retrieve, Balance
  Cues for Accessing and Coordinating the Use of Abilities and Lexicons
    Gauge, Modulate, Flexible/Shift, Generate, Associate, Retrieve
  Cues for Activating Working Memory in the Extended Immediate Time Frame
    Initiate, Sustain, Hold, Manipulate
  Cues for Coordinating the Multitasking of All Cognitive Capacities and Tasks
    Organize, Foresee/Plan, Balance, Flexible/Shift, Pace, Monitor, Correct
    Optional use: Time, Store

Table 6.4 (continued)   Executive Function Self-Regulation Cues
Used in Written Expression Production

Written Expression Skill Cues*
Text Editing/Revising Cues
Cues for Text Formation and Transcription (phased out once automaticity is achieved)
Focus/Select, Retrieve, Execute, Sustain, Monitor, Correct
Cues for Text Production Automaticity
Retrieve, Execute, Pace, Sustain, Monitor, Correct, Balance
Cues for Spelling
Retrieve, Execute, Monitor, Correct
Cues for Accessing and Coordinating the Use of Abilities and Lexicons to Generate Text Content
Gauge, Sustain, Hold, Manipulate, Retrieve, Generate, Associate, Organize, Plan/Foresee
Balance, Monitor, Correct
Cues for Activating Working Memory in the Extended Immediate Time Frame
Initiate, Sustain, Hold, Manipulate
Cues for Coordinating the Multitasking of All Cognitive Capacities and Tasks
Gauge, Organize, Foresee/Plan, Balance, Flexible/Shift, Monitor, Correct
Optional: Time, Pace
Additional Cues Needed for Reading Material
Cues for Sight Word Recognition
Focus/Select, Perceive, Inhibit, Retrieve, Monitor, Correct
Cues for Word Decoding
Focus/Select, Perceive, Inhibit, Retrieve, Monitor, Correct
Cues for Reading Rate
Pace, Retrieve, Balance
Cues for Accessing and Coordinating the Use of Abilities and Lexicons
Gauge, Modulate, Flexible/Shift, Generate, Associate, Retrieve
Cues for Activating Working Memory in the Extended Immediate Time Frame
Initiate, Sustain, Hold, Manipulate
Cues for Coordinating the Multitasking of All Cognitive Capacities and Tasks
Organize, Foresee/Plan, Balance, Flexible/Shift, Pace, Monitor, Correct
Optional use: Time, Store

*Note: The cues listed in this table represent those cues that are activated specifically for the direction of the written expression skill listed. Additional self-regulation cues that are already engaged to some degree to enable a general state of active engagement with the classroom routine no matter what the task (i.e., Perceive, Focus/Select, Initiate, Modulate, Inhibit) are not listed unless the task requires an increase over the typical level of use of these capacities.

Retrieve, Execute, Monitor, Correct, and Balance. These cues working in tandem assure that the writer maintains (Sustain cue) a consistent rate (Pace cue) of letter production (Retrieve and Execute cues), and that the rate is at the maximum speed that can be achieved while still maintaining (Balance cue) adequate (as judged by the writer) (Monitor cue) accuracy of letter formation (Correct cue). Note however, that in order to assess only graphomotor processing speed guided by the Retrieve, Execute, Pace, Sustain, Monitor, Correct, and Balance cues, the text to be produced must be a highly automated routine (e.g., writing the alphabet) or involve transcription (such as copying sentences). Tasks that require the child to self-generate text beyond these simple tasks necessitates the added use of text generation and spelling skills and the consequent addition of the executive function cues used to guide use of these skills. Even the copying of sentences, however, requires additional self-regulation cues in the form of increased use of the Focus/Select cue and the Monitor cue to attend to the material to be copied, possible increase in the use of the Sustain cue if the time period for writing increases, and the likely addition of the Modulate cue to adjust the level of effort as needed.

Spelling is a component skill that, while unique in terms of cognitive capacities required for effective performance, shares many features with both sight word recognition and word decoding skills. In fact, although traditionally only assessed as a single skill, spelling actually could be divided into automatic spelling of familiar words (similar to sight word recognition) and spelling of less familiar words based on the rules governing grapheme-phoneme (letter/letter cluster-sound) relationships (similar, but not identical to, word decoding). Both automatic spelling and rule-based spelling, however, make use of the Retrieve, Monitor, and Correct cues to guide production of correct spellings. Poor use of executive function cues when spelling can result in poor spelling production, which in turn can affect text generation. Poor spellers often restrict their use of words when writing to avoid using words they do not know how to spell, thereby reducing the overall quality of the text generation products (Berninger & Richards, 2002; Fletcher, Lyon, Fuchs, & Barnes, 2007).

Text generation and *text editing/revising* are unquestionably the most complex of the writing skills. Use of these skills requires near continuous integration of (1) all of the subordinate writing skills (text formation, text production speed and automaticity, spelling) and their executive function cueing needs with (2) additional cognitive capacities (idea generation, reasoning, visuospatial and language abilities; word knowledge, grammar and syntax knowledge, and general knowledge lexicons) and the associated executive cues that guide their access and use, as well as with (3) an additional set of executive functions responsible for cueing sustained extension of the immediate time frame (i.e., the need for active working memory engagement) and (4) an additional set of executive functions responsible for coordination and multitasking needs created by the writer's attempt to generate text beyond simple production or transcription (see Table 6.4).

Speed and automaticity of orthographic motor processing (referred to here as graphomotor processing) is the cornerstone to developing fluent text generation skills. As these motor routines become nonconsciously automated, they free up cognitive resources needed for generating and manipulating the language representation of ideas in working memory and translating those language-represented ideas into text on the page. As indicated in Table 6.4, a host of executive function cues are involved in the complex coordination and multitasking of all of the cognitive capacities involved in generating text. Editing and revising initially generated text requires even greater involvement of these and additional executive function capacities.

In addition to the coordination of all writing skills, the child must also bring into play the executive function cues needed to read text that is being produced during text generation and to reread the generated text during editing/revising. With the heavy involvement of the direction and use of reading skills when using these more complex writing skills, it is not surprising that many children who demonstrate learning and/or producing difficulties in reading also demonstrate difficulties with written expression learning and production. In situations where writing is being formally assessed with tasks other than free form writing, all of these capacities and the related executive functions are joined by an additional set of cognitive capacities and executive functions required for comprehending and responding to the format of the writing assessment.

Table 6.5 Executive Function Cascading Production Decrement Analysis Applied to Written Expression Assessment

Grapho-Motor Processing Decrement
Process Measures
PAL Alphabet Writing 8th Decile (71st–80th percentile range)
Process + Executive Function Measure
PAL Copying A 5th Decile (41st–50th percentile range)
Process + + Executive Function Measure
PAL Copying B 3rd Decile (21st–30th percentile range)
Written Expression Skill Decrements
Process Measures
PAL Alphabet Writing 10th Decile (91st–99th percentile)
PAL Copying A 9th Decile (81st–90th percentile)
PAL Copying B 9th Decile (81st–90th percentile)
Skill Measure
WIAT-II Spelling Standard Score 105 (63rd percentile)
Skill + Executive Function
Written Expression Standard Score 84 (14th percentile)
Process Measures
PAL Alphabet Writing 10th Decile (91st–99th percentile)
Process + Executive Function
PAL Copying A 6th Decile (51st–60th percentile)
PAL Copying B 6th Decile (51st–60th percentile)
Skill Measure
WIAT-II Spelling Standard Score 112 (79th percentile)
Skill + Executive Function Measure
WIAT-II Written Expression Standard Score 108 (70th percentile)
Skill + + Executive Function Measures
PAL Note Taking A 2nd Decile (11th–20th percentile)
PAL Note Taking B 2nd Decile (11th–20th percentile)
Classroom Writing Assignment Rubric Score 1 (Below Basic)

Assessment of Executive Functions Involved in Written Expression

Once again recalling the discussion of executive function assessment presented in Chapter 5, the cascading performance decrements presented in Table 6.5 illustrate an assessment strategy for helping to determine the contribution of executive function capacities to written expression problems. Text production and text transcription skills can be effectively assessed using the PAL Alphabet Writing and Copying A and Copying B tasks. The Alphabet writing task assesses the number of accurately formed letters produced in 15 seconds. The Copy A task assesses the number of letters copied from a sentence in 20 seconds, and the Copying B task assesses the number of letters copied from a paragraph in 90 seconds. Alphabet writing can be considered a baseline task as it minimizes as much as possible the need for self-regulation of the writing process. Copying A and Copying B require increased involvement of executive function capacities given the extended time frame and the need for the use of non-automated writing skills to copy unfamiliar text. Additional steps on the cascade can be filled with various measures of text generation and editing/revising skills including standardized measures of written expression from tests such as the WIAT-II, KTEA-II, TOWL-III or WJ-III, or classroom and/or homework assignments graded with a standard rubric.

It must be remembered that even though alphabet writing is used as a baseline measure, performing this task does require the use of executive function capacities to guide performance. When a child performs poorly on alphabet writing, a process-oriented approach is required to informally assess the degree to which executive difficulties are impacting performance. In these cases, careful observation of the child's efforts during the alphabet writing task can serve as a basis for generating hypotheses about which, if any, of the executive capacities is contributing to the child's poor performance. Further simplifying the text production process with informal tasks involving single letter production will provide additional sources of process-oriented information to further test hypotheses and develop recommendations for the type of instruction needed to help with improving the child's letter formation skills and quick and accurate production of written material.

Adequate performance on alphabet writing coupled with poor performance on Copying A and B and other writing tasks suggests that executive functions of one type or another are likely to be impacting written production. Adequate performance on alphabet writing, and Copying A coupled with poor performance on Copying B and other writing tasks raises the possibility of executive function difficulties, especially the Sustain cue and the Focus/Select cue. In the case of the pattern of adequate performance on alphabet writing, Copying A and Copying B coupled with poor performance on text generation tasks such as the WAIT-II Written Expression Subtest and classroom and homework assignments, the extent of executive function involvement in the lack of performance with text generation tasks is more difficult to determine, as the decrement in production could be due more to a lack of text generation skill than a lack of executive function involvement. In these cases, it must be established through process-oriented observation and performance on informal measures of text generation that the child does possess adequate text generation skills, but that these skills are not demonstrated when tasks require greater self-regulation of these skills. When adequate performance is demonstrated on all formal measures in the cascade, but poor performance is obtained on classroom and homework assignments, text generation skills have been sufficiently documented to warrant stronger hypotheses regarding the involvement of executive function difficulties in task performance.

Executive Functions and Mathematics

While executive functions are intricately involved in mathematics production, this involvement seems to have drawn the least attention of any academic area. This is likely related to the fact that it is now widely acknowledged that less is known about mathematics learning and learning disabilities than the other basic academic areas (Fletcher, Lyon, Fuchs, & Barnes, 2007). Drawing from the work of Berninger and Richards (2002), Temple (1998), Dehaene (1997), and Levine (1998), however, it is possible to construct a model of the mental capacities required in mathematics production similar to that developed for reading and written expression in the previous sections of this chapter. The diagram in Figure 6.5 offers a model of the mental capacities involved in mathematics production. As was the case with reading and writing, the diagram represents a dynamic interaction of multiple capacities, first to develop and utilize specific skills, and second, to use these skills in an integrated manner to accomplish math production. Also similar to the diagrams for reading and writing, the dotted lines enclosing the cognitive capacities indicate that executive function cues are required to effectively engage each of these components, and the arrows showing pathways between the various capacities represent the coordinated multitasking of executive function cues required to integrate all of the components of the writing process. Similar to the cases of reading and writing, we see that self-regulation capacities (1)

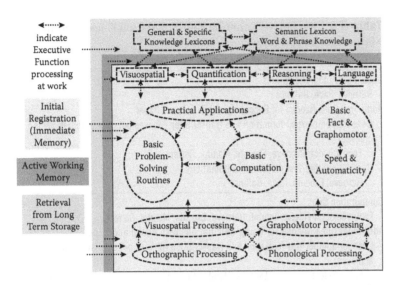

Figure 6.5 An Integrative Model Specifying Processes, Abilities, and Lexicons in Basic Mathematics.

apply specifically to the direction of specific cognitive processes, abilities, and lexicons as well as the individual math skills, and (2) apply generally to the multitasking and coordination of executive function capacities to integrate the various processes, abilities, lexicons, and skills to accomplish math production. As was the case with reading and writing, math problems (specifically poor basic fact automaticity, poor computation, poor problem solving, and/or poor practical applications), can result from, or be exacerbated by, disuse, or ineffective or inconsistent use, of the executive function capacities that direct all aspects of math processing.

Table 6.6 specifies the kinds of self-regulation executive function cues most likely to be utilized to direct efficient performance of each of the various cognitive capacities involved in math processing. As was the case with reading and writing, even the basic skills involved in producing computations require the integrated use of several self-regulation executive function cues. Throughout the elementary years of schooling, children learn procedures and calculation routines that enable them to solve a wide variety of computation problems, from simple addition with single digit numbers to complex multiplication and division of fractions and decimals. When performing these basic computations, executive function cues are needed to focus attention (Focus/Select cue) and direct the

Table 6.6 Executive Function Self-Regulation Cues Used in Mathematics Production

Mathematics Skill Cues*

Basic Fact Automaticity Cues
  Retrieve, Pace, Balance
Additional Cues Needed for Recording with Pencil and Paper
  Cues for number/text formation and transcription (phased out once automaticity is achieved)
    Focus/Select, Retrieve, Execute, Monitor, Correct
  Cues for number/text production automaticity
    Retrieve, Execute, Pace, Balance

Computation Cues
  Focus/Select, Perceive, Inhibit, Retrieve, Execute, Monitor, Correct
Additional Cues Needed for Doing Calculations with Pencil and Paper
  Cues for number/text formation and transcription (phased out once automaticity is achieved)
    Focus/Select, Retrieve, Execute, Monitor, Correct
  Cues for number/text production automaticity
    Retrieve, Execute, Pace, Balance
Additional Cues Needed for Doing Computations that Required Extended Time
  Cues for activating working memory in the extended immediate time frame
    Initiate, Sustain, Hold, Manipulate

Problem-Solving Cues
  Cues for basic fact automaticity
    Pace, Retrieve, Balance
  Cues for computation
    Focus/Select, Perceive, Inhibit, Retrieve, Execute, Monitor, Correct
  Cues for accessing and coordinating the use of abilities and lexicons to generate solutions
    Gauge, Modulate, Sustain, Hold, Manipulate, Retrieve, Generate Associate, Flexible/Shift
    Organize, Plan/Foresee, Balance, Monitor, Correct
  Cues for activating working memory in the extended immediate time frame
    Initiate, Sustain, Hold, Manipulate
  Cues for coordinating the multitasking of all cognitive capacities and tasks
    Organize, Foresee/Plan, Balance, Flexible/Shift, Monitor, Correct
    Optional: Time, Pace
Additional Cues Needed for Doing Calculations with Pencil and Paper
  Cues for number/text formation & transcription (phased out once automaticity is achieved)
    Focus/Select, Retrieve, Execute, Monitor, Correct
  Cues for number/text production automaticity
    Retrieve, Execute, Pace, Balance

Table 6.6 (continued) Executive Function Self-Regulation Cues
Used in Mathematics Production

Mathematics Skill Cues*
Practical Applications Cues
Cues for basic fact automaticity
Pace, Retrieve, Balance
Cues for computation
Focus/Select, Perceive, Inhibit, Retrieve, Execute, Monitor, Correct
Cues for accessing and coordinating the use of abilities and lexicons to generate solutions
Gauge, Modulate, Sustain, Hold, Manipulate, Retrieve, Generate, Associate, Flexible/Shift
Organize, Plan/Foresee, Balance, Monitor, Correct
Cues for activating working memory in the extended immediate time frame
Initiate, Sustain, Hold, Manipulate
Cues for coordinating the multitasking of all cognitive capacities and tasks
Organize, Foresee/Plan, Balance, Flexible/Shift, Monitor, Correct
Optional: Time, Pace
Additional Cues Needed If Reading Is Required
Cues for sight word recognition
Focus/Select, Perceive, Inhibit, Retrieve, Monitor, Correct
Cues for word decoding
Focus/Select, Perceive, Inhibit, Retrieve, Monitor, Correct
Cues for reading rate
Pace, Retrieve, Balance
Cues for accessing and coordinating the use of abilities and lexicons
Gauge, Modulate, Flexible/Shift, Generate Associate, Retrieve
Cues for activating working memory in the extended immediate time frame
Initiate, Sustain, Hold, Manipulate
Cues for coordinating the multitasking of all cognitive capacities and tasks
Organize, Foresee/Plan, Balance, Flexible/Shift, Pace, Monitor, Correct
Optional use: Time, Store
Additional Cues Needed for Doing Calculations with Pencil and Paper
Cues for number/text formation and transcription (phased out once automaticity is achieved)
Focus/Select, Retrieve, Execute, Monitor, Correct
Cues for number/text production automaticity
Retrieve, Execute, Pace, Balance
Additional Cues Needed if Extended Writing is Required (e.g., providing written verbal explanations of work)
Cues for number/text formation and transcription (phased out once automaticity is achieved)
Focus/Select, Retrieve, Execute, Monitor, Correct
Cues for number/text production automaticity
Retrieve, Execute, Pace, Balance
Cues for spelling
Execute, Retrieve, Monitor, Correct

Table 6.6 (continued) Executive Function Self-Regulation Cues Used in Mathematics Production

Mathematics Skill Cues*
Cues for accessing and coordinating the use of abilities and lexicons to generate text content
Sustain, Hold, Manipulate, Retrieve, Generate, Associate
Optional use: Organize, Plan/Foresee, Balance, Monitor, Correct
Cues for activating working memory in the extended immediate time frame
Initiate, Sustain, Hold, Manipulate
Cues for coordinating the multitasking of all cognitive capacities and tasks for writing
Organize, Foresee/Plan, Balance, Flexible/Shift, Monitor, Correct
Optional: Time, Pace

Note: The cues listed in this table represent those cues that are activated specifically for the direction of the math skill listed. Additional self-regulation cues that are already engaged to some degree to enable a general state of active engagement with the classroom routine no matter what the task (i.e., Perceive, Focus/Select, Initiate, Modulate, Inhibit) are not listed unless the task requires an increase over the typical level of use of these capacities.

retrieval (Retrieve cue) and execution (Execute cue) of learned procedures and calculation routines, and to provide self-generated feedback on the accuracy of graphomotor production of numbers and use of calculation procedures and routines (Monitor cue) and direct efforts to correct calculation errors and re-form poorly made numbers (Correct cue). Many children also require enhanced use of the Perceive and Inhibit cues to avoid working too quickly and making errors caused by missing important details such as the operation sign (doing addition instead of subtraction) or the placement of decimals.

Computation skills are greatly enhanced when the child can retrieve (Retrieve cue) basic math facts with speed and automaticity (Pace cue) and incorporate these facts into computation solutions without interfering with ongoing work (Balance cue). Longer and more complicated calculations may require extending work beyond the boundary of immediate registration of information, thereby necessitating the cueing of the need (Initiate cue) to hold information (Hold cue) in an effort to extend the immediate moment to allow more time (Sustain cue) for manipulating information (Manipulate cue) in active working memory. Note also the additional executive functions listed in Table 6.6 that need to be engaged when math work involves the use of pencil and paper.

The executive function requirements increase greatly when basic computation and fact retrieval skills must be integrated with math concept knowledge lexicons and abilities to figure out how to solve problems that extend beyond calculation procedures and routines, and to solve problems in the context of real world applications of math skills. As shown in Table 6.6, isolated problem solving and practical application of problem-solving skills requires the integration of (1) the subordinate basic computation and fact retrieval skills and their executive function cueing needs with (2) additional cognitive capacities (quantitative reasoning, non-quantitative reasoning, visuospatial and language abilities; mathematics concepts knowledge, and general knowledge lexicons) and the associated executive cues that guide their access and use, as well as with (3) an additional set of executive functions responsible for cueing sustained extension of the immediate time frame (i.e., the need for active working memory engagement) and (4) an additional set of executive functions responsible for coordination and multitasking needs created by the specific demands of the problem-solving and practical application contexts. Further engagement of additional self-regulation capacities is necessitated when pencil and paper are used in the work process and when requirements are made to show and explain work. In situations where math achievement is being formally assessed, all of these capacities and the related executive functions are joined by an additional set of cognitive capacities and executive functions required for comprehending and responding to the format of the mathematics assessment.

Assessment of Executive Functions Involved in Mathematics

Assessment of math skills has traditionally focused on measures of computation skills (e.g., KTEA-II Calculations Subtest, WIAT-II Numerical Operations Subtest, WJ-III Calculations Subtest), and measures of problem solving in the context of practical applications (e.g., KTEA-II Math Concepts and Applications Subtest, WIAT-II Math Reasoning Subtest, WJ-III Applied Problems Subtest). In addition to these, measures of speed and automaticity of recording basic math facts are available on the WJ-III (Math Fluency Subtest) and in the form of research-based measurement procedures.

Assessment for identifying the disuse, or ineffective or inconsistent use, of executive function cues in math production is conducted most effectively through application of the process-oriented approach to observing and interpreting task performance combined with clinical interviewing of the child immediately after task performance. Careful observation of the child while engaged in completing computations and solving problems enables the clinician to see if the child cues, or does not cue: (1) any particular strategies or calculation routines; (2) retrieval of well-known facts; (3) attention to operation signs, column placement, decimal point placement, etc; (4) checking of work for errors; (5) accurate correction of found errors; and (6) an adequate work pace that allows for effective completion of all work. After completion of work, a child can be asked to go over his or her and try to recall for the clinician the steps he used in completing both correct and incorrect problems. Although these reports are retrospective and sometimes do not match the observed behavior, they offer great insight into the child's mathematics knowledge base and can identify any discrepancies between what the child knows (i.e., has learned and stored) and what the child does (i.e., incorrect direction of the application of this knowledge resulting in procedural errors and incorrect responses).

In addition to the executive function cues listed in Table 6.6, children frequently must utilize additional self-regulation cues in order to perform effectively on math assessments. Increased use of the Initiate, Gauge, and Modulate cues are often necessary to enable the child to fully grasp what is expected in term of performance and to bring to bear the needed energy and persistence to complete tasks. Most measures of computation skills require the child to self-regulate all aspects of performance while doing "as many of these problems as you can." In these situations, there is increased need for use of the Sustain cue along with the Initiate, Gauge, and Modulate cues. It is not unusual for some children taking this type of self-regulated math test to underactivate various executive function cues and skip over problems, making no effort whatsoever to solve them, and yet, when prompted by the examiner to try these items, they complete them successfully.

Hypotheses about the impact of executive functions on math skill performance can be tested by employing the performance cascades illustrated in Table 6.7. When using this cascade, the strongest evidence for lack of adequate executive function involvement with task performance is obtained when a paradoxical cascading increment is observed. In a paradoxical increment, the child demonstrates better per-

Table 6.7   Executive Function Paradoxical Cascading Production
Increment Analysis Applied to Mathematics Assessment

Mathematics Paradoxical Increments
Skill + Effective Executive Function Use
KTEA-II Concepts & Applications Standard Score 114 (82nd percentile)
Skill + Ineffective Executive Function Use
KTEA-II Math Computation Standard Score 92 (30th percentile)
Skill + Effective Executive Function Use
KTEA-II Math Computation 2nd Administration
Standard Score 95 (37th percentile)
Skill + Ineffective Executive Function Use
KTEA-II Math Computation 1st Administration
Standard Score 73 (4th percentile)

formance on measures of problem solving and practical
applications that require greater use and coordination of
executive functions than on measures of computation skills
that require the coordination of far fewer executive functions.
In the example provided, the child earned a higher score for
the KTEA-II Applications and Concepts Subtest than for the
KTEA-II Math Computations Subtest. Although this pattern
suggests that executive function difficulties might be present, it is also possible that the applications problems utilized
simple computation routines while emphasizing the practical application aspects, as is the desired case in an attempt
to ensure that tests of practical applications are as distinct as
possible from tests of computation skills. Inferences generated for the results of a performance cascade analysis, therefore, need to be supported through observations derived from
process-oriented analysis of task performance that enables
the clinician to identify specific instances where computations were correctly completed when solving application
problems but performed incorrectly on a basic computation
skills test. In the example provided, the child demonstrated
the ability to understand the context of the math application
problems and effectively complete computations within that
context, but made errors with similar types of computations
when given a pencil and a record booklet containing computation problems and told to complete as many as possible.
It seems that in many cases where this paradoxical performance cascade points to executive function difficulties, the
format of the practical applications items (e.g., an explanation
of the problem and visual information showing the problem

or the elements to be used to solve the problem and presentation of each item individually by the examiner), offers many prompts to the student as to the specific executive function cues needed to complete the problem correctly. In contrast, the format of the computations tasks, e.g., independent work on a set of computation problems with no specific time limit and no explanation or set-up of each item, provides the student with no guides as to the type of executive function cues needed to guide effective performance.

Clinicians may also find the use of a short-term test/retest procedure to be an effective way of gauging the impact of executive function difficulties on math production. This technique involves administration of a computation skills test on one day, and readministration of the same computation skills test within the next day or two. The brief interval between the two administrations makes it highly unlikely that the child's scores will vary due to newly learned material, especially when the test is readministered the next day. Using this technique, the first author of this book has observed changes in Standard Scores on the WIAT-II Numerical Operations Subtest of more than 20 points. Process-oriented analysis of test results in these cases strongly implicated variation in the use of executive function cues as the major cause of performance changes. In these situations, lack of cueing or careful monitoring of performance lead to errors with easy computations on the first administration of the test that were not present in the second administration, as these same computations were completed correctly the next day. In some cases, the child is incredulous at the assertion that they incorrectly completed these same computations the day before—until shown his own work.

Executive Functions and Academic Production in the Upper Grades

As students move on to the middle, junior, and high school settings, any executive function difficulties they may be experiencing with the direction of basic academic skill production will be evident in content area classes. Additionally, these academic production limitations are likely to be joined by a host of production difficulties resulting from the significant demands for increased self-regulation of social, emotional, and academic functioning. The executive function demands imposed on students by their new teachers often are different from anything students have experienced so far in school. The novel requirements for many executive functions, especially the Organize, Foresee/Plan, Flexible/Shift, Gauge, and Time cues, may initially represent a nearly insurmountable barrier to academic success. Having difficulty adjusting to these extreme changes, a substantial number of students end up failing tests, assignments—even entire classes—for the first time in their lives. While many students work their way through an adjustment process made much more difficult by lagging maturation of executive function capacities, some never find a way to adapt to these increased demands for self-regulation. Their educational paths, frequently cluttered with failing grades and unexcused absences, far too often end short of high school graduation.

Entering the world of independent content area courses, students at the junior high and late middle school levels often find that they must quickly self-regulate the development of a host of new academic skills; note taking skills, study skills, test taking skills, project planning and organization skills. Each one requires a veritable constellation of executive capacities that involve the highest levels of coordination and multitasking. These increased academic demands are joined by equally challenging new requirements for directing effective social and emotional functioning both in and out of the classroom, and increased need for executive capacities at the self-realization and self-determination level.

Given the large number of executive function capacities and the multiple connections between executive functions and various cognitive capacities within each domain of functioning, coordination, and multitasking of all the executive functions to meet the demands of the school setting can represent a great challenge to any child. Some children are able to maintain effective self-regulation when the demands for multitasking of executive functions are minimal, but experience great difficulties when their control capacity is exceeded by the demands of a situation. Other children can demonstrate much greater capacity for multitasking executive functions, but only when the need to do so is anticipated well in advance or when the demands occur in a familiar setting. The need for multitasking is a critical capacity for effective functioning in the upper grades. This contextual factor should always be considered when evaluating a child's executive function capacities, especially when encountering children who do demonstrate self-regulation capacities, but who find it difficult to coordinate their use on a large scale.

In the upper grades, direct formal assessment can sometimes mask the presence of executive function difficulties because of relatively limited task focus and time frames for task performance. Some students, for example, can effectively plan and organize a one minute task administered as part of a formal assessment, but are unable to plan and organize a large scale project to meet the requirements of a course. This example illustrates the significant difference between the use of the Plan and Organize cues of the self-regulation level and the long-term planning cues of the self-determination level. The need to consider contextual factors beyond the immediate testing situation as well as executive function capacities at multiple levels when assessing students in the upper grades necessitates the use of indirect formal and informal assessment techniques to obtain information from parents and teachers. Information from these sources will be critical for accurate identification of executive function difficulties, especially those that involve self-determination and self-realization difficulties and/or contextual constraints such as difficulty with multitasking or sleep inertia symptoms.

CASE VIGNETTES REVISITED

For each of the children in our case vignettes, information related to the assessment of executive functions involvement in academic skill production is provided.

Case of Justin

Although Justin is not considered to be a child with a learning disability, the results of academic testing completed with Justin did reflect the effects of executive function difficulties on academic production as evidenced in a number of cascading production decrements (e.g., KTEA-II Nonsense Word Decoding Standard Score 114, 82nd percentile but TOWRE Pseudoword Decoding Efficiency Standard Score 100, 50th percentile) and paradoxical increments (e.g., KTEA-II Math Computation Standard Score 92, 30th percentile but Math Concepts and Applications Standard Score 112, 79th percentile).

In the case of reading skills, process-oriented analysis of Justin's performance and discussion with Justin about reading habits revealed that Justin has a tendency to become less careful with his attention to orthography when he feels rushed.

Under time pressure, Justin is much more likely to misperceive letters in words, resulting in misreading of less familiar words. This results in reduced accuracy of text processing and often necessitates rereading of sentences to get the correct meaning. When time pressures are not present, Justin is much less likely to experience these difficulties and comprehension of text comes much faster for him. In the case of math, Justin frequently misperceives operation signs and other visual details (decimal points, negative value sign, labels for quantities such as lbs, oz, cm, mm). As a result, his final answers contain detail errors and often do not accurately reflect his knowledge of the computation algorithms and procedures used in his calculation efforts.

Case of Kevin

The lack of concern with academic problems expressed by Kevin's teachers seemed appropriate based on the results of the achievement assessment included as part of the comprehensive assessment done with Kevin. Results of testing indicated average levels of performance in all academic skill areas and no difficulties with executive functions related to skill use. Kevin was proud of his efforts with academic tasks and responded very positively to verbal praise given for his high level of engagement with tasks. It was observed, however, that when Kevin was confronted with achievement tasks that he believed he could not perform, he would simply refuse to continue with his efforts, even when encouraged to do so.

Case of Caroline

During the individual assessment conducted with Caroline, earned scores were much lower than might be expected with the WIAT-II math and written expression tasks given the results of the cognitive measures administered and from prior school reports that suggested solid acquisition of academic skills. Performance of math tasks yielded scores only in the average range (Numerical Operations Standard Score 101; Math Reasoning Standard Score 98) with errors occurring due to inattention to the operational sign in basic calculations and difficulty in sustaining attention when solving longer math problems, even though she periodically used pencil and paper to help keep track of her work. The Written Expression Subtest score also fell in the average range (Standard Score 99) with Caroline demonstrating solid writing fluency but difficulty with organizing sentences in a succinct manner and minimal sustained effort during the production of a persuasive essay.

Case of Brett

The academic assessment activities completed with Brett revealed adequately developed phonological and orthographic processing capacities, but as anticipated, relatively severe problems with executive function-driven graphomotor production. The K-SEALS was chosen as an additional means of assessing number, letter, and word readiness and vocabulary development because of its quick-take administration format where each question is presented on a single easel page, allowing for quick changes in stimuli that help to maintain the interest and engagement of highly distractible children. Brett responded well to the K-SEALS format and was able to display an adequately developed skill knowledge base earning scores in the above average range for the Vocabulary and the Numbers, Letters & Words subtests.

Case of Morgan

Use of formal achievement testing and informal process-oriented observation and analysis revealed the extensive nature of the effects of Morgan's executive function self-regulation difficulties on her reading and writing production. Morgan's difficulties with focusing and sustaining attention for orthography were reflected in her poor performance with the PAL Receptive Coding (2nd Decile, 11th to 20th percentile range) and Expressive Coding (3rd Decile, 21st to 30th percentile).

When executive function demands were increased, Morgan demonstrated a number of cascading decrements in her ability to use reading skills. These included decrements in the application of reasoning with verbal information during multitasking for reading comprehension (WISC-IV Similarities and Comprehension Scaled Score 14, 91st percentile but WIAT-II Reading Comprehension Standard Score 90, 25th percentile), decrements in phonological processing efficiency when attempting to apply learned decoding rules (NEPSY Phonological Processing Scaled Score 13, 84th percentile and Repetition of Nonsense Words Scaled Score 12, 75th percentile, but WAIT-II Pseudoword Decoding Standard Score 96, 39th percentile), and decrements in processing speed when required to read familiar words or apply decoding rules (NEPSY Speeded Naming Scaled Score 10, 50th percentile and PAL RAN Words 4th Decile, 31st–40th percentile, WIAT-II

Pseudoword Decoding Standard Score 96, 39th percentile, but TOWRE Sight Word Efficiency Standard Score 84, 14th percentile and TOWRE Phonemic Decoding Efficiency Standard Score 74, 4th percentile).

Likewise, increases in executive demands in the writing process produced a cascading decrement in Morgan's ability to use writing skills (PAL Alphabet Writing and Copy A 10th Decile, 91st to 99th percentile, but PAL Note taking A 4th Decile, 31st to 40th percentile range, PAL Note taking B 3rd Decile, 21st to 30th percentile range, and WIAT-II Written Expression Standard Score 74, 4th percentile). A decrement was also observed in Morgan's capacity for orthographic processing when task demands increased the need for quick, efficient attention to orthography. For this production cascade, the WISC-IV Symbol Search Subtest (Scaled Score 11, 63rd percentile) was used as a measure of nonsense orthography processing and contrasted with the results of the PAL Receptive Coding (2nd Decile) and Expressive Coding task results. Although Morgan could register and discriminate among orthographic-like symbols at a reasonable pace when doing symbol search, she was unable to apply this capacity to real words and nonsense words when she was required to focus attention and make orthographic discriminations at a very rapid rate more consistent with the rate used to discriminate words while reading.

Overall, Morgan demonstrated difficulties with executive direction of her superior reasoning abilities when tasks were complex and/or required multitasking and coordination of visual and auditory processing. These difficulties were especially evident when she was engaged in reading comprehension and writing activities, including note taking and difficulties with maintaining a consistent work pace, with a tendency to slow down considerably when performing a task for more than 15 seconds.

Although Morgan has been well-instructed in decoding rules and word analysis techniques, she demonstrated a lack of adequate use of word analysis techniques and decoding rules when attempting to read unfamiliar or less frequently encountered words. She demonstrated difficulty with rapid naming of letters, numbers, and words and with executive control of verbal production when required to inhibit or switch responses, and read both word lists and passages at a very slow rate. Morgan demonstrated difficulty with attending to the details of orthography (the visual features of letters and words), resulting in the misreading of many common sight words and a reduction in the ability to comprehend what was read. Morgan also demonstrated difficulties holding visual representations of words in working memory long enough to produce correct spellings of words despite her ability to read these same words and demonstrated difficulties with the proper use of punctuation, word spelling, and quantity and quality of production when required to write for extended periods of time.

Morgan's executive function difficulties are making it very hard for her to demonstrate consistent production with individual reading and writing tasks due to the difficulties she experiences with the integrated multitasking needed for effective reading comprehension and composition writing.

Case of Alex

The assessment work conducted with Alex revealed no executive function-related difficulties with academic production in reading, writing, or math, and Alex applied these skills effectively in his daily routines in the home.

SUMMARY

This chapter provided an overview of the involvement of executive functions in academic skill production. In order to identify the impact of executive function difficulties on academic functioning, it is necessary to have a shared framework for conceptualization of the mental capacities involved in skill development in the areas of reading, writing, and mathematics. This chapter provided basic definitions of various mental capacities that play roles in academic functioning and models were provided that specify the mental capacities used, and the interrelationships among these capacities, when engaging academic skills. The self-regulation capacities likely to be involved in academic production were specified for reading, writing, and math as well as methods for assessing executive function difficulty involvement in academic skill production problems. The distinction between learning difficulties and producing difficulties was discussed in more detail.

7

Interventions for Executive Function Difficulties

In the previous chapter, we discussed methods for assessing executive functions in the context of a multidimensional conception of executive function capacities. Assessments conducted from this perspective enable the clinician to provide a clear description of executive function difficulties that a child might be experiencing and the specific contexts in which these difficulties are most likely to affect the child's functioning. Such clear, contextually based descriptions form the basis for planning and implementing interventions designed to help the child improve functioning through increased use of executive function capacities. This chapter will offer a general perspective on intervention for executive function difficulties and describe various approaches that can be utilized in intervention efforts.

CONCEPTUAL BASIS FOR EXECUTIVE FUNCTION INTERVENTION

Any attempt at intervention for executive function difficulties depends on the proper conceptualization of the problem. Proper conceptualization requires a thorough appreciation of the nature and impact of executive function difficulties. Adopting an effective approach to case conceptualization involves three critical keys that hinge on answering three questions about the nature of executive function difficulties.

Key 1: Executive Function Difficulties Are Associated with Suboptimal Brain Function

The first question related to case conceptualization that a professional working with children with executive function difficulties must answer is, "Are the observed executive function difficulties a matter of disuse through conscious choice or a matter of nonconscious brain dysfunction?" As discussed in

Chapter 4, because executive control is heavily involved in demonstrating learning through production, in complying with requests of others, and in the effective performance of everyday tasks, executive difficulties usually manifest as "producing disabilities." The nature of this disability can be exasperating to parents, teachers, and anyone else involved in dealing with the consequences of the child's inability to meet expectations.

Although it might appear to be the case that the child is consciously choosing how to perceive, feel, think, and act when a lack of production is observed, proper conceptualization of executive function difficulties requires an acknowledgment that the source of the executive function problems is most likely a result of less than optimal nonconscious brain function. Most importantly, clinicians must help parents and teachers, as well as themselves, realize that the executive difficulties that are so exasperating to them are just as exasperating to the child, with the only difference being in the nature of the reactions that are expressed.

Parents, teachers, and others involved with a child with executive function difficulties must be careful not to attribute the particular production deficits they observe to character flaws or consciously chosen states of mind, such as laziness, lack of motivation, apathy, irresponsibility, or stubbornness. Rather, it must be understood that the behaviors that they are observing emanate from difficulties that are rooted in brain function, that the child's current state of brain function very likely was not a matter of conscious choice, and that immediately changing that current state of brain function most likely is not within the consciously controlled skill set of the child. This insight is especially hard to keep in mind when the child's internally commanded behaviors are so glaringly different from what they exhibit when externally commanded to produce, and when their reaction to comments pointing out this state of affairs seems callous, disrespectful, vindictive, or even hateful. In these situations, it seems so natural to attribute the lack of on-demand production to negative qualities such as lack of responsibility, apathy, passive aggression, or outright defiance. Avoiding such negative attributions, even when confronted with statements from the child strongly suggesting that they are true, is the first essential key to proper conceptualization of the executive function problems that must be addressed.

With a more appropriate conception of the nature of the executive function problems, difficulties can be clearly stated in behavioral terms, which indicate a behavior that can be changed through intervention. The goal here is twofold: first, to help the parents and professionals to understand the nature of the deficit so that, secondly, through proper intervention, the child or adolescent can be assisted in changing the behavior from negative to positive.

Key 2: Brain Function Can Be Altered Through Intervention

The second question related to case conceptualization that must be answered is, "Is the less than optimal brain functioning associated with the observed executive difficulties an unalterable condition resulting from permanently damaged neural networks or is it an alterable condition caused by underutilization or underdevelopment of neural networks?" While it is certainly true that in cases of more severe brain damage neural networks have been altered or damaged to the point where little change in the current level of executive function capacity is likely, these cases are much more the exception than the rule. In the absence of clear evidence that the child was born with severe brain damage or severe traumatic brain injury since birth, it is best for professionals to assume that children possess the neural capacity to alter their current state of brain function. The important assumption here is that internal change that would enable the child to demonstrate the desired self-regulation capacities is possible. Working from the initial assumption that change is possible is the second essential key to proper conceptualization of the problem. This optimistic stance enables the clinician to develop an intervention plan with the goal of positive change rather than the goal of simply managing a suboptimal state of functioning. A lack of progress over time toward positive goals, however, may necessitate the inclusion of behavior management strategies to deal with a child's current lack of executive control.

Key 3: Interventions Can Activate the Use of Intact Brain Function

The third important question that should be asked during case conceptualization is, "Are the observed executive function difficulties the result of disuse of already developed neural capacities or the result of a delay in the natural progression of neural network development?" If the difficulties are the result of disuse of existing neural capacities, then an intervention plan focused on positive behavior change goals will be based on teaching the child how to activate these neural networks, either consciously or nonconsciously, to achieve positive goals. In this situation, the amount and rate of progress toward positive goals will be constrained only by other contextual factors such as the level of functioning of other cognitive capacities (e.g., the child's capacity to benefit from language-based learning). Assuming that the child can be taught how to access internal mechanisms of self-regulation to achieve the positive behavior goals is the third essential key to proper conceptualization of problems that must be addressed.

If the difficulties are more related to delays in the natural progression of development of neural networks that enable increased executive control, then progress toward positive goals is likely to be slower and less consistent than might be expected even when other contextual factors are not creating any conditions that might constrain progress. It should be apparent to the reader that this third important question cannot be definitively answered at the outset of an intervention, but rather that the answer emerges over time based on the nature of the child's response to intervention. If intervention attempts progress over time with less than the desired results, even after modifications in the strategies used to obtain results, the presence of developmental delays becomes much more likely. The answer to this third question, therefore, does not alter the initial assumption of the need to develop positive goals for behavior change and the need to teach the child ways to achieve these goals. Rather, it enables all involved in intervention efforts to maintain hope for future results and offers the encouragement needed to maintain patience with the slow rate of progress that might be occurring. Although as time progresses, the lack of progress might suggest that the child is not capable of developing self-regulation capacities, in the absence of clear physical evidence of severe neural dysfunction, the best course of action is to maintain a positive outlook and continue to encourage and assist the child in working toward positive change goals.

ADDITIONAL ISSUES RELATED TO INTERVENTION CONCEPTION

Along with the three critical keys to conceptualizing interventions, a number of other issues should be kept in mind when planning and implementing interventions. These include balancing the teaching of internal control with requirements for external control, the executive function environment in which interventions will be implemented, the use of rewards and punishment during intervention, maturation of frontal lobe neural circuits, and consequences for unacceptable behavior.

Balancing the Teaching of Internal Control with Requirements for External Control

Although the goal of any intervention should be to increase the child's capacity for internally directed self-regulation, some children will require external controls for regulating existing behavior problems in the form of a behavior management plan. Effective interventions, therefore, often will involve finding the proper balance between teaching the child strategies and techniques that will affect internal change for improving self-regulation, while simultaneously supplying the requisite external controls that might be needed to support the child and manage behavior as long as severe self-regulation difficulties are being manifested. As a child learns to increase the use of existing executive capacities, or experiences developmental shifts which increase the capacity to exert executive control over functioning, the external controls can be lessened gradually with the goal of eventually being eliminated altogether. Careful monitoring of progress during the intervention period is required to enable the clinician and the child's parents to make the necessary decisions about the timing and extent of alterations made to external control contingencies.

The Executive Function Environment in Which Interventions Will Be Implemented

Executive function interventions do not occur in a vacuum, nor are they implemented by flawlessly performing automatons. The effectiveness of any intervention attempt will depend greatly on the executive function capacities of the clinician and those most closely associated with the child—family, friends, teachers, administrators, etc. A caring environment populated with individuals who exhibit at least average levels of executive development can help the child in many ways. Not only can these individuals model good use of executive functions in their own daily behavior, they are more likely to be able to help with the implementation of a consistent intervention plan and be counted on to react appropriately to the executive miscues of the child. In addition, they can also model appropriate ways to handle the executive function oversights or lapses that are a part of the normal functioning of us all. Appreciating that no one is flawless in their perceiving, feeling, thinking, and acting, and that mistakes can be made and handled gracefully and without conflict is an especially important lesson for children with executive function difficulties. For the clinician, there are few situations more challenging than being faced with planning an intervention for a child whose parents are experiencing as many, or even more, executive function difficulties than the child.

The Use of Rewards and Punishment During Intervention

Nearly all externally developed and monitored behavior management plans make use of rewards and/or punishment for performance, or lack of performance, of target behaviors. When dealing with children who exhibit executive function difficulties, the use of rewards and punishments should be thought through very carefully. The use of rewards and punishment assumes, either implicitly or explicitly, that the child already possesses the executive skills required to cue perception, feeling, thought, or action in a manner that will produce the target behavior, and that the lack of production of the target behavior is a matter of conscious choice. The rewards and punishments therefore are intended to serve as external sources of motivation to help generate within the child the desire to engage in the target behaviors. As the reader should now realize, in the case of children with executive difficulties, the assumption of control through conscious choice is a faulty one.

While some children may be able to identify what it is that they should be doing, their executive function deficits make it difficult for them to cue themselves sufficiently or consistently in order to engage in the target behaviors. In these situations, because the neural mechanisms needed to produce the target behavior are not yet under the conscious or nonconscious control of the child, the likelihood of attaining rewards is small while the likelihood of accruing punishment is great. The use of rewards and punishments for these children typically leads to frustration, anger, or withdrawal with the result being additional, possibly more extreme, behavior problems. The problem in these situations is that the child does not possess the skills necessary to achieve the target behaviors. As a result, no amount of reward or punishment will enable the child to meet the expectations of the program. When results are not achieved in these circumstances, it is often the child rather than the program that is thought to be at fault.

Although the use of rewards and punishments are not effective with children who have not yet developed either nonconscious or conscious control of the executive capacities required to achieve target behaviors, there certainly exists a substantial number of children with executive function difficulties for whom rewards and punishments can be effective. Unlike those children who do not yet possess the executive function capacities required to produce the target behaviors and/or who are unable to consciously or nonconsciously engage executive functions to attain rewards or avoid punishment, these children do possess the requisite executive function capacities and are able, at least nonconsciously, to activate the needed executive capacities when rewards or punishment are introduced and consistently applied. The lack of production evidenced by these children prior to the implementation of a behavior management program, however, is typically not the result of a lack of motivation to engage in the target behaviors. Rather, these children are often very motivated to demonstrate the target behaviors despite their lack of success in doing so prior to the start of the program. In these cases, the behavior management program offers a source of consistent, frequent feedback about the effectiveness of performance, thereby enabling these children to engage in the proper level of self-monitoring needed to assure adequate production. For these children, the feedback component of the management program can be a powerful tool for producing the desired behaviors.

Because clinicians are not likely to know beforehand whether a child exhibiting executive function difficulties will, or will not, respond as desired to a behavior management program using rewards and/or punishments, the use of such programs should be carefully monitored. If, after a reasonable trial period, the program does not appear to be working, program modifications such as reducing the time between demonstrating the desired behavior and receiving a reward should be tried. If such modifications are not effective, clinicians are advised to try to develop intervention programs that are not dependent on the use of rewards or punishment rather than assume that the child's behavior is unalterable.

Even when rewards and punishment produce the desired results, it should be realized that programs that rely strictly on rewards and punishment to produce the desired results are only external forms of control. They do not teach children to become consciously aware of, reflect on, and internalize the control of their behavior; they simply reward the presence of the behavior and/or punish its absence. While rewards and/or punishment can play a role in a good intervention program, the ultimate goal of helping the child to internalize executive control will require conscious attention to teaching of the use of the skills and providing a cueing system for knowing when to employ the skills.

Maturation of Frontal Lobe Neural Circuits

Given that executive function capacities follow a developmental progression dependent on the maturation of the neural circuitry of the frontal lobes, perhaps the most powerful intervention tool is time in itself. Over time, most children and adolescents gradually improve in their ability to demonstrate self-activation, self-regulation, self-realization, and self-determination. As noted in Chapter 4, problems arise when cultural expectations impose arbitrary timelines on brain function development. As Gioia, Isquith, Guy, and Kenworthy (2000) point out, the final endpoint of executive function development varies by individual, as does the order and timing of the developmental progression of these capacities. For many children faced with overly aggressive expectations for brain maturation, a little time may be all that is needed to achieve the desired levels of self-direction. For others with more substantial developmental delays, the ultimate solution to the executive difficulties being experienced may simply be much more time.

Recall in Chapter 4 the discussion of the proposition that children with ADHD typically experience about a 30% delay in development of specific self-regulation capacities. For those who are responsible for helping the child achieve transition to an independent state of self-direction, adjusting to the idea that their child will not demonstrate many aspects of self-direction typical of a 20-year-old until about the age of 30 might not be met with a great deal of enthusiasm. On the other hand, knowing that the executive difficulties that their child is experiencing do not represent a permanent state of mental functioning should be a significant relief. One of the goals of working with children experiencing executive function difficulties should be to help family members develop a perspective that engenders hope for the future. Discussing

the developmental nature of most executive function difficulties offers the clinician an opportunity to help the family
reframe the issues in a more positive way that can greatly
help to accomplish this goal.

While maturation is likely the single most significant factor in determining the ultimate resolution of executive function difficulties, this does not mean that clinicians and family
members should adopt a wait and see approach to dealing
with the problems being experienced in the present moment.
Certainly, energy and effort should be put into developing
and implementing interventions in the present that attempt
to produce positive behavior changes in current areas of difficulty. Appreciating the likelihood of a slow trajectory of neural development for the child, however, provides the impetus
for professionals and parents to remain patient with less than
optimal results from intervention efforts and to maintain
hope for improved functioning in the future. By implementing
intervention efforts rather than simply waiting for maturation
to run its course, professionals and parents are providing the
child with a knowledge base relevant to utilizing executive
functions that has the potential to be an invaluable resource
that can be tapped when increases in neural development
make increased use of executive capacities possible.

Another important implication of maturation of executive
functions relates to the viability of the two primary intervention stances. The less developed the neural processes, the more
likely it is that external control will play a major role in any
intervention efforts. Younger children, brain injured children,
and cognitively impaired children with significant executive
function difficulties all typically require interventions that
are focused on external controls for improving executive functioning. Children with less severe executive difficulties who
are approaching or who have entered adolescence are much
more likely to be able to respond to interventions that focus
on internalizing executive control processes. If intervention
must begin with external controls, those responsible for implementing the intervention should pair external control with
discussion of the use of the external control techniques and
the reasons for their use in an effort to make the child more
aware of the type of control that is needed in that situation,
and encouragement for the child to attempt to self-initiate the
desired forms of executive control. If the child begins to demonstrate the capacity to self-regulate, approaches focused on

internalizing self-regulation can be introduced into intervention efforts.

Consequences of Unacceptable Behavior

As discussed earlier, many children who experience difficulties with executive functions are not capable of the level of self-regulation of behavior needed to avoid rule infractions. When attempting to structure interventions for children with executive function difficulties, it may be difficult for some authority figures to accept that consequences (i.e., punishments) that are to be applied for rule infractions should be altered in any way for these children. The beliefs that making exceptions to rules simply teaches children that they can get away with any form of decadent behavior in which they choose to engage and that it is unfair to all of the other law-abiding children to allow certain children to break rules without serving the prescribed consequences are deeply held, unshakeable ones for many people, especially those in positions of authority where enforcement of laws and legal policies is a major part of their job function. Clinicians are likely to find negotiation with these authority figures to be the most difficult aspect of their efforts to structure an environment that will enable the child to stay positively engaged with society in general. It is hoped that the readers of this book would recognize the need to make exceptions to some rules in order to preserve the opportunities for these children to make contributions to society in the future. A little understanding in the present moment can often pay large dividends in the distant future. It should also be understood that the authors are not making a case for excusing all forms of unacceptable behavior, no matter how severe or harmful. In fact, we support the application of consequences for behavior that causes great harm to others, even if that behavior was carried out by a child whose neural functions are clearly deficient. However, we strongly advocate for the humane treatment of these children in the sense that the consequences should be of a reasonable nature and not overly harsh.

As we have just discussed the role of maturation and consequences for children with deficits in executive functions, a logical next step might be to question the feasibility of retention as an intervention. To some, retention is a logical and natural consequence of a failure to produce in the classroom. In addition, some espouse the use of retention in order to give a student additional time to mature. While such course of action may seem reasonable and well intentioned, the use of retention as an intervention does not have an evidence base to suggest that it is effective for any specific population. In fact, the research on retention (Jimerson, 2001) suggests it is a practice that may produce more harm than potential benefit. Nevertheless, the issue of retention continues to be a "Hot-Button" issue among educators. Those in favor of, as well as those opposed to, the practice vehemently defend their positions in debates, which often raise the ire of the participants and result in impassioned discussions. In spite of this, many educators are able to cite anecdotal cases where they feel retention has been beneficial. In Jimerson's (2001) meta-analysis of the research studies on retention published in the 1990s, it was reported that only 5% of the studies found results that are more favorable for students who were retained. The remaining 95% of the studies analyzed demonstrated either no difference between groups that were retained and those who were socially promoted, or a worse outcome for the children who were retained. While this meta-analysis suggests that retention may be beneficial for a small subset of students, it is not yet clear who may benefit. Until there is an evidence base to effectively differentiate those who may benefit from retention from the vast majority of those for whom it does not benefit, or for whom it is actually harmful, retention is not a general intervention practice that can be ethically supported for students with executive deficits.

SUGGESTED GENERAL GUIDELINES FOR PLANNING AND IMPLEMENTING INTERVENTIONS

In light of the discussion of the three critical keys and related issues relevant to conceptualizing intervention, the following general guidelines are offered to help guide the planning and implementation of interventions for executive function difficulties experienced by children:

1. Provide the child with as rich an "executive function environment" as possible; engage the assistance of family members and others who have frequent contact with the child who are capable of modeling effective executive function use and of encouraging the development of similar capacities in the child.
2. Initially assume the position that the executive function difficulties that the child is experiencing are the result

of nonconscious disuse of existing executive capacities, and that the child can be taught to consciously or nonconsciously activate these capacities to achieve positive behavior change.

3. Develop an intervention plan that focuses on making the child aware of the executive capacities needed to achieve desired behavior goals and on teaching the child how and when to activate the use of the needed executive capacities with the ultimate goal being internalization of the self-regulation routines needed for effective functioning.

4. Develop and apply, as needed, interventions involving external control of behaviors resulting from executive function difficulties. Monitor the use of the interventions closely to determine when to begin the gradual or complete withdrawal of external control in order to allow for the demonstration of the use of newly developed internally driven executive capacities.

5. Maintain and model attitudes of hope, perseverance, and patience with intervention efforts, realizing that in many cases, gains may be minimal and may require prolonged periods of time to achieve.

6. Maintain, and foster in others, reasonable expectations for behavior change and sensible and reasonable consequences for unacceptable behavior that stems from the child's executive function deficiencies.

INTERVENTIONS FOR EXECUTIVE FUNCTION DIFFICULTIES: AN OVERVIEW OF THE STATE OF THE ART

In order to adequately engage intervention practices, a general understanding of the state of the art on interventions for executive function difficulties experienced by children is necessary. Given the lack of widespread knowledge of the nature of executive functions and the complexity of what comprises executive function difficulties, it should not be surprising to readers to find that there is minimal evidence-based literature available that addresses executive function interventions. While understanding that the current body of research and clinical practice literature does not address evidence-based interventions for executive function problems, it is important to realize that a wealth of data exists that is likely to be helpful in developing interventions for children who exhibit executive function difficulties. Current sources of evidence-based information can be found—even though the executive function nomenclature discussed in this book may not be used by the various authors of these sources. These sources cover a wide range in terms of professional fields and perspectives.

Intervention Strategies Specifically Dealing with Developing Internal Control

As mentioned earlier, the primary goal of interventions for executive function difficulties should be the internalization of directive capacities. Although not specifically presented as interventions for children with executive functioning difficulties, a number of therapeutic approaches have been highly efficacious in addressing many aspects of self-regulation difficulties.

Perhaps the best researched of these is *Cognitive Behavior Therapy*. Although this technique was not originally conceptualized as a treatment for executive function difficulties, it is now clear from the research that this technique enables individuals to gain access to frontal lobe self-direction neural mechanisms (Schwartz, 1996; Goldberg et al., 2004). Cognitive Behavior Therapy is a clinical technique that utilizes training of executive control processes to improve a client's control of their feelings, emotions, thoughts, and actions. Cognitive behavioral approaches have been highly effective in helping children and adults gain executive control over their perceptions, thought patterns, emotional reactions, and overt behaviors. CBT strategies can increase the child's explicit awareness of inner cueing and regulating functions. For example, a child with a severe anxiety disorder who learns to control the anxiety without using medication has learned how to use internal capacities to exert executive control over the neural processes that produce or maintain the anxious feelings. Excellent resources for specific CBT approaches and strategies for use with children can be found in Friedberg and McClure's *Clinical Practice of Cognitive Therapy with Children and Adolescents* (2002) and Mennuti, Freeman, and Christner's *Cognitive Behavioral Interventions in Educational Settings* (2006).

Variations on the general cognitive behavior approach, such as Jeffrey Schwartz's (1996) approach to treating obsessive-compulsive disorder, Ross Greene's (2001; 2006) strategies for dealing with explosive (easily frustrated, highly inflexible) children, Myrna Shure's (1992) *I Can Problem-Solve* education program for children, and McGinnis and Goldstein's (1984) skill-streaming series also are intervention approaches that are specifically designed to address self-regulation executive function difficulties.

While a relatively new extension of CBT, mindfulness based cognitive behavior therapy (Brown & Ryan, 2003; Hayes, Follette, & Linehan, 2004; Segal, Williams, & Teasedale, 2002) and other mindfulness practices (Kabat-Zinn, 1994, 2005, Siegel, 2007) also appear to be efficacious in fostering increased well-being. As an adjunct activity, there is increasing suggestion that yoga, tai chi, and similar practices might also provide increased well-being and, in fact, the mainstream literature increasingly touts physical activity as having a positive impact not only on physical health, but also cognitive functioning, with executive function improvement specifically noted (e.g., Carmichael, 2007).

Other examples of interventions geared to deal with executive function deficits of self-regulation include motivational interviewing techniques (Miller & Rollnick, 2002), and motor planning and motor praxis training conducted by occupational and physical therapists. Social problem-solving therapy (Nezu & Perri, 1989) has been found to be efficacious as an approach for dealing with stressors. Carol Gray's Social Stories program (Gray, 2002) employs scaffolding techniques to make explicit what those without executive and cognitive deficits find relatively routine and implicit. Originally designed as an intervention to deal with the self-regulation deficits of children diagnosed with Autism, variations of the Social Stories approach could be used with children (especially young children) who lack a developmentally appropriate "theory of mind" (realization of self and others) needed to size up a situation in order to know how to respond.

Meta-analyses of the efficacy of social skills training (Gresham, Cook, & Crews, 2004) have noted significant behavioral improvements for identified or at-risk behavior disordered children. The effect may be particularly powerful if the treatment is provided to young children with early onset behavioral regulation difficulties (Webster-Stratton & Reid, 2003; Antshel, 2005). For older children and those with more entrenched or long-standing executive function difficulties, the training program may need to be more extensive (Gresham, Van, & Cook, 2006). Most literature related to the use of social skills training continues to suggest, however, that such training for behavioral difficulties needs to be conducted in the natural setting to allow for better generalization and maintenance.

From the education literature, Reuven Feuerstein's (1980) instrumental enrichment technique, emphasizing mediated learning and teaching how to think about thinking, is perhaps the most ambitious attempt to improve the executive function capacities of children who appear to have limited cognitive capacities. *Metacognition*, a term appearing in the educational and cognitive psychology literature that refers to how children think about thinking, overlaps greatly with the concept of executive functions. For example, metacognitive strategies for teaching skills such as reading comprehension can be viewed as attempts to teach children how to use executive control processes to guide their thinking about what they are reading.

A substantial body of educational research has supported the use of cognitive strategy training, metacognition, self-regulated learning, and self-monitoring as effective approaches for helping children develop the capacity to develop and use self-regulation and self-realization executive functions (Apthorp & Clark, 2007; Borkowski & Muthukrishna, 1992; Case, et.al., 1992; Gaskins & Elliott, 1991; Harris & Graham, 1996; Hartman, 2001; Kurtz & Borkowski, 1987; Mastropieri & Scruggs, 1991; Miranda, et. al, 1997; Pressley & Woloshyn, 1995; Scheid, 1993; Schraw, 1998; Schunk, 1989; Scruggs & Mastropieri, Wood & Murdock, 2002; Wood, et. al, 1995; Zimmerman, 1989, 1990).

Intervention Strategies Specifically Dealing with Developing External Control

The most prevalent evidence-based intervention data related to external control of executive capacities comes from the ADHD literature, which places great emphasis on the well-documented efficacy of psycho-stimulant medication for dealing with significant hyperactive-impulsive symptomatology, but which also presents research on the effectiveness of behavior management programs (Barkley, 2006; Reid & Barkowski, 1987; Teeter, 1998).

For instance, Russell Barkley's book *Attention-Deficit Hyperactivity Disorder: A Handbook for Diagnosis and Treatment* (2006) describes behavior management interventions for a number of executive function difficulties typically exhibited by individuals with ADHD, and his book *Taking Charge of ADHD* (2000) provides many practical suggestions for parents and teachers for managing the behavior of children with

ADHD. Clare Jones' *Attention Deficit Disorder: Strategies for School-Age Children* (1996) and Phyllis Teeter's *Interventions for ADHD: Treatment in Developmental Context* (1998) also describe intervention techniques targeting specific executive function problems exhibited by children with ADHD.

As discussed in Chapter 4, however, the reader is cautioned not to oversimplify the problems associated with executive function difficulties by considering them to be synonymous with ADHD symptomatology. Individuals with ADHD experience difficulties with some, but not necessarily all, of the self-regulation capacities identified in earlier chapters. In fact, a diagnosis of ADHD alone does not provide the clinician much direction in determining what intervention approaches are likely to be most effective. Also as discussed in Chapter 4, although nearly all DSM diagnoses are accompanied by some aspect of execution functioning difficulties, the DSM diagnosis itself is likely to provide very little information relative to the specific executive function deficits that a particular child may be experiencing.

In addition to the ADHD literature, clinicians working with survivors of traumatic brain injuries have developed a number of external control strategies to help manage the often severe executive function deficits that these children exhibit. The Interventions section of the *BRIEF Software Portfolio* (Isquith et al., 2002) provides an excellent overview of executive function interventions primarily gleaned from the traumatic brain injury (TBI) literature (Levine, et al., 2000; Marlowe, 2001; Ylvisaker, 1998; Ylvisaker, & Feeney, 1998; Ylvisaker, Szekeres, & Feeney, 1998).

Additional Sources of Intervention Information

A number of other sources offer information that addresses both internal self-regulation and external control strategies of a more general nature, or simply offer good ideas that can serve as starting points for generating more individualized strategies. Mel Levine's *Developmental Variations and Learning Disorders* (1998) contains recommendations for a wide variety of executive function difficulties in the chapters addressing Attention, Memory, Higher Order Cognition, Social Ability, and Reading.

While most of the previously mentioned authors discuss interventions for executive function difficulties without using the executive function nomenclature, the Dawson and Guare book, *Executive Skills in Children and Adolescents* (2004), is one of the few guides published to date that specifically addresses interventions for executive function difficulties in the context of both the home and the classroom.

A new text by Michael Posner and Mary Rothbart (2007) entitled *Educating the Human Brain* addresses brain function and educational curricula and has great promise for becoming a cornerstone for thought in developing classroom educational practices that address executive functions, although, as mentioned in Chapter 5 of this book, Posner chooses to refer to the various executive function capacities of the frontal lobes under the single label of attention mechanisms.

Although the specific literature on executive function interventions is lagging far behind the basic research literature, there are some indications that this may change in the future with the continued publication of research articles such as those by Watson and Westby (2003) on strategies for addressing the executive function impairments of students prenatally exposed to alcohol and other drugs, and Singer and Bashir (1999) on executive functions, self-regulation, and language learning disabilities, and books such as *Executive Function in Education,* a volume edited by Lynn Meltzer (2007). The intervention section of the Executive Function Annotated Bibiliography located on the CD accompanying this book can be consulted for additional sources of information about interventions for executive function difficulties.

THE ENVIRONMENT ARENA OF INVOLVEMENT: A NEW FRONTIER FOR INTERVENTION?

For most readers, it was likely not very difficult to envision the type of self-regulation difficulties manifested in the intrapersonal, interpersonal, and/or the symbol system arenas to which the intervention techniques discussed in this section would clearly apply. Much less likely, however, is that readers found it easy to envision the application of these interventions to executive function difficulties as they are manifested in the environmental arena. And yet, the environmental arena executive function difficulties exhibited by some children are likely to be the greatest cause of damage to property and significant, and sometimes tragic, injury to these children and those around them. Executive function difficulties exhibited in the environment arena are the reason why parents keep childproof paraphernalia installed in households long after it would be considered developmentally appropriate; why the accident rate of ADHD teenagers is considerably higher than the general same-age population; and why there is an audible reminder to fasten the seatbelt when car ignitions are engaged. Although often overlooked, interventions for addressing self-regulation difficulties in the environment arena could well be the most critical in terms of benefit to the child and family, and society in general.

Once attention is focused on the environment arena, the natural tendency is to think of the impulsive, often risky, behaviors exhibited by many ADHD children such as Brett. However, it would be misleading to suggest that most executive function difficulties in the environment arena involve inadequate use of the inhibit cue. Even the expansion of the list to include the Foresee/Plan, Gauge, Modulate, and Sustain cues as suggested by the examples described above would be too limiting. In fact, all 23 of the self-regulation capacities play a role in the child's ability to effectively navigate and manage their surrounding environment. Failure to use the Perceive cue to spot a warning sign for a detour; failure to use the Initiate or the Execute cue to engage a motor plan when a stopped car unexpectedly appears on the horizon; failure to use the Inhibit cue to stop from swinging the bat when the ball is clearly out of the strike zone; failure to locate a missing item due to lack of use of the Organize cue to direct an effective search. All these are examples of executive function difficulties that, if exhibited with great frequency, can reduce the likelihood of desired outcomes. Although self-regulation difficulties that are manifested in the environment arena are often overlooked as targets for intervention, the fact of the matter is that many of the same intervention strategies used to deal with executive function difficulties in the other arenas can be applied just as effectively to improve a child's performance and quality of life. It is our hope that readers of this book will not overlook the need to address executive problems in what is perhaps the most important of all the arenas of involvement.

SPECIFIC INTERVENTION STRATEGIES FOR EXECUTIVE FUNCTION DIFFICULTIES

Based on a review of the sources discussed in the previous section, a set of specific strategies that have been most effective in producing positive behavior change and improving self-regulation capacities can be identified. The executive function intervention strategies discussed in this section are organized into two general categories: intervention strategies for developing internal control and intervention strategies for applying external control. All of the strategies described here, with the exception of pharmacology, are applicable to efforts to improve the use of the full spectrum of executive function capacities for directing perceptions, feelings, thoughts, and actions within the intrapersonal, interpersonal, environment, and symbol system arenas of involvement and across multiple settings (e.g., home, school, and community).

Intervention Strategies for Developing Internal Control

Intervention strategies for developing internal control help children improve their use of self-regulation cues without the assistance of others. The ultimate goal of these strategies is to enable the child to demonstrate age-appropriate executive function capacities.

Increasing Awareness

As the research findings of Posner (Posner & Rothbart, 2007) and cognitive behaviorists such as Segal, Williams, and Teasdale (2002) and Singh (2007) have demonstrated, focused awareness can be a powerful tool for developing the capacity to self-monitor and affect changes in perceptions, feelings, thoughts, and actions. Although it might be assumed that a certain level of brain maturation is required to engage in exercises for developing greater self-awareness, Myrna Shure's work with the I Can Problem Solve program (1992) suggests that even young children can increase their capacity for self-awareness through the use of more concrete problem-solving activities. When possible, the use of videotaping technology can be a powerful tool for increasing awareness by providing children with concrete examples of their behavior and its effects on others.

Modeling Appropriate Use of Executive Functions

Social modeling strategies have been used to alter children's social behavior (Quinn, Kavale, Mathur, Rutherford, & Forness, 1999), and the research in this area suggests that social modeling strategies are likely to be an effective means of helping children consciously or nonconsciously engage executive function capacities to self-direct functioning within all four arenas.

Teaching Specific Executive Functions as Skills Routines

Although applied primarily in cognitive strategy training approaches focusing on improvement of academic functioning (as noted in the section referencing interventions for increasing internal control), these techniques can be adapted to address executive difficulties in the intrapersonal, interpersonal, and environment arenas as well. As in the academic arena where the task is dismantled into its component pieces and the child is given explicit self-direction cues (i.e., a plan of attack or action to complete or accomplish the task), this same scaffolding can be provided for a child's interactions with others, awareness of self, or navigation of the environment.

Using Verbal Mediation

As Barkley (1997) has noted, the capacity for generating internalized language is perhaps the single most effective tool for improving self-regulation capacities. CBT approaches are particularly effective examples of the use of self-talk to increase self-control. Social story techniques also make great use of mediated language to generate changes in behavior.

Using Verbal or Nonverbal Labeling

One of the significant strengths of many CBT-oriented approaches such as Ross Greene's (2001; Green & Albon, 2006) methods for helping children develop greater self-regulation is the emphasis on developing a common vocabulary that can be used to describe the child's internal experiencing of perceptions, feelings, and thoughts and linking these mental experiences to routines for behavior control. In the case of children who are more visually oriented in their thinking and/or who have significant language impairments, nonverbal labels can serve a similar function (e.g., mentally picturing the image of a stop sign to represent the inhibit cue).

Teaching the Use of Internal Feedback

Some children with executive function difficulties need assistance with learning how to generate and/or cue the use of internal perceptions, feelings, or thoughts to provide themselves with feedback about their perceptions, feelings, thoughts, or actions within one or more of the four arenas of involvement. Although many intervention approaches, including CBT, rely heavily on "self-talk" as a source for internal feedback, such feedback can come in the form of nonverbal mental processes involving perceptions, feelings, and thoughts.

Establishing Self-Administered Rewards

Some children with executive function difficulties need assistance with identifying and/or cueing positive sources of self-reinforcement that could include specific perceptions, feelings, thoughts, or actions. Once identified, these self-rewards can be administered when self-regulation goals are met. Not surprisingly, many children with executive function difficulties are likely to require a period of external prompting to learn when and how to self-cue these internal reward mechanisms.

Intervention Strategies for Maintaining External Control

Intervention strategies for maintaining external control help children improve their self-regulation through the direct assistance of others. The ultimate goal of these strategies is to produce greater self-regulation as a result of externally guided positive behavior change.

Pharmacological Treatment

As mentioned earlier, psycho-stimulant medication use is perhaps the most common form of intervention for ADHD symptomatology. Although the use of medication enables many children to demonstrate increased use of some self-regulation capacities, it is likely a gross oversimplification to suggest that the medication is directly acting on the frontal lobe executive components of the activated neural networks. In fact, some research suggests that psycho-stimulant medications are primarily acting on portions of the activated neural network located in other parts of the cerebral cortex and/or subcortical regions (Hoeppner, et al., 1997; Hale, et al., 1998; Hale, Fiorello, & Brown, 2005). Whatever the specific brain mechanisms at work, the observable effects for children who benefit from the use of these medications very often is improved use of some self-regulation capacities, especially the Focus/Select, Sustain, and Monitor cues.

Structuring the Environment

The ADHD and TBI literatures as well as the education literature on classroom management and individual behavior management programs contain many references to approaches that involve careful structuring of the environment to reduce the demands for frequent self-regulation. For some children with executive function difficulties, the problems they encounter relate more to the inability to handle the number and frequency of the executive controls that must be used much more so than the engagement of individual executive capacities. For these children, modifying the executive demands by structuring the environment and implementing consistent behavior management plans can greatly reduce the number of executive function-related problems these children exhibit.

Structuring Time

As is the case with structuring the environment, providing aids for time management such as consistent schedules for activities, the use of clocks and timers, and building time monitoring into activities can greatly aid students who have difficulties self-regulating the use of the Pace and Time cues.

Externalizing Cues for Effective Processing

Perhaps the most widely used external control intervention for executive function difficulties—though unacknowledged as such—is external prompting for, or direct delivery of, self-regulation cues. This form of intervention is used in virtually every setting within all four arenas of involvement. Parents, teachers, work supervisors, administrators, and even peers engage in self-regulation prompting. As will be discussed in Chapter 8, much of what is considered good teaching practice involves a great deal of prompting for and/or delivery of self-regulation cues.

In some cases, the prompting process needs to be made a more concrete part of the child's environment in order to encourage performance of actions in the proper sequence for adequate work production. Such concrete prompts include making lists of the steps to be completed, and the specific order of completion of the steps, for a task; posting to do lists where they are sure to be seen; or providing and checking homework assignment books.

Providing Feedback

For some children who exhibit executive function difficulties, especially those with ADHD, providing immediate and frequent feedback about the effectiveness of performance can be a highly effective means of increasing the likelihood of further engagement of self-regulation capacities as well as a means for helping with the transition from external control to internal command.

Providing Rewards

Although there is little question that the use of eternally administered rewards can increase the likelihood of meeting program goals for positive behavior change, the use of rewards should be carefully planned and monitored for the reasons discussed extensively earlier in this chapter.

Aligning External Demands with Internal Desires

As noted in Chapter 4, for many children with executive control problems directing externally demanded production is much more difficult to accomplish than directing internally commanded production. This observed fact could be capitalized on in situations where flexibility can be exercised with external demands. When possible, making externally demanded production requirements match internally commanded desires for production would increase the likelihood of the child's effective use of self-regulation capacities to achieve the desired outcomes.

APPLYING INTERVENTION STRATEGIES TO THE 23 SELF-REGULATION CAPACITIES

In addition to applying to all domains of functioning within all arenas of involvement across multiple settings, all of the internalizing and externalizing strategies (except pharmacological intervention) discussed in the previous section can be applied to aid in the development and increased use of all 23 of the self-regulation capacities described in the McCloskey Holarchical Model of Executive Functions introduced in Chapter 3. An example of the application of these various strategies to one of the 23 self-regulation functions—the Modulate cue—is presented in Table 7.1.

Interventions for Executive Function Difficulties Impacting Academic Skill Production

This section discusses the application of the general intervention strategies introduced in this chapter to executive function difficulties that significantly impact academic skill production in reading, writing, and math.

Table 7.1 Applications of Internalizing and Externalizing Intervention Strategies to Improve Use of the Modulate Cue

Intervention Strategy	Applied to the Modulate Cue
Developing Internal Control	
Increase awareness	Engage in direct discussions with the child/children to increase awareness of the fact that it is possible to control the intensity of effort put into perceiving, feeling, thinking, and acting and that this is called cueing Modulation. Explain how intensity can relate to how much effort you put into taking information in from the environment (e.g., how much effort you put into seeing something or listening to hear a sound, or how intensely you would sense the pain if you got hurt), how strongly you feel about things, how much effort you put into thinking about things, and how much effort you put into doing things. Explain how we modulate the intensity of perceptions, feelings, thoughts, and actions in relation to ourselves (e.g., the intensity of our own feelings about ourselves), in relation to others (e.g., the intensity of our feelings about others and/or the intensity of our feelings when we are around others) in relation to the environment (e.g., how much effort we put into looking for things on a nature walk), and in relation to what we do in school (e.g., how much effort you put into doing a writing assignment in class or at home). Explain that we use the Modulate cue a lot throughout most days, but that we usually are not directly aware of knowing when to use it or of using it, but that when we want to, we can become aware of when to use it and then use it. Provide examples of when the Modulate cue needs to be used, e.g., at a party when everyone is having fun and talking loudly, you still need to know how loud is too loud and use the Modulate cue to make sure that you do not get too loud. Continue the discussion with more examples and opportunities for the child/children to practice the use of the Modulate cue with the four domains of functioning within each of the four arenas of involvement.
Modeling appropriate use of executive functions	Model appropriate use of the Modulate cue throughout the school day, e.g., do not overreact emotionally to things that happen in the classroom. As time and opportunity permit, monitor your own use of the Modulate cue and point out and describe to the child/children situations in which you effectively used it. Allow time for the child/children to discuss the situation with you.

Table 7.1 (continued)   Applications of Internalizing and Externalizing Intervention Strategies to Improve Use of the Modulate Cue

Intervention Strategy	Applied to the Modulate Cue
Developing Internal Control	
Teaching specific executive functions as skills routines	Teach the child how to engage in a self-regulation routine for becoming aware of the need to use the Modulate cue and then using it.
	Teach the child a "Modulate" routine that combines the Monitor cue (already taught) with the Modulate cue to do an "intensity check" of perceptions, feelings, thoughts, and actions and then combine the Correct cue with the Modulate cue to make intensity adjustments as needed.
	Use simulated examples, such as the party situation, to provide the child/children opportunities to practice use of the Modulate routine.
	Provide multiple examples involving all four domains of functioning and all four arenas of involvement, e.g., "When you are alone, you can use this routine to modulate your own thoughts, for example ____." "When you are with others, you can use this routine to modulate your feelings, for example ____." "When you are walking down the street, you can modulate your perceptions, for example ____." When you are doing homework, you can modulate your actions, for example ____."
Using verbal mediation	Model the use of verbal mediation strategies by talking through a problem out loud. Be sure to describe to your students the thought process beyond the strategies that are being implemented. Orally describe problems that you encounter and the thought processes enlisted to resolve the problem.
Using verbal or nonverbal labeling	Pair verbal and nonverbal cues for emotional modulation through the analogy of a volcano as a metaphor for recognizing building emotional intensity. Help the child envision two ends of an emotional intensity continuum; at one end is a dark, silent featureless uninteresting mountain of rock that shows no activity while at the other end is an exploding volcano that causes great damage to everything around it. Work with the child/children to learn to regulate the intensity level of their "emotional volcano" with the goal of keeping their volcano from exploding, but also from becoming dormant and inactive. (Note that this metaphor also can be used to help develop the Balance cue.)

Table 7.1 (continued) Applications of Internalizing and
Externalizing Intervention Strategies to Improve Use of the
Modulate Cue

Intervention Strategy	Applied to the Modulate Cue
Developing Internal Control	
Teaching the use of internal feedback	Use teaching exercises to build the use of internal feedback for each domain of functioning within each arena of involvement. For example, the following exercise could be used to develop the use of internal feedback with intrapersonal perception of kinesthetic sensation: During times of low intensity, take students through progressive muscle relaxation exercises to build awareness of internal states and tensions (i.e., undesired levels of intensity). Help students to recognize what maintaining too much intensity in different parts of their body (holding tension) feels like. Have students practice releasing the unwanted intensity (tension) through deep-breathing and muscle relaxation.
Establishing self-administered rewards	Students monitor their own perceptions, feelings, thoughts, or actions and provide themselves with an appropriate reward when the criterion for reinforcement has been met. Allow students to select the specific reward that they will administer to themselves. For a student who has difficulty modulating voice volume in the classroom, allow the child to select from a list of rewards that will be self-administered when the student's voice volume remains within an acceptable range for an entire class period. Using a note card placed on the child's desk, the child self-records teacher feedback about the adequacy of voice volume during specific time segments within the class period. If the criterion of adequate voice volume control during all time segments within the class period is met, the student self-administers the agreed-upon reward. Gradually increase the amount of time during which appropriate voice volume is required before a reward can be self-administered.
Maintaining External Control	
Structuring the environment	Structure the environment to match the level of intensity desired in specific domains of functioning and specific arenas of involvement. For example, at bedtime, establish a routine to help the child modulate intensity of all domains of functioning within the intrapersonal arena to prepare for sleep. The routine could include bath time, hygiene routines (e.g., brushing teeth, and story time in bed with dimmed lighting in the room).
Structuring time	Build into the day specific times for teaching about, modeling and discussing, and practicing use of the Modulate cue.

Table 7.1 (continued)   Applications of Internalizing and
Externalizing Intervention Strategies to Improve Use of the
Modulate Cue

Intervention Strategy	Applied to the Modulate Cue
Maintaining External Control	
Externalizing cues for effective processing	Throughout the day, provide positive, clear, and specific cues for engaging the Modulate cue. Depending on the level of Modulate capacity of the child/children, these cues can vary from specific substitution cues (e.g., "You are too noisy right now, please use your indoor voices") to scaffolded engagement cues (e.g., "How's the intensity level in here?").
Providing feedback	Provide positive feedback when the child appropriately cues effective modulation of perception, emotion, thought, or action (e. g., "I like how you realized that your voice was getting very loud and started talking much more quietly without my having to ask you to do so"; or "Thank you for speaking more softly when I asked you to do so.") Note that these examples could also represent a form of verbal reward for exhibiting desired positive behavior.
Providing rewards	Provide positive reinforcement and rewards for the effective use of the Modulate cue. Identify appropriate rewards and establish reinforcement contingencies that are obtainable and realistic. For students who talk too loudly in class, work with them on a positive cue, such as "time to use your inside voice." Explain to the students the meaning of the cue and the appropriate response (appropriate range of acceptable voice volume) expected when they hear the cue. Reward students for appropriate use of an inside voice. If necessary, develop a positive reinforcement system that rewards the use of inside voice volume. Break the day into developmentally appropriate time segments. Provide positive reinforcement for appropriate response to the cue for voice modulation. Initially reinforce the students for appropriately responding to the external cue. Gradually move to rewarding students for "catching" themselves and spontaneously modulating their voice volume. This transition is an important step toward getting students to self-modulate and reward themselves for learning how to be in control of voice modulation.
Aligning external demands with internal desires	Make an effort to match external demands for use of the Modulate cue with internal desires to use the Modulate cue. For example, provide a work break that allows for heightened activity and greater outward emotional expression at a point when it is apparent that children need such a break.

204 Assessment and Intervention for Executive Function Difficulties

Interventions for Executive Function Difficulties Impacting Reading

It should come as no surprise to readers that many of the most effective reading intervention programs make implicit or explicit use of strategies designed either to provide external executive function cue substitutes or to encourage students to internally cue themselves to make use of executive function cues. Table 7.2 shows how strategies for increasing executive function self-cueing or externally substituting for lack of executive function self-cueing can be incorporated into the design and implementation of reading intervention plans. In the following paragraphs, specific issues related to word reading accuracy, reading rate, and reading comprehension are addressed. Even the best teachers using the best programs for teaching word recognition and decoding skills are sometimes mystified by students' inaccurate applications of these skills; misuse of decoding rules that the teachers know they have previously learned and used effectively; inaccurate pronunciation of words that they know are in these students' sight word pronunciation lexicons. As noted in the previous section, these students' are not effectively using the Inhibit, Perceive, and/or Focus/Select cues to effectively process the orthography of the words on the page prior to cueing retrieval of pronunciations. The lead author of this book has been able to demonstrate improvement in word reading accuracy of students classified as reading disabled using various combinations of the executive function-driven strategies listed in Table 7.2.

Children who exhibit poor use of the Pace cue when attempting to read words quickly often show a curious pattern of performance. These students read slowly, then increase their rate when the teacher guides them, then return to their slow pace when the guidance is removed. Reading programs that focus on improving reading rate for these students employ various strategies including guided repeated oral reading, paired reading, speeded word reading training, and the neural impress method. All of these techniques begin by externalizing the Pace cue by having someone or something other than the student set the pace for word reading rate. Gradually, through hundreds of practice trials, these students learn to adjust their internal Pace cueing to match the rate established by the use of the external Pace cues. Gradually, the external Pace cues are faded and finally removed when the student has nonconsciously internalized

Table 7.2 Applications of Internalizing and Externalizing
Intervention Strategies to Improve Reading Skills

Intervention Strategy	Applied to Improving Reading Skills
Developing Internal Control	
Increase awareness Using verbal or nonverbal labeling Using verbal mediation	Engage in direct discussions with the student(s) to increase awareness of executive functions (in a general or more specific sense, depending on the age and learning capacities of the child) and the role they play in directing the use of reading skills. Use metaphors and analogies to increase the child's/children's understanding of individual executive function cues or a cluster of cues that are used simultaneously when using a specific reading skill or all reading skills at one time. When observing the child perform a specific reading skill, offer feedback about when the child is, or is not, effectively using executive functions to cue performance. Explain how executive functions are usually used nonconsciously, i.e., without our thinking about their use or telling ourselves that we need to use them, but that when we want to we can consciously think about their use and tell ourselves when to use them. Explain that in the reading instruction you will be doing with the student(s), use of executive functions might start out being a conscious process guided by the teacher, but will eventually become a process that is nonconsciously activated by the student(s) themselves. Develop and share with the student(s) (or include the student(s) in development of) goals for increased, nonconscious use of executive function cues while performing specific reading skills.
Modeling appropriate use of executive functions	Model nonconscious, effective use of executive functions to cue word reading, decoding, and reading rate while reading to the child. Also demonstrate poor reading skill use resulting from ineffective use of executive cues; point out how the inefficiencies were caused by lack of use of executive function cues; and show how to improve performance by using the needed cues. Demonstrate comprehension of what you read by stating your understanding to the student(s). Explain how effective use of executive function cues enabled you to comprehend the text you read. Also demonstrate common errors in comprehension and explain how these errors can be caused by ineffective use of executive function cues and how use of the proper executive function cues can prevent them from occurring.

Table 7.2 (continued) Applications of Internalizing and Externalizing Intervention Strategies to Improve Reading Skills

Intervention Strategy	Applied to Improving Reading Skills
Developing Internal Control	
Teaching specific executive functions as skills routines	Teach the student(s) how to engage in a self-regulation routines for specific reading skills. Create a list of the cues (specifically the ones that the child frequently does not use) that can be consciously activated and when in the reading process they need to be activated for effective use of the skill.
Teaching the use of internal feedback	Teach the student(s) how to use self-talk and self-monitoring routines to become aware of when to use specific executive function cues in reading and to be aware of when they are using, or not using, the needed cues.
Establishing self-administered rewards	Help the student(s) learn how to self-reward for effective use of executive function cues when using reading skills.
Maintaining External Control	
Structuring the environment externalizing cues for effective processing	While presenting a reading lesson, monitor the child's reading and offer cues that replace the need to internally activate executive functions. These would include prompts such as: "Look carefully at every letter of that word, now try to sound it out." "Stay focused on what you are reading." "Follow my finger across the page and read the words as quickly as my finger is moving." "As you read this paragraph, remember to apply the 'meaning strategy' you learned." Within the classroom, provide multiple forms of external prompts that signal the child to use executive function cues when reading.
Structuring time Externalizing cues for effective processing	Help the student(s) improve awareness of the amount of time it takes them to read sentences and passages and to read and comprehend sentences and passages. Provide time guidelines and prompts to monitor how long reading activities are taking. Set time limits for specific reading activities and provide time-related prompts to help students maintain awareness of the passage of time.
Providing feedback	Provide the student(s) with feedback about their efforts to self-regulate the use of executive function cues when reading. Provide the student(s) with feedback about the effectiveness of their efforts to respond to external cues when reading.

Table 7.2 (continued)   Applications of Internalizing and
Externalizing Intervention Strategies to Improve Reading Skills

Intervention Strategy	Applied to Improving Reading Skills
Maintaining External Control	
Providing rewards	Provide positive reinforcement and rewards for the effective self-regulation of the use of executive function cues while reading. Use identified reinforcers and establish reinforcement contingencies that are obtainable and realistic.
Aligning external demands with internal desires	Help the student(s) to develop internal sources of motivation for wanting to improve their reading. Find ways to help them realize the connection between good reading skills and the activities for which they have the greatest interest. Allow time for the student(s) to bring to class and read materials of their own choosing. As much as possible, build lesson plans around the reading materials of greatest interest to the student(s).

a Pace cue setting more consistent with the average of age or grade level peers, and is able to maintain growth in adjusting that setting consistent with the growth experienced by same-age or same-grade peers.

The complex nature of reading comprehension offers numerous ways for executive function difficulties to impact students' reading production. Multidimensional cognitive strategy instruction techniques (Pressley & Woloshyn, 1995) and specific self-monitoring routines (Borkowski & Muthu-krishna, 1992; Case, et. al, 1992; Gersten, Fuchs, Williams & Baker, 2001; Jitendra, Hoppes, & Xin, 2000; Rosenshein & Meister, 1997) are effective means of helping students develop a greater capacity for using executive function cues during reading comprehension.

Interventions for Executive Function Difficulties Impacting Written Expression Problems

As was the case in the area of reading, many of the most effective writing intervention programs make implicit or explicit use of strategies designed either to provide external executive function cue substitutes or to encourage students to internally cue themselves to make use of executive function cues. Table 7.3 shows how strategies for increasing executive function self-cueing or externally substituting for lack of executive

Table 7.3 Applications of Internalizing and Externalizing Intervention Strategies to Improve Written Expression Skills

Intervention Strategy	Applied to Improving Writing Skills
Developing Internal Control	
Increase awareness Using verbal or nonverbal labeling Using verbal mediation Providing feedback	Engage in direct discussions with the student(s) to increase awareness of executive functions (in a general or more specific sense, depending on the age and learning capacities of the child) and the role they play in directing the use of writing skills. Use metaphors and analogies to increase the child's/children's understanding of individual executive function cues or a cluster of cues that are used simultaneously when using a specific reading skill or all reading skills at one time. When observing the child perform a specific writing skill, offer feedback about when the child is, or is not, effectively using executive functions to cue performance. Explain how executive functions are usually used nonconsciously, that is, without our thinking about their use or telling ourselves that we need to use them, but that when we want to we can consciously think about their use and tell ourselves when to use them. Explain that in the writing instruction you will be doing with the student(s), use of executive functions might start out being a conscious process guided by the teacher, but will eventually become a process that is nonconsciously activated by the student(s) themselves. Develop and share with the student(s) (or include the student(s) in development of) goals for increased, nonconscious use of executive function cues while performing specific writing skills.
Modeling appropriate use of executive functions	Model nonconscious, effective use of executive functions to cue written expression skill use while writing as the student(s) observe. Talk through the writing process and explain how effective use of executive function cues enabled you to compose what you wrote. Also demonstrate poor writing skill use resulting from ineffective use of executive cues; point out how the inefficiencies were caused by lack of use of executive function cues; and show how to improve performance by using the needed cues. Also demonstrate common errors in writing and explain how these errors can be caused by ineffective use of executive function cues and how use of the proper executive function cues can prevent them from occurring.

Table 7.3 (continued)   Applications of Internalizing and
Externalizing Intervention Strategies to Improve Written Expression
Skills

Intervention Strategy	Applied to Improving Writing Skills
Developing Internal Control	
Teaching specific executive functions as skills routines	Teach the student(s) how to engage in self-regulation routines for specific writing skills. Create a list of the cues (specifically the ones that the child frequently does not use) that can be consciously activated and when in the writing process they need to be activated for effective use of the skill.
Teaching the use of internal feedback	Teach the student(s) how to use self-talk and self-monitoring routines to become aware of when to use specific executive function cues in writing and to be aware of when they are using, or not using, the needed cues.
Establishing self-administered rewards	Help the student(s) learn how to self-reward for effective use of executive function cues when using writing skills.
Maintaining External Control	
Structuring the environment Externalizing cues for effective processing	While presenting a writing lesson, monitor the child's writing and offer cues that replace the need to internally activate executive functions. These would include prompts such as: "What are you going to write about?" "Stay focused on what you are writing." "How do you write the letter 'r'?" "What punctuation mark do you put at the end of a declarative sentence?" "As you write your paragraph, remember to apply the composition writing strategy you learned." Within the classroom, provide multiple forms of external prompts that signal the child to use executive function cues when writing.
Structuring time Externalizing cues for effective processing	Help the student(s) improve awareness of the amount of time it takes them to produce letters, words, sentences, and passages. Provide time guidelines and prompts to monitor how long writing activities are taking. Set time limits for specific writing activities and provide time-related prompts to help students maintain awareness of the passage of time.
Providing feedback	Provide the student(s) with feedback about their efforts to self-regulate the use of executive function cues when writing. Provide the student(s) with feedback about the effectiveness of their efforts to respond to external cues when writing.

Table 7.3 (continued) Applications of Internalizing and Externalizing Intervention Strategies to Improve Written Expression Skills

Intervention Strategy	Applied to Improving Writing Skills
Maintaining External Control	
Providing rewards	Provide positive reinforcement and rewards for the effective self-regulation of the use of executive function cues while writing. Use identified reinforcers and establish reinforcement contingencies that are obtainable and realistic.
Aligning external demands with internal desires	Help the student(s) to develop internal sources of motivation for wanting to improve their writing skills. Find ways to help them realize the connection between good writing skills and the activities for which they have the greatest interest. Allow time for the student(s) to write about topics of their own choosing. As much as possible, build writing lesson plans around the writing topics of greatest interest to the student(s).

function self-cueing can be incorporated into the design and implementation of written expression intervention plans.

Developing the handwriting—the gateway skill for written production using pen/pencil and paper—of young children presents a tremendous challenge to kindergarten and first grade teachers charged with this task. Helping young children with relatively poor executive capacities automate the complex process of handling a writing implement and staying focused while retrieving recently stored kinetic melodies is no small feat. Not surprisingly, programs designed to help students develop automatic handwriting skills focus on creating in the student a conscious awareness of the motor processes involved in forming letters (Levine Rubell, 1999; Olsen, 2008). Knowing the requirements of the task makes it much more likely that a young child will know what executive functions need to be used and when they need to be used when attempting to produce printed letters. Of course, even knowing this does not necessarily guarantee success for children who are far behind their peers in executive function control of attention and effort, motor memory, and motor production. For these students, intervention strategies will be almost exclusively focused on the use of external control substitutes during closely supervised guided practice sessions. In this area more than any other, recognizing the constraining effects of maturation on skill development is necessary not just when working with young children, but also when working with late elementary, middle, junior, and senior high school and college age students.

Patience with slower rates of development and less than expected production are necessary to help students remain engaged with efforts to improve production with this very difficult skill. While it is critical to develop the capacity to communicate language through the motor systems that control the hands, it is essential to keep in mind that manipulating pens or pencils is not the only source of production of printed material. Although the belief is strong that handwriting strengthens the capacity for depth of processing of language when writing (Berninger & Richards, 2002), it is unclear whether this supposed advantage holds for children whose brains, from near-birth on, are continually exposed to the use of keyboards as a form of written language communication. What is certainly clear, however, is that the use of keyboarding skills, besides being the most viable alternative to handwriting, also happens to be the written production method for which mastery is almost universally demanded in the world of work.

Whether or not students learn to communicate their thoughts through printed and/or cursive handwritten script in early elementary school, there is no doubt that from junior high school age on, they will be required to communicate those thoughts by keyboarding text. Recognition of this fact should inform decisions about what text production skills students are taught to automate and at what age they are taught to automate them, especially in the case of a student who consistently struggles with text production using pencils and pens despite adequate instruction to improve these skills.

Beyond the development of text transcription skills, a central technique of programs designed to help students improve written expression skills is the provision of highly structured, explicit strategies for generating, editing, and revising text. These programs make use of externally cued structures to scaffold the writing process in the absence of more internally directed cueing capacities. These scaffolds include strategy routines for idea generation, preplanning and organization of ideas, generation of text, monitoring text production for accuracy, and reviewing and revising produced text. The Self-Regulated Strategy Development (SRSD) model of Graham and Harris (2005) exemplifies this type of scaffold strategy instruction approach. The model (Graham, Harris, & Troia, 2000) includes planning by delineating what is required for the writing process (engaging the Gauge, Modulate, Plan/Organize, and Retrieve cues); conferencing on goals and strategies (activating the Initiate, Gauge, Modulate, Generate, Associate, Plan/Organize, and Retrieve cues); modeling the strategy; putting the strategies to be employed in memory by use of mnemonics (engaging the Store cue and developing a knowledge base to be accessed later by the Retrieve and Execute cues); actual employment of the strategies (engaging the Retrieve, Execute, Monitor, and Correct cues in conjunction with the Hold, Manipulate Generate, and Associate cues); and, finally, independent practice with the goal of skill generalization (self-regulation of all of the cues listed in Table 7.3). The efficacy of the SRSD approach is well-documented (Graham & Harris, 2005; De La Paz & Graham, 2002; Graham, Harris, & Troia, 2000; Troia & Harris, 2002); its efficacy is likely due not only to the fact that automatization of these individual components is emphasized, but also to the fact that the skills learned model the use of the executive function capacities required to direct the writing process. Additional study by De La Paz, Swanson, and Graham (1998) also noted the efficacy of a structured and routine approach that externally cues the process of reviewing and revising text. Graham (1997) highlighted the degree to which the subskills used in the revising process needed to be identified before students could develop real improvement in their ability to revise what they had written. Ferretti, MacArthur, and Dowdy (2000) also contributed to the findings relative to the efficacy of explicit planning and goal-setting along with instruction in cognitive and self-regulated strategies for persuasive writing.

The acquisition of handwriting, spelling, and composition (idea generation, text generation, revising, editing) skills involves a complex developmental progression. The acquisition of sufficient writing skills over the grades requires the coordination of multiple executive functions to oversee the multitasking of cognitive skills used in the production of written material. Interventions for individuals with written expression weaknesses need to address the underlying skill deficits that contribute to the poor task attainment. For those with executive deficits, achieving fluency in the lower-level skills of handwriting and spelling allow for greater attention to the more complex processes involved in composition. At this more complex level, interventions need to help students learn how to self-regulate—through scaffolding routines and modeling—the coordination of the cognitive skills required for planning, organizing, generating, editing, and revising a written product.

Interventions for Executive Function Difficulties Impacting Math Problems

Comparable to the areas of reading and written expression, effective mathematics instruction programs make implicit or explicit use of strategies designed either to provide external executive function cue substitutes or to encourage students to internally cue themselves to make use of executive function cues. Table 7.4 shows how strategies for increasing executive function self-cueing or externally substituting for lack of executive function self-cueing can be incorporated into the design and implementation of mathematics intervention plans.

As was the case with handwriting, automaticity of graphomotor production of numbers and mathematics symbols is critical to the effective development of computation skills (Berninger & Richards, 2002). Students exhibiting executive function difficulties with control of the production of numbers and symbols will require intervention efforts similar to those provided for handwriting. Students who make computation errors such as misreading operation signs or transposing numbers are experiencing difficulties with the Perceive, Inhibit, and/or Focus/Select cues in a manner similar to students who have difficulty attending to orthography when reading, and would benefit from the use of strategies similar to those recommended for readers with such difficulties.

Helping students improve the use of executive functions for efficient production with procedural routines for computation and problem solving is analogous to the situation encountered in helping students be writers that are more productive. Similar to the cognitive strategy interventions that attempt to enable students to self-regulate the complex processes involved in writing, interventions for improved math computation and problem-solving production focus on cognitive strategy instruction routines (Jitendra & Hoff, 1996; Kelly & Carnine, 1996) designed to increase the self-cueing capacities of the student.

Table 7.4 Applications of Internalizing and Externalizing Intervention Strategies to Improve Math Computation and Problem-Solving Skills

Intervention Strategy	Applied to Improving Math Skills
Developing Internal Control	
Increase awareness Using verbal or nonverbal labeling Using verbal mediation Providing feedback	Engage in direct discussions with the student(s) to increase awareness of executive functions (in a general or more specific sense, depending on the age and learning capacities of the child) and the role they play in directing the use of math skills. Use metaphors and analogies to increase the child's/children's understanding of individual executive function cues or a cluster of cues that are used simultaneously when using a specific math skill or multiple math skills at one time. When observing the child perform a specific math skill, offer feedback about when the child is, or is not, effectively using executive functions to cue performance. Explain how executive functions are usually used nonconsciously, that is, without our thinking about their use or telling ourselves that we need to use them, but that when we want to we can consciously think about their use and tell ourselves when to use them. Explain that in the math instruction you will be doing with the student(s), use of executive functions might start out being a conscious process guided by the teacher, but will eventually become a process that is nonconsciously activated by the student(s) themselves. Develop and share with the student(s) (or include the student(s) in development of) goals for increased, nonconscious use of executive function cues while performing specific math skills.
Modeling appropriate use of executive functions	Model nonconscious, effective use of executive functions to cue math skill use while doing math calculation or problem solving as the student(s) observe. Talk through the math skills, routines, and procedures you applied and explain how effective use of executive function cues enabled you to complete the work. Also demonstrate poor math skill use resulting from ineffective use of executive cues; point out how the inefficiencies were caused by lack of use of executive function cues; and show how to improve performance by using the needed cues. Also demonstrate common errors in math calculation and problem solving and explain how these errors can be caused by ineffective use of executive function cues and how use of the proper executive function cues can prevent them from occurring.

Table 7.4 (continued) Applications of Internalizing and
Externalizing Intervention Strategies to Improve Math Computation
and Problem-Solving Skills

Intervention Strategy	Applied to Improving Math Skills
Developing Internal Control	
Teaching specific executive functions as skills routines	Teach the student(s) how to engage in self-regulation routines for specific math skills. Create a list of the cues (specifically the ones that the child frequently does not use) that can be consciously activated and when in the math calculation or problem-solving process they need to be activated for effective performance.
Teaching the use of internal feedback	Teach the student(s) how to use self-talk and self-monitoring routines to become aware of when to use specific executive function cues in math calculation and problem solving and to be aware of when they are using, or not using, the needed cues.
Establishing self-administered rewards	Help the student(s) learn how to self-reward for effective use of executive function cues when using math skills.
Maintaining External Control	
Structuring the environment Externalizing cues for effective processing	While presenting a math lesson, monitor the child's work and offer cues that replace the need to internally activate executive functions. These would include prompts such as: "Look at the operation sign; it tells you to subtract this time, not add." "Stay focused on your work." "How do you write the number 3?" "Remember, you will need to use regrouping to do this one." "As you attempt to solve this problem, remember to use all the steps in the process you learned." Within the classroom, provide multiple forms of external prompts that signal the child to use executive function cues when doing math calculations or solving math problems.
Structuring time Externalizing cues for effective processing	Help the student(s) improve awareness of the amount of time it takes them to complete calculations or solve problems. Provide time guidelines and prompts to monitor how long math activities are taking. Set time limits for specific math activities and provide time-related prompts to help students maintain awareness of the passage of time.
Providing feedback	Provide the student(s) with feedback about their efforts to self-regulate the use of executive function cues when using math skills. Provide the student(s) with feedback about the effectiveness of their efforts to respond to external cues when using math skills.

Table 7.4 (continued) Applications of Internalizing and Externalizing Intervention Strategies to Improve Math Computation and Problem-Solving Skills

Intervention Strategy	Applied to Improving Math Skills
Maintaining External Control	
Providing rewards	Provide positive reinforcement and rewards for the effective self-regulation of the use of executive function cues when using math skills. Use identified reinforcers and establish reinforcement contingencies that are obtainable and realistic.
Aligning external demands with internal desires	Help the student(s) to develop internal sources of motivation for wanting to improve their math skills. Find ways to help them realize the connection between good math skills and the activities for which they have the greatest interest. Allow time for the student(s) to apply math to practical situations of their own choosing. As much as possible, build math lesson plans around the practical applications of greatest interest to the student(s).

Intervention for Executive Function-Related Academic Production Difficulties in the Upper Grades

Clinicians who develop an understanding of executive functions and how they impact behavior and academic production can apply this knowledge to help parents, teachers, administrators, and other school staff in understanding the increased demands the upper grades place on students and ways that they can help students adjust more effectively to these increased demands. These include:

1. Orientation sessions and extended orientation periods to help students become aware of, and adjust to, the increased executive function demands of new settings.
2. Availability of, or mandatory scheduling of, study skills courses to help students become more consciously aware of the kinds of executive function capacities that will be required for success in the new setting and to help them develop skill-based routines and cognitive strategies that they can apply when studying.
3. Demonstration, usually embedded in content area courses, of the steps in planning and organizing long-term projects, and guided practice through the steps before assignment of large-scale, independent projects.
4. Direct instruction in test taking skills.

5. Direct instruction in note taking skills.
6. Peer tutoring programs that offer assistance with homework, studying for tests, and planning and organization of large-scale projects.
7. Provision of systems to improve home-school communication, such as homework hotlines and posting homework assignments and grades on-line at a school website.
8. Practice of good classroom test construction principles by teachers, such as avoiding "executive function traps" on tests, realizing the effects of test question format on performance.
9. Thoughtful use of reward/punishment systems as incentives to complete homework; for example, providing extra points for on-time completion of homework rather than loss of points for not completing homework on time.

CASE VIGNETTES REVISITED

We now revisit our case studies while considering the strategies discussed in this chapter for helping children internalize self-control and for substituting external control for a lack of internal control.

Interventions for Justin

Although it is clear that maturation of self-regulation capacities is playing a major role in Justin's school problems, the answer to these problems is not to simply wait until his frontal lobes have caught up with those of his peers (if that were ever the case). Justin's capacity for self-determination is far outpacing his development of self-regulation capacities, and his self-determined strong interests in art and computer programming are leading him down a path that does not share a great deal in common with standard junior high school academic coursework. Justin's teacher's are unaware of his interests and talents and are focused on Justin's lack of production in their classes. The lack of positive feedback from school and the lack of opportunity to share his talents with his teachers are increasingly creating a rift between Justin's internal desires and the external demands of the traditional school setting. Although Justin is a gifted artist and has already begun to focus on a career goal, his artistic and technical interests do not necessarily challenge him to utilize the full range of self-regulation capacities that are likely to be needed on the job, even in his chosen field. This fact, coupled with the need for Justin to at least graduate from high school with passable grades in order to further his career interests, makes it important to help Justin develop his self-regulation capacities and apply them to the task of maintaining at least a minimal level of involvement and production in the traditional academic courses that need to be completed successfully.

Considering Justin's growing disengagement with school and his belief that it has nothing to offer him, it is not likely that he will attempt to solve his difficulties through self-initiated actions. Although Justin's strengths are his capacity for self-awareness and self-determination, he has not been able to make the connection between success in school now and success in his desired career later. Work with Justin will need to help him develop an appreciation of the need to maintain engagement with school. At this point in time Justin can describe his self-regulation difficulties, but he does not appreciate their source. Given this fact, he is more likely to benefit from an increased awareness of what self-regulation executive functions are and how they impact his functioning. Justin is capable of appreciating the need to increase his effectiveness with these capacities, and he would benefit from knowing that improvement may be possible with an appropriate investment of effort on his part and guidance from sources that appreciate the nature of his difficulties and what could be done to assist him.

While modeling might have an impact on Justin, the junior high school structure of classes makes it less likely that this technique could be effectively applied in any organized way. Justin's parents do their best to model planning and organization in the home, but the tension that has been building between Justin and his parents makes it more likely that he will see their guidance as a form of nagging rather than as helpful guidelines for behavior.

Teaching executive function routines as skills could work well for Justin in the form of a study skills course. The course could have a particularly positive impact if it is taught from the perspective of helping students develop internal self-regulation capacities for cueing the use of skill routines. Justin clearly has language skills and self-awareness capacities that would enable him to benefit from the use of verbal mediation and verbal labeling strategies to increase his understanding of executive functions and how to effectively use them to improve his academic production. The study skills course would also be an appropriate mechanism for addressing Justin's difficulties with the use of the Focus/Select, Sustain, Monitor, and Correct cues that were the likely sources of Justin's difficulties with attention to detail when performing math calculations, as these types of errors have been reported as typical of Justin's test-taking behavior.

The internal feedback Justin generates is mostly negative; he has a number of negative feelings and thoughts about himself in terms of school production, and these often contribute greatly to preventing him from taking positive action. Justin would benefit from assistance in developing more positive thought patterns and learning how to provide positive feedback to himself.

In terms of external substitutions for self-control, Justin's parents need to recognize that Justin requires a great deal of assistance in dealing with his developmental delays in brain functioning. Justin's slow initiation problems need to be addressed with great patience. Even under the best of conditions, Justin has great difficulty initiating activity and adjusting his pace when responding to external demands. This is partly due to the strong nature of his internal desires and the growing gap between these internal desires and the majority of the external demands that are being made on him. Expectations for immediate response to commands are likely to generate much frustration. A more effective approach to getting Justin to comply with requests would involve developing a system for gradually transitioning into activities involving a series of prompts with positive rewards tied to faster engagement times and reduced number of prompts used.

Justin would benefit from more structure in home routines. While both of Justin's parents and his sisters exhibit great flexibility and good self-management, Justin lacks any consistent structure to help him overcome his lack of planning and organization and his relatively inflexible approach to problem solving. He needs a specific place designated as his study area, limited access to his computer and art materials, and a specific time schedule for homework and chores. Even with more structure, Justin will require frequent verbal prompts to remind him of the routines and to help him with organization and planning. Increased home-school communication would help Justin's parents to know what is due and when. Justin's parents could develop a positive reinforcement system where Justin would be rewarded for doing homework and chores.

An observation made after the time spent with Justin and his parents is that nearly all of the conversations and interactions between Justin and his parents have a negative tone and relate back to his academic production difficulties. Explanation of the nature of executive function development and the executive function difficulties that Justin was encountering helped his parents gain a greater appreciation of the sources of Justin's behavior and enabled them to develop a more positive communication style when discussing these difficulties. It was also recommended that the family establish a time and a place, most likely a meal out at a restaurant, where they could have a positive conversation during which school topics would be out of bounds.

Interventions for Kevin

With Kevin's explosiveness, there is a greater sense of urgency for the provision of interventions—as his behavior has direct impact on classroom functioning and his safety and that of his peers. Also, there is concern relative to how he is perceived by himself as well as others, as one with Kevin's profile is likely to have his issues interpreted as character flaws and/or the result of bad parenting. As indicated by the principal's growing impatience with Kevin, he is likely on the fast track to being labeled "emotionally disturbed." As noted by Ross Greene in *Treating Explosive Kids* (Greene & Albon, 2006), children like Kevin are the most commonly referred for mental health assistance although, paradoxically, they often are the most poorly understood. In Kevin's case, the fact that a behavioral management system appeared to be working—at times—increases the perception of others that he could better manage his behavioral and emotional reactions to situations if he really wanted to. However, from the interviews with Kevin's parents, his teachers, and the school psychologist as well as from the findings of the direct assessment process, a more careful analysis reveals that Kevin exhibits significant executive function difficulties in the interpersonal and intrapersonal arenas that skew his perceptions, feelings, and thoughts and the actions that follow these miscues.

The idea of a functional behavior assessment was certainly a good place to start in attempting to deal with Kevin's problematic behaviors, but the actual assessment and the subsequent behavior support plan failed to take into account a number of factors. Most importantly, setting events and antecedents and predictors were not adequately explored in the assessment or integrated into the support plan. In truth, however, Kevin's teacher was not really ready to take on the manipulation of antecedent conditions to the degree needed to help Kevin avoid meltdowns.

In retrospect, one might question why Kevin's problems are only now being addressed by the school-based team. Looking back on Kevin's history, his explosive tendencies were recognized as early as first grade, but the teacher was very good at applying the needed external controls in her classroom that year to enable Kevin to learn and progress academically without any significant incidents. Made aware of Kevin's problems by the first grade teacher, the school principal had hand-picked Kevin's second, third, and fourth grade teachers, all of whom could effectively apply the needed external controls to regulate Kevin's classroom behavior even while believing that Kevin and his parents were the exclusive owners of the problems. None of these very effective teachers attempted to alter Kevin's behavior through changes in internal processes and no individual or group-counseling services were provided because the teachers were able to handle Kevin's classroom behavior. Unfortunately for Kevin, the principal had finally run out of flexible, tolerant, nurturing but firm teachers to whom he could assign Kevin. In retrospect, given the poor match between Kevin and his teacher's classroom management style, the early-year emergence of behavior difficulties was highly predictable.

Now charged with implementing a behavior support plan, Kevin's fifth grade teacher displayed no tolerance for any of Kevin's difficulties and frequently chastised him excessively in front of his peers as a way to maintain classroom control, the result being to simply make things worse. An additional problem with the intervention plan was that the entire intervention was attempted in the confines of the school with no input from Kevin's parents. The minimal contact with the parents since the second grade incident mentioned earlier had left the impression (later found to be inaccurate) that the parents were overindulgent and made excuses for Kevin's behavior to avoid dealing with the problems that resulted. From that point on, they were not included in discussions of Kevin's behavior and were never engaged in efforts to change Kevin's behavior in a positive way.

While functional assessment is an appropriate technique to use for behavior problems, when these problems persist over time and require extensive external control on a daily basis, other factors that might be contributing to the behavior problems need to be considered more carefully. While maturation is certainly an issue with Kevin, the nature and severity of his problems suggested that there might be more from a biological perspective that needed to be addressed. The executive function-oriented functional assessment completed with Kevin clearly indicated the issue of AD/HD needed to be explored with a physician to determine if pharmacological intervention would be appropriate. The high ratings on all scales indicating hyperactivity and inattention were not surprising. As Barkley has noted, AD/HD and conduct disorder have a significant overlap (2005). Kevin's problems were never viewed from a perspective of AD/HD or executive function difficulties; rather, they were attributed primarily to the choices of a spoiled child who was not appropriately disciplined at home, resulting in negative spillover into the school environment.

In Kevin's case, the severity of the behavior problems stemming from his self-regulation executive function difficulties combined with his lack of capacity for self-awareness necessitate intervention efforts that are initially focused exclusively on external control such as that provided in earlier grades. Ideally, the psychological report on Kevin would be shared with a physician familiar with the symptoms of AD/HD and appropriate modes of treatment. Whether or not medication were prescribed, a new behavior support plan would need to be drawn up that did a better job of considering setting events and antecedents and identifying ways that the setting events and antecedents could be altered to help reduce the likelihood of explosive episodes. The plan would need to be developed in conjunction with Kevin's parents and home-school communication would be an essential part of the program's implementation with parents maintaining consistency at home and following through with consequences as needed. Kevin's teacher would need to receive training that would provide her with the skills needed to alter her classroom management practices in a manner that would enable her to implement the revised behavior support plan. The fact that Kevin's behaviors had been effectively managed for four years by general classroom teachers strongly suggests that Kevin could remain in a general education classroom provided that the teacher could implement external controls effectively. Kevin's executive function difficulties were explained to his parents and teachers at a meeting of the school-based team. Up to that point, the parents' reaction to Kevin's behavior problems was to apply extremely severe consequences, including physical punishment. Because Kevin's problems were as evident in the home setting as in the school setting, the family would be well-served by seeking help from a mental health professional familiar with techniques similar to those used by Ross Greene in his treatment of explosive children.

Finally, it needed to be explained to Kevin that his behavior problems stem from the way his brain functions and that if he could acknowledge this fact, it is very possible that he could be taught how to control his brain functions so that he would experience fewer problems in school and at home, and more of his fellow students would like him and would be more likely to include him in activities and games. Although Kevin is not yet ready to effectively process this information, it needs to be offered at regular intervals in order to try to help Kevin improve his capacity for self-realization and self-regulation. Additional strategies for developing Kevin's internal control will not be very effective until Kevin develops increased awareness of these capacities and increases his willingness to participate in efforts to help him improve self-control. Until this happens, external control strategies will need to remain in place to assure that Kevin's behavior remains within acceptable limits.

Interventions for Caroline

As noted from results of her assessment, while Caroline demonstrates an inability to effectively engage many self-regulation executive function capacities (most notably Perceive, Initiate, Sustain, Organize, Retrieve, Foresee/Plan, Monitor, Correct) in all four domains, her poor self-regulation of functioning in the intrapersonal, self-control arena has been most problematic. Caroline is "her own worst enemy" in that her difficulties, in part, focus on her relationship with herself—her internal conversations or lack thereof. Intervention efforts at this point in time need to focus on that internal dialogue with the intent of changing its content and themes.

While antidepressant medication appears to have alleviated some of Caroline's depressive symptoms, it has not appeared to significantly alter her negative self-perceptions. Understanding this is important for laying out an intervention plan in that, while Caroline may benefit from an increased awareness of what executive functions are and how they impact her functioning, she is quite likely to view any such instruction or dialogue as another way of telling her what she is doing wrong. Caroline is much more likely to hear the message of needed change if she is able to interpret it from a more positive vantage point. Caroline appears to be a good candidate for cognitive behavior therapy, which attempts to help individuals gain executive control over perceptions, thought patterns, emotional reactions, and overt behaviors. For Caroline, the key is to develop more accurate and positive self-perceptions. This goal could be approached through cognitive techniques that create some cognitive dissonance regarding her actual versus perceived cognitive abilities, challenge the validity of her negative self-perceptions, and that positively alter her self-assessments of what she is able to do. Other behavioral techniques, particularly activity scheduling, may also be instrumental to changing Caroline's self-perceptions, particularly if she is supported in the engagement of tasks for which she has some degree of competency and that involve peer interaction.

Once the negative self-dialogue is significantly reduced, Caroline may be more amenable to learning about what executive capacities she has in sufficient abundance and which she is in need of increasing. Certainly, the message that improvement in her functioning may be possible with investment of effort on her part and understanding and guidance of others is an important one for her to hear. With her strong cognitive abilities, she may be intrigued by the nature of executive function capacities and able to engage in considerable discussion relative to the concept and application. The goal of this knowledge would be to help Caroline develop self-awareness around how she is perceiving, feeling, thinking, and acting at any given moment and to better recognize whether those perceptions, feelings, thoughts, and actions are appropriately helpful for the situation. With structured intervention in problem-solving techniques, she would be better equipped to size up alternative responses, thoughts, feelings, and perceptions.

While this learning process is taking place, Caroline is likely to require significant cueing from those around her. Caroline's parents will need to not only educate themselves relative to the nature of their daughter's self-regulation difficulties, but will need to help her develop self-cues or provide external prompts for her difficulties in perceiving, initiating, sustaining, organizing, retrieving, planning, monitoring, and correcting. Family meetings, which take on a problem-solving rather than person-blaming tone, may be essential. Family members may want to develop a self-care plan, which accommodates Caroline's slow-to-activate morning state. As no other family member appears to have similar morning difficulties, a schedule that gives Caroline last "dibs" on the shower, etc., may be the most productive and least conflict-producing. Working with Caroline to develop a plan of action for long-term assignments, helping her to locate and use a site conducive to doing homework, helping her estimate the amount of time and energy required for task completion, and providing monitoring and correcting assistance are all likely components of this parental support. While Caroline currently appears somewhat vested in improvement, should her parents' intervention become a source of considerable discord, they may want to enlist the services of a tutor or "coach," who is well versed in knowledge executive function, to provide the requisite cues and strategies.

Caroline may also need similar "coaching" in the interpersonal realm, which may be derived from a sympathetic and more executively mature peer, from participation in a group intervention where similar-aged peers can discuss typical concerns, or through participation in activities, that stress a lack of competition and a focus on wellness and mindfulness, such as yoga or tai chi.

Interventions for Brett

Although we typically do not harbor expectations for high levels of vigilance or self-awareness for 5-year-olds, Brett illustrates the relative nature of such developmental appraisals. Compared to Brett, most of his same-age peers are an exceptionally vigilant and self-aware bunch! When observing Brett in action, we realize just how much executive function development has already occurred by the age of 5, as well as how much more is needed for truly independent functioning.

Because of Brett's age and the severity of his impulsiveness in terms of guiding perceptions and actions in the environment and when engaged with fine motor tools required for success in school, Brett is in need of almost constant external control. While maturation is certainly an issue with Brett, the nature and severity of his problems, like those of Kevin, strongly suggest the need to consider biological factors. The executive function-oriented comprehensive assessment completed with Brett clearly indicated the issue of AD/HD needed to be explored with a physician to determine if pharmacological intervention would be appropriate. The high ratings on all scales for areas related to hyperactivity, impulsivity, and inattention were not unexpected given the interview information gathered and Brett's behavior during the interview session. What is surprising, to some degree, is the fact that Brett's difficulties do not affect his social interactions with other children or adults (except to exasperate them with his daredevil maneuvers) and that he does not demonstrate much in the way of emotional impulsivity or frustration at having his impulses thwarted. It almost seems as though, on some level, Brett does have some degree of awareness of the dangerous situations his actions create.

Ideally, the psychoeducational report on Brett should be shared with a physician familiar with the symptoms of AD/HD and appropriate modes of treatment. Whether or not medication were prescribed, a functional assessment and behavior support plan should be completed to assure that Brett's risky behaviors are controlled as effectively as possible in the school setting, and a similar plan should be in place in the home for similar reasons. Parent training is likely to be an important component of this behavior support plan, as such participation is found to be efficacious, especially in conjunction with medication, in managing child behavioral difficulties (Edwards, 2002). The focus of such training would be to help Brett's parents restructure his environment to enable him get around in a safer, more deliberative manner. Using Ross Greene's delineation of priority setting for behavioral improvement is especially helpful in regard to Brett's situation, as his behavior appears at times overwhelm and exhaust his parents. Because of this, Brett's parents also are encouraged to seek support groups that focus on dealing with children diagnosed with AD/HD as well as work to provide themselves with "child-free times." While Brett may not be able to actively engage the self-awareness capacities needed to self-regulate, it is likely to be helpful to introduce him to the language of self-regulation by cueing him to:

- Stop and plan what he needs to do before he engages in a motor act (crossing the street, entering a classroom, playing a game, etc.)
- Perceive what is going on in his environment
- Calm down (modulate) his activity level

- Gauge what speed or activity level or attention he needs for the specific task
- Inhibit his actions to be able to make an alternative choice
- Pace his motor speed to match the task demands
- Monitor his motor actions by acknowledging what happens
- Correct his motor act when he bumps into, knocks over, etc. items, by retracing his steps

Also, although Brett is young and cannot really be expected to simply "get with the program," there is much that could be done here in the way of educating him about the dangerous consequences of his actions. Use of a program such as Myrna B. Shure's I Can Problem-Solve or the Dina Dinosaur Treatment Program (Webster-Stratton & Reid, 2003) could help to lay the groundwork for Brett to develop a greater capacity for self-regulation in the environment. Work with a physical therapist would likely be of great help to Brett in helping develop the executive control needed to develop better fine motor coordination and pencil-handling skills.

Interventions for Morgan

Morgan is at an age where she is likely to benefit from an intervention plan that includes strategies for helping her develop internal control as well as strategies that provide external control. Her increasing self-awareness and self-determination capacities provide a basis for helping Morgan develop an understanding of the nature of her executive function difficulties and the things she can do to help improve her self-regulation capacities. All of the internalizing strategies presented in this chapter could be utilized to provide Morgan with the tools she needs to engage in greater self-regulation of her reading and writing production. Especially helpful would be teaching the use of executive functions as part of skill routines. Modeling, verbal mediation, verbal labeling, developing internal feedback, and learning to use self-administered rewards could all be used to support the learning of these skill routines.

Morgan's difficulties with focusing and sustaining attention and effort make it necessary to use external control strategies to assure the necessary level of engagement with reading and writing tasks. To achieve this end, all of the external control strategies could be applied. Morgan especially needs a structured environment and help with structuring her use

of time. External cueing including lists of steps for performing academic skill routines and verbal prompts would be of
benefit. Feedback about performance and aligning external
demands with internal desires should also be considered.
Morgan is very motivated to succeed, and verbal praise should
be sufficient reward for maintaining engagement.

The question of AD/HD was raised by both school staff
and Morgan's parents. The fact that most of Morgan's symptoms relate to inattention and are extremely narrow in their
impact (symbol system arena only) would lead some professionals to immediately discount the possibility of the existence of an AD/HD condition. It must be noted, however, that
many hyperactive symptoms were observed during the individual assessment and reported by the resource room teachers.
Morgan's parents, while not endorsing Hyperactivity/Impul-
sivity items on the ADHD-IV rating scale, did report a history
since early elementary school of the type of fidgety behavior
observed during the individual assessment. The psychologist
evaluating Morgan (the first author of this book) also noted that
Morgan's pattern of test results, executive function difficulties
and her academic production problems were very similar to
those of a number of other late elementary-age female students
who had been diagnosed with AD/HD and had responded very
well to the use of psychostimulants. Based on the information gathered in the assessment process and the psychologist's
previous experiences with children with profiles similar to
Morgan's, it was recommended that the parents provide a copy
of the psychoeducational report to a physician familiar with
the symptoms and treatment for AD/HD to determine if medical treatment would be an option for Morgan. Morgan's case
is somewhat different from the others we have considered
in that her executive function difficulties are limited almost
exclusively to the regulation of academic production in basic
skill areas related to reading and writing. These difficulties
were addressed in detail in the discussion of Morgan's academic assessment results presented in Chapter 6. Additional
information related to specific intervention efforts to help deal
with Morgan's academic difficulties in the school context is
presented in the Case Vignette section of Chapter 8.

Interventions for Alex

As was the case with Justin, Alex is clearly demonstrating
significant delays in the development of executive function
capacities. Unlike Justin, however, the delays are focused

much more at the self-awareness and self-determination levels than at the self-regulation level. Now in his early twenties, Alex still has not developed the capacity to harness his self-regulation capacities to goals beyond immediate gratification of urges or to plan or organize beyond the present day. Alex also is seriously lagging behind in the development of self-analysis capacities that would help him to reflect on his situation in a meaningful way. Despite many discussions about these areas of need with Alex, and his brief participation in a cognitive behavior therapy program, he has not yet developed the degree of self-awareness needed to affect real change. Given Alex's history, it was apparent that a greater degree of external control needed to be in place in order to help him become more engaged with activities likely to help produce meaningful change. In terms of knowledge bases, it was apparent that Alex lacked much in the way of vocational maturity, having little understanding of the world of work or what it takes to become engaged and succeed in a job of any sort. Complicating matters was Alex's physical condition that appeared to be related to stress. The psychologist and Alex mutually agreed on a goal of gainful employment within 4 weeks as the primary goal of their collaborative efforts. The plan included check-ins with the psychologist every other day to update on what activities Alex had completed in his job search. Additional goals related to improved sleep habits, improved diet with meals at regular times, and a daily exercise routine. After 8 months, Alex's sleep habits and diet had improved significantly and he continued to exercise regularly, but did not find a job. After failing to find employment, an alternate goal of researching and selecting a career area and enrolling in school for training in that area was set with an 8-week time goal. Unfortunately, that goal was not attained either even after extensions of the time line. During the 8-month period, Alex was provided with external prompts and close monitoring of his activities, but these efforts were not successful in producing the desired changes in behavior. At this point, it seemed clear that something more was needed. The specific option selected will be discussed at the end of the next chapter.

SUMMARY

At the beginning of this chapter, we noted that any attempt at intervention for executive functioning difficulties depends on the proper conceptualization of the problem, which evolves from a thorough assessment and clear description of the difficulties as well as the contexts in which they occur. Given the multidimensional nature and impact of executive functioning difficulties, it is not surprising that interventions need to be varied and responsive to the particular domain, arena, and self-regulation difficulty. Just as the concept of executive functions is not a unitary trait, interventions cannot be packaged in a "one size fits all" program. However, we do propose that there is universality in the way that an intervention plan is approached and that is with the adoption of three critical key points: Executive function difficulties are associated with suboptimal brain functions, not a by-product of conscious choice; brain function, and thus executive functions, can be altered through intervention; and interventions can activate the use of intact brain functions. The key to effective intervention requires a balance between teaching strategies and techniques that will affect internal change, while supplying the necessary external scaffolds and supports. While this external support system may include rewards and punishment, use of such needs to take into careful consideration the capacity of the child to cue the engagement of the needed executive function. If the capacity is not there, the use of rewards is not likely to be effective.

General guidelines for an intervention plan involve providing the child with a rich executive function environment, where there is effective modeling and cueing; developing a plan that focuses on increasing the child's awareness of the executive functions needed to achieve the desired goal and when to use them; providing requisite external controls; and maintaining and encouraging others to maintain reasonable expectations and an attitude of hope, patience, and perseverance. Keeping these general guidelines in mind, we provided specific intervention strategies for developing internal control and increasing external control. Additionally, we provided an example of how to use these strategies to improve the use of the self-regulation capacities.

Specific interventions for executive function difficulties come from multiple and diverse sources, some of which do not specifically use the executive function nomenclature. For approaches designed to increase internal control, we highlighted the approaches of Cognitive-Behavioral Therapy and mindfulness practices; problem-solving training; McGinnis and Goldstein's skill-streaming series; Greene's approach for dealing with explosiveness; and Schwartz's approach for dealing with obsessive-compulsive disorder. Social skills training and social stories provide explicit scaffolding supports for those with executive function difficulties in the interpersonal arena. For academic difficulties, we briefly note the work from instrumental enrichment, metacognition, and cognitive strategy training, but will discuss in Chapter 8 more specific interventions for executive function difficulties in the symbol system (academic) arena. For approaches designed to increase external control, we note the interventions emanating from ADHD and TBI literature. Finally, we ask the reader to consider the impact of executive function difficulties in the environmental arena, where the need for explicit interventions may be most critical.

If, in turning to this chapter on interventions, the clinician had hoped for a "recipe" for correcting executive function difficulties, he or she may be frustrated by the complexity of the conceptualization and the need to view interventions in an equally multidimensional manner. While there is no magic formula or recipe, the existing literature points to intervention strategies that are likely to be effective and already in the skill set of many clinicians. For this reason, we encourage the reader to employ a mindset of hope and perseverance both in formulating an accurate conceptualization of the child's executive function difficulties as well as in developing an appropriate and comprehensive intervention plan of action.

8

Executive Functions in the School Setting

Previous chapters have defined executive functions, discussed their role in guiding all aspects of daily functioning, and described assessment and intervention methods for dealing with executive function difficulties. This chapter will discuss how to take the information presented in earlier chapters and apply it to the school setting. Clinicians who develop an understanding of executive functions and how they impact behavior and academic production can apply this knowledge to their work in the school setting in a number of important areas, including:

- Sharing knowledge to help parents and school staff understand the role of executive functions in children's behavior and academic performance
- Helping teachers use their understanding of executive functions to enhance group or individual instruction
- Identifying the role of executive functions in social and emotional functioning and using that knowledge to guide behavior assessment and the development of interventions for behavior problems
- Identifying the role of executive functions in academic skill production and using that knowledge to enhance assessment of academic problems and the development of interventions
- Helping guide the implementation and evaluation of interventions that incorporate knowledge of executive functions to enhance effectiveness
- Advocating for system level change in schools to improve student academic performance and behavior by taking into account what is known about executive functions

Each of these areas will be discussed in more detail in the specific sections of this chapter.

SHARING KNOWLEDGE OF EXECUTIVE FUNCTIONS

Clinicians who have acquired a good working knowledge of executive functions can share this information with parents, teachers, administrators, and other school staff to help increase awareness of this important concept and its application to instruction, assessment, and intervention activities. The goal here should be to understand how these concepts can be integrated into existing ideas about instruction, assessment, and intervention rather than as a replacement for existing ideas. The ideas presented in this book can be viewed as a set of important insights into a specific set of neuropsychological capacities that can be woven into existing knowledge and practices to enhance effectiveness. When information about executive functions has been shared effectively with staff, the reaction should not be: "I used to think he had behavior problems; now I see he really has executive function problems" but rather: "I can see how his behavior and/or academic problems reflect a lack of executive control, and I now have some good ideas about what I can do to help him improve his behavior and/or academic production."

An important goal of sharing information about executive functions should be to help teachers realize the extent of the executive function demands they make on students and how these demands can be overwhelming for children who are experiencing slower than average development of executive function capacities. As discussed in Chapter 4, maturation plays a large role in determining the extent to which a child can handle the self-regulation expectations teachers have for their classes. Recognizing the wide variation in executive function maturation levels within same-age and same-grade students is the starting point for differentiating instruction in a manner that allows more children the opportunity to succeed.

Much of what children do throughout the day in school is nonconsciously directed, even when performance is highly effective. This state is not restricted to children, however; rather, it is the natural state of functioning for most of us. A major focus of sharing information about executive functions should be to raise parents, teachers, school staff, and students' conscious awareness of the specific executive function capacities needed for effective academic performance and social and emotional functioning. Making all students aware of the academic goals and behavioral expectations that are in place in the school setting should go hand-in-hand with increasing awareness of executive functions and the need to engage them. Students who are consciously aware of goals and expectations are much more likely to find ways to engage executive function capacities to assist in achieving these goals and expectations. Students who find these goals and expectations difficult to achieve will require compassionate assistance in making as much progress as possible given the maturation-based constraints they are likely to be encountering in their efforts to succeed.

Another important goal of sharing knowledge about executive functions should be to help parents, teachers, and school staff distinguish between learning difficulties and producing difficulties. The contrast between these two concepts was introduced in Chapter 4 and discussed at length in Chapter 6. When teachers and administrators understand this important contrast, school-based decision-making teams can be much more effective in accurately identifying the nature of a child's difficulties in school and in developing and implementing interventions that address the identified problems.

APPLYING KNOWLEDGE OF EXECUTIVE FUNCTIONS TO ENHANCE GROUP AND INDIVIDUAL INSTRUCTION

Once knowledge of executive functions has been shared with teachers and a basis for meaningful dialogue about the concept has been established, clinicians can assist teachers in finding ways to incorporate this knowledge base into instructional practices. Observation of the teacher's delivery of instruction can be a good way to initiate this process. These observations provide clinicians with much insight into how teachers do, or do not, utilize strategies either encouraging the internalizing of self-regulation or externally guiding students in situations where self-regulation is not forthcoming.

The instructional practices used by teachers reflect the extent to which they are aware, implicitly or explicitly, of the executive function capacities of the children in the classroom and the techniques they can use to assist children in handling the self-regulation demands related to expectations for classroom behavior and academic production. Teachers' incorporation of knowledge of executive functions into their teaching practices is reflected in the extent to which they exhibit the applications listed in Table 8.1. Teachers and school administrators may realize that many of the applications listed in Table 8.1 have been described in the educational literature as teaching practices most likely to produce behavior improvement and academic gains (e.g., Marzano, Pickering, & Pollock, 2001; Marzano, 2003; Marzano, Marzano, & Pickering, 2003). This fact only serves to underscore the important point that knowledge of executive functions can be incorporated into existing knowledge bases to enhance understanding of what works in classroom instruction and behavior management and why it works from the perspective of brain development.

Ideally, teachers will apply their knowledge of executive functions to help students increase their use of self-regulation capacities in developmentally appropriate ways. This is especially the case for older students in middle, junior, and senior high schools. Younger students (especially early elementary school) and children with more pronounced executive function difficulties, however, exhibit far fewer self regulation capacities. Appreciation of this fact is reflected in teachers' effective use of techniques to externally direct students in their efforts to demonstrate appropriate classroom behavior and academic production. As discussed in Chapter 7, teacher delivered prompts are the most frequent strategy employed as an external substitute for internally cued self-regulation. Clinicians conducting observations of teachers to help them improve the effective use of external cueing techniques may find the Executive Function Classroom Observation Checklist (EFCO) provided on the CD accompanying this book to be a valuable resource.

APPLYING KNOWLEDGE OF EXECUTIVE FUNCTIONS TO PROBLEM BEHAVIOR ASSESSMENT AND INTERVENTION

Current best practices (O'Neill, Horner, Albin, Sprague, & Newton, 1997; Knoster & McCurdy, 2002) advocate the use of functional assessment techniques to identify and analyze behavior problems. Functional assessment techniques are effectively employed to identify setting events and antecedents that trigger problem behaviors, clearly describe the negative behavior to be changed, specify positive replacement behaviors, and

Table 8.1   Applying Knowledge of Executive Functions in
Classroom Instruction Practices

Applying Knowledge of Contextual Factors Impacting Executive Function Use by:
Making children consciously aware of goals of academic instruction and behavioral expectations
Finding ways to help students become conscious of executive functions and how they are used to help with learning, production, and behavior control
Aligning external demands with students' internal desires when possible to maximize student motivation and improve behavior and academic production
Adjusting classroom routines and assignments to take into account the effects of slow maturation of executive functions that some students will be experiencing
Recognizing that medical conditions and medication use can affect executive function capacities, which students in their class have medical conditions or are taking medication, and watch for and deal with any observed fluctuations in executive function use
Recognizing the need to cue students to apply knowledge learned in one setting to another setting
Adjusting content and teaching methods to take into account observed patterns of fluctuation in energy and stamina and their effects on students' use of executive functions
Reducing task complexity (thereby decreasing the degree of executive function coordination required) for students who have difficulty with multitasking
Allowing for alternative methods of assessment of mastery of objectives, recognizing that certain assessment formats rely heavily on specific types of executive functions that might present difficulties for some students
Applying Knowledge of Strategies for Externally Controlling Behavior and Cueing Production by:
Making use of verbal and nonverbal prompts when necessary
Providing feedback about progress toward goals and to reinforce appropriate behaviors and adequate academic production
Providing rewards as needed to help students achieve goals, exhibit appropriate behavior, and demonstrate adequate academic production
Structuring the classroom environment to allow for self-regulation by those who can use internal control cues, and prompting and direction for those who require external cues
Structuring time and students' awareness of time as needed
Applying Knowledge of Strategies for Helping Students Increase Self-Regulation by:
Helping students become aware of executive functions and how they are used to cue and direct perceptions, feelings, thoughts, and actions

Table 8.1 (continued) Applying Knowledge of Executive Functions in Classroom Instruction Practices

Helping students develop a vocabulary for describing executive functions that can be used by the teacher and students to communicate about executive functions and how and when to use them
Helping students become aware of when they are using, or when they could be using, executive functions to self-regulate behavior and academic production
Helping students become aware of when the teacher is cueing regulation of behavior and academic production because students are not doing so themselves
Helping students to be consciously aware of "self-talk" and how to use self-talk to cue and direct perceptions, feelings, thoughts, and actions
Helping students learn how to use self-talk to give themselves feedback about the adequacy of behavior and academic production
Helping students understand the idea of self-administered rewards and helping them generate self-rewards
Modeling effective use of self-regulation capacities and explaining to students how this self regulation was achieved
Developing and applying routines that teach students how to self regulate behavior and production

specify consequences that exist for both positive and negative behaviors. Once the elements are known, interventions can be planned that alter the event settings and antecedents thereby avoiding the occurrence of problem behaviors. These alterations to antecedents are accomplished by those working with the student. Additionally, functional assessment emphasizes the external structuring of consequences to encourage the occurrence of positive behaviors and avoidance of negative ones. This structure of traditional functional assessment is perfectly suited to situations where external control is required to obtain and maintain acceptable behaviors. As stated by experts in the field of functional behavior assessment (O'Neill, Horner, Albin, Sprague, Storey, & Newton, 1997):

> Behavior support plans are designed to alter patterns of problem behavior. The process by which this is done, however, involves change in the behavior of family, teachers, staff, or managers in various settings. Plans of behavior support define what *we* will do differently. It is the change in our behavior that will result in improved behavior of the focus person. (p. 65)

The purpose of traditional functional assessments and behavior support plans is to effect change in as efficient and effective a manner as possible. They are not intended to explain or provide an understanding of reasons why the setting events or antecedents cause the behaviors that lead to the unwanted consequences. They are simply designed to change the behavior from undesirable to desirable. Traditional functional assessment procedures do not offer much in the way of conceptualizing intervention strategies that will enable the child to transition from external control situations to internal self regulation which, as we have stated, is the ultimate goal of interventions intended to deal with problems related to executive function difficulties.

Because of their strong emphasis on observable behaviors, functional assessments typically do not provide a conceptual basis for understanding the root causes of why setting events and antecedents result in problem behaviors even when the negative consequences associated with the problem behaviors are completely undesirable from the student's perspective as well as everyone else's. While some strict behaviorists might argue that it is unnecessary to speculate on such causal issues, parents, teachers, and students themselves find such explanations to be central to their attempts to make sense of things. A functional assessment infused with knowledge of executive functions makes it clear that the origin of the problem behaviors lies in brain functions over which the student does not have conscious control. Understanding this fact helps parents, teachers, and students realize that the behaviors being exhibited typically are not conscious, premeditated acts defiantly carried out in the presence of a clear awareness of the consequences they will produce. Rather, these behaviors are the result of inadequate activation of executive function capacities that are necessary for regulating perceptions, feelings, thoughts, and actions. In other words, the problem behaviors are not simply a matter of personal choice or a means to achieve desired consequences. Acknowledgment of the neuropsychological origins of problem behaviors provides parents, teachers, and school staff with a conceptual framework that engenders understanding and compassion rather than negatively biased attributions regarding the student's character and moral fiber.

Informed by knowledge of executive functions, the functional assessment model can be revised as in Figure 8.1. In this model, executive function difficulties result in ineffective reg-

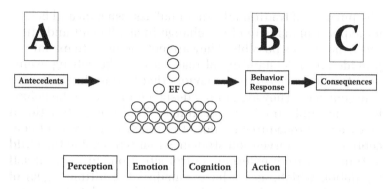

Figure 8.1   An Executive-Driven Functional Assessment Model.

ulation of perceptions, feelings, thoughts, and actions leading to undesired behavioral responses to setting events and/or antecedents thereby producing undesired consequences. Whereas traditional behaviorally-oriented functional assessment can be viewed as an A-B-C (Antecedents-Behaviors-Consequences) model, executive-driven functional assessment can be viewed as an A-EF/PETA-B-C (Antecedents-Executive Function miscuing of Perceptions, Emotions, Thoughts, Actions-Behavior-Consequences) model.

It should be noted that models such as school-based problem-solving consultation (Kratochwill, Elliott, & Callan-Stoiber, 2002) have been developed to broaden the theoretical underpinnings and applications of behaviorally-oriented functional assessment techniques, especially to address issues of social competency in addition to behavior problems. These models, however, typically do not address in detail the need to expand on the strict behavioral conceptions of problems and their solutions in the manner that is being advocated here through the use of an executive-driven functional assessment model.

Clinicians conducting executive-driven functional assessment may find the Executive Function Student Observation Form (EFSO), provided on the CD accompanying this book, to be a useful tool. The EFSO provides a format for interpreting the content of a classroom observation from the perspective of classroom executive function demands and the type of self-regulation capacities a student does or does not demonstrate to meet these demands. The observation form also enables the observer to note strategies the teacher does, or does not, use to engender use of internal control or to externally direct behavior and academic production. The EFSO can be reviewed prior to the observation to prepare the observer for the types of judgments that will need to be made after observation data has been recorded. During the observation period, the clinician should take good notes on what the child does as well as what the teacher and other children are doing. After the observation, the clinician should complete the EFSO using the notes taken during the observation period.

Approaches to Behavior Problem Intervention

As noted earlier, traditional behaviorally oriented functional assessments result in the development of behavior support plans. These behavior support plans clearly involve external control strategies rather than strategies for developing internal self-regulation capacities that would enable the student to take control of the situation. Certainly, in cases where executive function difficulties are severe and the problem behaviors are extreme, or when dealing with young children (early elementary age), such behavior support plans are likely to be the most effective means of producing positive behavior change. In these situations, executive-driven functional assessment can identify the executive function difficulties that are the source of the behavior problems. Subsequently, part of the intervention plan would be to help parents and teachers understand the nature of these executive function difficulties, their impact on the student's behavior, and the reasons why external control strategies are required. Additionally, understanding the executive function difficulties producing the problem behaviors will help those charged with delivering the intervention adopt an appropriate perspective during such implementation.

Realizing that the student's behaviors are not intentionally driven enables those involved with the child to maintain a compassionate but firm attitude when required to deliver any negative consequences that might be specified in the plan. All too often when a traditional behavior support plan is required, the implicit message communicated to parents and the student is: Since you (student) have chosen not to take control of your own behavior, we will now take control for you. When using an executive function-oriented behavior support plan, a very different, explicit message is delivered to all involved in the process, including the parents and student: The child is experiencing executive function difficulties; that is, he is having trouble with (state the specific executive function difficulties). These difficulties most likely are being caused by a lack of maturation of some parts of the child's brain. These difficulties are making it hard for the child to control behavior. We are going to provide the child with a program that will help him (or her) control behavior while he (or her) is here in school.

Implementing interventions that are based on external control strategies can often be very labor intensive or require major adjustments to settings and/or complex adjustments to manipulate antecedent conditions and careful monitoring of behavior to ensure that appropriate consequences follow behaviors. While such interventions are sometimes implemented in general education classrooms, they are much more likely to involve special settings in order to effectively manage the student's executive function difficulties. Such settings include special education programs for children with social/emotional difficulties, alternative schools, and residential placements.

In cases where the executive function difficulties are less severe and the student is older (late elementary through high school age), the outcomes of the executive function-oriented functional assessment can serve a greater number of roles in planning and implementing intervention efforts. These roles can include identifying the executive function difficulties producing the problem behaviors and subsequently explaining to parents, teachers, school staff, and the student: (1) the nature and role of the executive function difficulties and their role in producing the problem; (2) why external control strategies might be needed at the outset of the intervention; (3) that the ultimate goal of the intervention plan is to help the student internalize control and engage in self-regulation; (4) that the intervention plan will include a transition stage during which the student will be taught ways to improve self-regulation; (5) that the student will be guided through a process of moving from external control of behavior to internal control of perceptions, feelings, thoughts, and actions.

When dealing with older students experiencing less severe executive function difficulties, intervention efforts can make use of the specific strategies discussed in Chapter 7 for helping to develop internal control. The less severe nature of these difficulties also makes it more likely that interventions can be effectively implemented by teachers in general education classrooms with the support of a consultant, or through individual or group counseling or resource room settings.

Most classroom-wide behavior management techniques make use of behavioral principles similar to those employed in the development of individual behavior support plans (Marzano, Marzano, & Pickering, 2003). As was the case with individual behavior management, classroom behavior management can be enhanced in important ways through application of knowledge of executive functions.

It can be seen that the expanded A-EF/PETA-B-C executive-driven model for interventions (Figure 8.1) focuses not just on behaviors, but on the perceptions, feelings, thoughts, and actions that lead to the behaviors and the executive control capacities that cue and direct all of these. The executive-driven model also has the ultimate goal of self-regulation rather than maintenance of external control. Interventions based on the executive-driven model do not say that problem behavior is a matter of choice and the solution is for the student to make better choices—or else. Ultimately, the goal of an executive-driven intervention is to get to the point where, in fact, the student actually *is* making good choices, not just about behavior, but also about perceptions, feelings, and thoughts associated with behaviors. Something, however, needs to happen on the way from not making any choices to making good choices. That something will be an intervention program that will be suited to the particular executive function capacities, or lack of executive function capacities, of the student. For some students, intervention will be a more straightforward matter of educating them in the effective use of executive function capacities they already possess. In other situations, intervention will be a matter of trying to help the student develop greater executive function capacities, possibly needing to start with external control strategies and gradually working toward internal control. In the worst-case scenarios, intervention will be a matter of substituting for a severe executive function capacity deficit through external control. Whatever path intervention efforts take, and whatever the outcome, adopting an executive-driven model will ensure sensible and humane treatment of the child along the way.

APPLYING EXECUTIVE FUNCTION KNOWLEDGE TO ACADEMIC PROBLEM ASSESSMENT AND INTERVENTION

In Chapter 4, we discussed the concept of arenas of involvement, which enabled us to make distinctions among executive function difficulties that specifically impact the use of symbol systems for learning and communicating, including their use in reading, writing, and doing math (symbol system arena), and executive function difficulties that impact other aspects of functioning (intrapersonal, interpersonal, and environment arenas). In Chapter 5, we discussed the fact that nearly all direct, formal assessments of executive functions are focused on difficulties related to the symbol system arena. While research has established that poor performance on some formal measures of executive functions can be linked to poor academic skill production, these links are highly specific and not clearly generalizable. There is some research supporting the connection between production decrements on some executive function measures using academic content and academic skill production problems. For example, Berninger (2005) offers evidence for the connection between executive function measures involving word reading and letter/word writing and reading problems and writing skill production problems. Consistent with the professional literature and our clinical experiences, Chapter 6 emphasized those aspects of executive function assessment that can be directly related to academic skill production problems. The discussion emphasized the use of cascading production decrements and increments evidenced in a child's production on academic skill assessment tasks.

Executive function difficulties can have a wide variety of negative effects on production in all academic areas. In the elementary grades, these effects are most prominent in the impact they have on the demonstration of written expression, reading, and mathematics skill production. In the upper grades, executive function difficulties with basic skill production often persist and are joined by difficulties with organization and planning and completion of projects and homework as well as inadequate regulation of the use of study skills, note-taking, and/or test-taking skills.

Applying the idea of knowledge integration rather than replacement, clinicians can appreciate that assessment and intervention for executive function difficulties associated with academic production problems should not be viewed as stand-alone activities. For example, there really is no specific intervention for "executive function reading problems," but rather interventions that take into account the impact executive function difficulties may have on a child's ability to demonstrate reading skills. Likewise, assessment of executive functions involved in academic production therefore should be viewed as an integrated part of whatever type of assessment is being conducted—functional, curriculum-based, or psychoeducational—rather than a unique form of assessment unto itself. As noted in the initial section of this chapter and consistent with the detailed discussions provided in Chapter 6, executive function concepts should be integrated into existing frameworks for academic assessment rather than be considered as a separate, stand alone area of assessment.

In the upper grades, some of the direct formal measures of executive function that assess direction of mental capacities such as reasoning and verbal fluency can be very helpful in understanding some students' lack of production in terms of classroom participation or test taking. The authors of this book have frequently employed the WCST as a tool for helping teachers understand how children with exceptional reasoning capacities are unable to cue the use of these reasoning capacities when ambiguous directions are offered for cueing task performance. Additionally, showing the contrast between a student's effective expressive language production for semantic fluency tasks and ineffective production for letter fluency tasks has enabled many teachers to understand how a talkative student can become "tongue-tied" when faced with the need to quickly retrieve highly specific information.

APPLYING KNOWLEDGE OF EXECUTIVE FUNCTIONS WHEN IMPLEMENTING AND EVALUATING INTERVENTIONS

A detailed discussion of procedures for evaluating the effectiveness and outcomes of intervention efforts is beyond the scope of this chapter. This section, however, will provide a brief discussion of intervention implementation and evaluation issues specific to dealing with executive function difficulties. As noted in Chapter 7, interventions can be designed specifically to address the difficulties a child might be having with the use of one or more executive functions. As discussed in Chapter 5, however, it is important to remember that executive functions do not exist in a vacuum—they are involved in cueing and directing specific perceptions, feeling, thoughts, and actions in various settings throughout the day. In the school setting, executive functions are being used to cue and direct social and emotional functioning and academic production. Considering the school setting context, it is more likely that executive function difficulties, if acknowledged appropriately, will be addressed in conjunction with intervention efforts focused on specific social, emotional, or academic problems. The integration of executive function issues into interventions for behavior and academic problems has been a major focus of Chapter 7 as well as sections of this chapter. Whether the intervention is designed to address specific executive function difficulties or to address executive function difficulties in relation to specific social, emotional, or academic problems, the effectiveness and outcomes of these efforts need to be evaluated.

Interventions that take into account, and program for, the effects of executive functions on social, emotional, and academic functioning will typically require progress monitoring and outcome measures that go beyond basic curriculum-based academic skills measures or standard behavior rating scales. Clinicians charged with the responsibility of developing and implementing intervention evaluation plans may find the following references to be helpful with the details of developing procedures for progress monitoring and outcome evaluation that focus on measures that address more than just standard academic or behavioral outcomes: the Outcomes: Planning, Monitoring, Evaluating system (Outcomes: PME; Stoiber & Kratochwill, 2001a), the Functional Assessment and Intervention System (FAIS; Stoiber & Kratochowill, 2001b), and the Academic Intervention Monitoring System Guidebook (AIMS Guidebook; Elliott, DiPerna, & Shapiro, 2001).

Goal Attainment Scaling (GAS) is a methodology well suited to developing measures to evaluate interventions that incorporate executive functions conceptions in their design and implementation (Kiresuk, Smith, & Cardillo, 1994; Stoiber & Kratochwill, 2001a; Stoiber & Kratochwill, 2001b; Elliott, DiPerna, & Shapiro, 2001). Goal attainment scaling involves the construction of individual items designed to evaluate specific program objectives. To maintain technical adequacy, GAS-constructed measures need to include five plausible and scorable levels of outcome accompanied by clear, detailed criteria for scoring at each of the levels of outcome (Cardillo & Choate, 1994). Examples of GAS-constructed measures appear in Table 8.2 and are discussed in more detail later in this section.

Setting goals for intervention efforts is a critical component of any intervention plan. Consistent with the discussion of executive functions throughout this book, clinicians should realize the importance not only of setting goals for the specific outcomes desired from intervention programs, but also

Table 8.2   GAS-Constructed Measures for Monitoring Progress in a Reading Intervention Program

Level of Attainment	Criterion for Determining Level of Attainment
Decoding Learning	
Much less than expected −2	Has no recollection of being taught the decoding rules that were presented during instruction that week; has difficulty relearning and applying these same rules during new instruction sessions.
Somewhat less than expected −1	Cannot state the decoding rules learned during instruction that week, but quickly recognizes them and can apply them when they are reintroduced during new instructional sessions.
Expected level of outcome 0	Can state the decoding rules learned during instruction that week and can apply them to decode words presented during instruction that week.
Somewhat more than expected +1	Can apply the newly learned decoding rules to decode unfamiliar words in lists presented after instruction sessions that week.
Much more than expected +2	Can apply the newly learned decoding rules to decode unfamiliar words in textbooks used in general education reading lessons that week.
Immediate Decoding Production Accuracy	
Much less than expected −2	Accurately applies the newly learned decoding rules 0 to 20% of the time when attempting to decode unfamiliar words in lists and in textbooks used in general education reading lessons that week.
Somewhat less than expected −1	Accurately applies the newly learned decoding rules 21 to 40% of the time when attempting to decode unfamiliar words in lists and in textbooks used in general education reading lessons that week.
Expected level of outcome 0	Accurately applies the newly learned decoding rules 41 to 60% of the time when attempting to decode unfamiliar words in lists and in textbooks used in general education reading lessons that week.
Somewhat more than expected +1	Accurately applies the newly learned decoding rules 61 to 80% of the time when attempting to decode unfamiliar words in lists and in textbooks used in general education reading lessons that week.
Much more than expected +2	Accurately applies the newly learned decoding rules 81 to 100% of the time when attempting to decode unfamiliar words in lists and in textbooks used in general education reading lessons that week.

Table 8.2 (continued)   GAS-Constructed Measures for Monitoring Progress in a Reading Intervention Program

Level of Attainment	Criterion for Determining Level of Attainment
Long-Term Decoding Production Consistency	
Much less than expected −2	Never reaches the criterion of applying the newly learned decoding rules 81 to 100% of the time when attempting to decode unfamiliar words in lists and in textbooks used in general education for one week.
Somewhat less than expected −1	Accurately applies the newly learned decoding rules 81 to 100% of the time when attempting to decode unfamiliar words in lists and in textbooks used in general education reading lessons on consecutive weeks.
Expected level of outcome 0	Accurately applies the newly learned decoding rules 81 to 100% of the time when attempting to decode unfamiliar words in lists and in textbooks used in general education reading lessons on 2 consecutive weeks.
Somewhat more than expected +1	Accurately applies the newly learned decoding rules 81 to 100% of the time when attempting to decode unfamiliar words in lists and in textbooks used in general education reading lessons on 3–4 consecutive weeks.
Much more than expected +2	Accurately applies the newly learned decoding rules 81 to 100% of the time when attempting to decode unfamiliar words in lists and in textbooks used in general education reading lessons on 5–6 consecutive weeks.

of sharing those goals with students. As noted earlier in this chapter, making students consciously aware of the intentions of intervention efforts increases the likelihood that students will engage, consciously or nonconsciously, any self-directive capacities available to them in an effort to achieve these goals. While goal sharing improves student participation and increases the likelihood of success of intervention efforts, it is imperative that students find the goals worthwhile and acceptable (Miller & Rollnick, 2002).

Executive functions are the mental capacities that enable us to function effectively in the complex physical and cultural environments we have shaped around us. In the school setting, effective social, emotional, and academic functioning all depend on the use of developmentally appropriate executive function capacities. Possessing age-appropriate executive function capacities, however, is not a guarantee that they will be used effectively. Even the most capable of students sometimes need assistance to work out exactly how to apply their executive function capacities to the task at hand. When students with good executive functions experience social, emotional, or academic problems, interventions are typically highly informal, short-lived, and very effective.

On the other hand, when social, emotional, or academic difficulties are identified, but the students exhibiting these problems are experiencing executive function difficulties, the likelihood is much greater that the problems will be dealt with through formal intervention processes. The compromised nature of these students' executive function capacities, however, reduces the likelihood that intervention goals will be achieved quickly, and often greatly impacts the day-to-day effectiveness of intervention efforts. Table 8.3 provides a list of the types of ineffective behaviors likely to be exhibited in the school setting by students exhibiting difficulties with one or more of the 23 self-regulation executive functions. As Denckla (2007) has noted, the single most consistent finding across children who exhibit executive function difficulties of one type or another is the inconsistent nature of their behavior and/or academic production. This fact weighs heavily on teachers and other school staff attempting to implement interventions. These professionals frequently express great exasperation with executive deficient students' inabilities to consistently demonstrate skills that they know the students have learned and have used effectively at one or more times in the past. What these observations of teachers and staff corroborate is the essential distinction between producing and learning discussed at various points in this book. Staff who work with students exhibiting executive function difficulties see that the students are learning the skills being taught. The exasperating part is that these students do not demonstrate consistently the use of these skills; that is, they do not produce in a consistent manner after learning has taken place. This does not reflect a breakdown in the skill learning process, but rather a breakdown in the on-demand cueing of skill production.

An understanding of the inconsistencies that result from students' executive function difficulties can greatly assist teachers and other school staff in developing the frame of mind needed to maintain consistent intervention efforts with these students. When attempting to monitor progress and the

Table 8.3 Ineffective Behaviors Likely to Be Exhibited in School Settings by Students Experiencing Difficulties with One or More of the 23 Self-Regulation Executive Functions

Self-Regulation Cue	Observed Behavior Related to Inefficient Use of Self-Regulation Cue
Perceive	Does not see signs, directions, etc; does not hear directions; does not make use of materials; unaware of own emotions, thoughts, and/or actions
Focus/Select	Does not attend to information being presented
Initiate	Slow to get started with tasks; perceptions, thoughts, and emotional reactions seem to come slowly
Gauge	Has difficulty "sizing up" what is needed in the way of ability and skill to complete a task
Modulate	Has difficulty regulating the intensity of perceptions, feelings, thoughts, and/or actions
Inhibit	Has difficulty resisting the urge to perceive, feel, think, or act when such resistance is necessary
Sustain	Has difficulty working on tasks for extended periods of time; has difficulty sustaining perceptions, feelings, and/or thoughts for extended periods of time
Interrupt/Stop	Has difficulty interrupting or stopping perceptions, feelings, thoughts, and/or actions
Flexible/Shift	Has difficulty shifting and re-orienting focus of perceptions, feelings, thoughts, and/or actions
Hold	Has difficulty holding onto information for more than a few seconds
Manipulate	Has difficulty actively working with information that is being held in mind
Store	Does not seem to realize when it is necessary to store information so it will be available for later use
Retrieve	Does not seem to know when it is necessary to retrieve information and/or what information should be retrieved
Organize	Has difficulty organizing perceptions, feelings, thoughts, and/or actions
Foresee/Plan	Has difficulty looking ahead or anticipating what will be next
Generate	Does not seem to pick up on when it is necessary to come up with a new idea or try a novel solution to a problem
Associate	Does not seem to pick up on when it is necessary to make connections between information, or to know what kinds of connections between information could be made
Balance	Has difficulty finding the balance between extremes

Table 8.3 (continued)   Ineffective Behaviors Likely to Be
Exhibited in School Settings by Students Experiencing Difficulties
with One or More of the 23 Self-Regulation Executive Functions

Self-Regulation Cue	Observed Behavior Related to Inefficient Use of Self-Regulation Cue
Pace	Is not able to adjust the rate of perceiving, feeling, thinking, and/or acting to meet immediate requirements
Time	Seems unaware of the passage of time; is very poor at estimating the passage of time or estimating how long it takes to do things
Execute	Has trouble effectively using routines that most children the same age have automated
Monitor	Has trouble keeping track of, or checking the accuracy of, perceptions, feelings, thoughts, and/or actions
Correct	Has trouble correcting errors of perception, feeling, thought, and/or action

effectiveness of interventions with students exhibiting executive function difficulties, clinicians need to consider two key issues: (1) how should decisions be made about whether or not progress is being made, and (2) how long should intervention efforts continue without major modification if the student is not demonstrating progress?

How Should Decisions Be Made About Whether or Not Progress Is Being Made?

Assuming that reasonably reliable and effective measures have been selected or developed for use, the key to determining whether or not progress is being made will depend on how the collected data are analyzed and interpreted. Figure 8.2 shows the bi-weekly results of progress monitoring of the word reading accuracy of an elementary grade student with executive function difficulties who was receiving decoding instruction through a small group resource room intervention program. Note the fluctuations in the accuracy rate across several weeks of data collection. The teacher requested assistance in interpreting the student's performance because the teacher did not believe that the assessments were accurately reflecting the student's knowledge and daily use of the decoding rules being taught. The parents were becoming distraught with the student's lack of consistent performance when reading at home and believed that the data collected reflected a lack of learning, and therefore questioned the adequacy of the selected

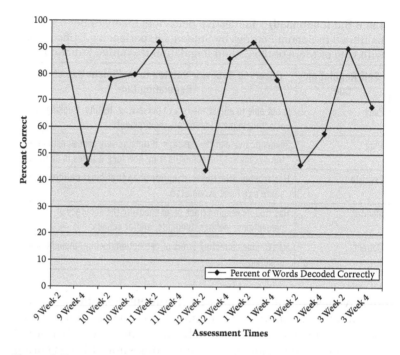

Figure 8.2 Percent of Words Decoded Correctly by Morgan.

intervention to develop the student's word reading skills. In this instance, two methods were being used to determine progress: (1) averaging across all bi-weekly measures to date to produce what was thought to be an average rate of growth in decoding skill compared to the original baseline measure, and (2) identifying the degree of accuracy on the most recent administration of the measure. The logic underlying interpretation of results was that if instruction is effective, the average accuracy score will be significantly higher than the baseline score. In addition, the most recent measure of accuracy will reflect the total increase in decoding accuracy to date, because the bi-weekly measures were cumulative in their coverage of decoding rules being taught.

Given the student's inconsistent performance, however, large gains at one time were often being negated by large losses at the next time, making averaging of data a questionable practice. Equally questionable, given the most recent drop in performance on the last administration of the decoding accuracy measure, was the assumption that the most recent administration would reflect the sum total of the student's knowledge about, and application of, decoding rules.

Given this student's executive function difficulties with use of the Perceive, Inhibit, Focus/Select, Modulate, and Sustain cues, the inconsistent performance reflected in the biweekly measures and the student's home reading were not surprising. The teacher's observations of more effective use of learned strategies by the student are a valid counterpoint to the methods being used to determine student progress in this case. In assessing the adequacy of the intervention, a number of factors were taken into consideration:

1. Prior to consultation with the lead author of this book, the student's specific executive function difficulties had not been identified or acknowledged as a factor that might be affecting reading intervention efforts in school or reading performance at home.
2. Commensurate with the first point, no consistent strategies were being applied either to externally substitute for the student's lack of executive function self cueing or to help the student improve capacity for self regulating.
3. The distinction between learning and production needed to be taken into consideration, meaning that separate goals, separate intervention strategies, and separate evaluation measures were needed to address these two distinct dimensions of the academic problem.

Based on these considerations and the results of the comprehensive psychoeducational evaluation that documented the executive function difficulties of the student, the revised intervention and evaluation plan included the following components:

1. In addition to teaching word decoding skills, intervention efforts would include the use of specific strategies for providing external cues for increased accuracy of production. Additionally, strategies for improving the student's capacity for internal control of the executive capacities needed for developing greater consistency in skill production would be gradually incorporated into instruction. The executive function strategies to be used in this case were drawn from those shown previously in Table 7.2.

2. Curriculum-based, bi-weekly measures of word reading accuracy were to be continued, but the results of these measures would be used in conjunction with teacher observations to complete, on a weekly basis, two GAS-constructed measures. A third GAS-constructed measure was to be used to assess the long-term consistency of accurate application of decoding rules. These GAS-constructed rating scales are shown in Table 8.2.

The use of the GAS-constructed Decoding Learning measure enabled the teacher to effectively document progress in learning and applying the various decoding rules as they were being taught. The Immediate Decoding Production measure was used weekly as a measure of the consistency of application of learned decoding rules. The Long-Term Decoding Production measure was designed to be used weekly after a 5-week period to provide a weekly assessment of fluctuations in long-term consistency. Both the Immediate Decoding Production measure and the Long-Term Decoding Production measure enabled the teacher to assess the effectiveness of executive function strategies for improving accuracy and consistency of decoding skill production.

The example presented here illustrates the complexity of the issues involved in designing and implementing interventions for students who exhibit academic production executive function difficulties. The example also provides a specific case that represents some important principles to keep in mind when developing, implementing, and evaluating interventions for these students, including:

1. Identify and describe the executive function difficulties exhibited by the student and their impact on behavior and/or academic production.
2. Develop intervention strategies that take into account the effects of executive function difficulties on production.
3. Make clear the distinction between learning and producing, and the need to consider them as two distinct but integrated elements of a single intervention program.
4. Develop program evaluation measures using GAS techniques that enable parents, teachers, and other school staff to evaluate the effectiveness of intervention elements designed to improve learning and elements designed to improve production.

Many school-based teams gather significant amounts of data related to student progress, but struggle in their efforts to figure out how to use that information to make decisions about whether or not a student has made progress, or if the amount of progress made represents an adequate response to intervention. GAS measures are well-suited for the team decision-making process because they require, as a part of scale construction, clearly stated evaluation criteria for what constitutes progress and how progress will be assessed. Note that all GAS scales specify a mid-point that represents acceptable, expected progress (0). This is joined by two points (+1, +2) that represent improvement above what would be expected, and two points (–1, –2) that represent less than expected improvement. The scaling properties of GAS measures therefore give a clear indication of whether or not progress has been made and the extent of the progress, or lack thereof. Because of these design features, use of properly constructed GAS measures can greatly improve team decision making related to issues of response to intervention.

How Long Should Intervention Efforts Continue Without Major Modification If the Student Is Not Demonstrating Progress?

How long to persist with intervention efforts is perhaps the most difficult question that school-based teams will face. Even when the difference between learning and production is clearly understood and assessment techniques have been adapted to take into account inconsistencies in production related to executive function difficulties, limited progress toward academic goals may be observed in some cases. Although no definitive answer can be provided in these cases, further consideration of additional factors can help clinicians organize thinking about this issue. Table 8.4 depicts a matrix representing an expansion of the concept of learning and producing difficulties. The matrix takes into account the contributions of the additional factors of cognitive abilities and cognitive processes. The matrix helps school-based teams consider the effect that the combination of these factors is likely to have on student learning and production. Selection of curricular materials and teaching methods should be done with the combination of these factors in mind. For example, while many reading programs address the development of specific reading skills very effectively, not all of them are well suited for

Table 8.4 Matrix for Considering the Severity of Impairment and Response to Intervention Prognosis for Word Decoding Skill and Comprehension Skill Development

Phonological Processing	Self-Regulation Executive Function Capacities	Ability to Reason with Verbal Information	Resulting Condition
Deficient	Adequate	Adequate	• Slower acquisition of decoding skills due to phonological processing deficits likely to be off-set and minimized through compensatory efforts involving effective executive functions and/or effectively remediated through appropriate intervention efforts that address the phonological processing difficulties (ages 4–8) and/or explicitly, systematically teach decoding skills (ages 6–Adult). • Effective use of executive functions enables consistent skill gains and consistent demonstration of the use of decoding skills that are being taught and learned. • Adequate ability to reason with verbal information supports development of comprehension skills when reading passages with mostly familiar words; comprehension likely to be enhanced through improved word decoding skill development when reading passages with less familiar but now decodable words.
Adequate	Adequate	Deficient	• Adequately developed phonological processing capacities enable development of decoding skills; appropriate instructional efforts that explicitly and systematically teach decoding skills are likely to be needed. • Effective use of executive functions should enable consistent skill gains and consistent demonstration of the use of decoding skills that are being taught and learned. • Deficits in ability to reason with verbal information are likely to minimize the benefits of adequate word decoding skills on comprehension when reading passages with less familiar but decodable words. Comprehension skills constrained by reasoning limitations.

Deficient	Deficient	Adequate	• Acquisition of decoding skills likely to be slowed by phonological processing deficits; decoding skills can be learned through appropriate intervention efforts that address phonological process deficits (ages 4–8) and/or explicitly, systematically teaching decoding skills (ages 6–Adult). • Ineffective use of executive functions likely to result in inconsistent skill gains and inconsistent demonstration of the use of decoding skills that are being taught and learned as well as inconsistent demonstration of comprehension when reading passages. • Adequate ability to reason with verbal information supports development of comprehension skills when reading passages with mostly familiar words; comprehension likely to be enhanced through improved word decoding skill development when reading passages with less familiar but now decodable words.
Adequate	Deficient	Deficient	• Adequately developed phonological processing capacities enable adequate development of decoding skills through appropriate instructional efforts that teach decoding skills. • Ineffective use of executive functions likely to result in inconsistent skill gains and inconsistent demonstration of the use of decoding skills that are being taught and learned as well as inconsistent demonstration of comprehension when reading passages. • Deficits in ability to reason with verbal information are likely to minimize the benefits of word decoding skills on comprehension when reading passages with less familiar but decodable words. Comprehension skills constrained by reasoning limitations.
Deficient	Adequate	Deficient	• Acquisition of decoding skills likely to be slowed by phonological processing deficits; decoding skills can be learned through appropriate intervention efforts that address phonological processes (ages 4–8) and/or explicitly, systematically teach decoding skills (ages 6–Adult). • Effective use of executive functions should enable consistent skill gains and consistent demonstration of the use of decoding skills that are being taught and learned. • Deficits in ability to reason with verbal information are likely to minimize the effects of improved word decoding skills on comprehension when reading passages with less familiar but now decodable words. Comprehension skills constrained by reasoning limitations.

Table 8.4 (continued) Matrix for Considering the Severity of Impairment and Response to Intervention Prognosis for Word Decoding Skill and Comprehension Skill Development

Phonological Processing	Self-Regulation Executive Function Capacities	Ability to Reason with Verbal Information	Resulting Condition
Deficient	Deficient	Deficient	• Acquisition of decoding skills likely to be slowed by phonological processing deficits; decoding skills can be learned through appropriate intervention efforts that address phonological processes (ages 4–8) and/or decoding skills (ages 6–Adult). • Ineffective use of executive functions likely to result in inconsistent skill gains and inconsistent demonstration of the use of decoding skills that are being taught and learned as well as inconsistent demonstration of comprehension when reading passages. • Deficits in ability to reason with verbal information are likely to minimize the effects of improved word decoding skills on comprehension when reading passages with less familiar but now decodable words. Comprehension skills constrained by reasoning limitations.
Adequate	Deficient	Adequate	• Adequately developed phonological processing capacities enable adequate development of decoding skills through appropriate instructional efforts that teach decoding skills. • Ineffective use of executive functions likely to result in inconsistent skill gains and inconsistent demonstration of the use of decoding skills that are being taught and learned as well as inconsistent demonstration of comprehension when reading passages. • Comprehension skills likely to be adequate but inconsistently applied when reading passages with mostly familiar words and inconsistently enhanced through improved word decoding skill development when reading passages with less familiar but now decodable words.

students who demonstrate limited ability to reason with verbal information, severe process deficits, and executive function difficulties.

APPLYING KNOWLEDGE OF EXECUTIVE FUNCTIONS TO ADVOCATE FOR SYSTEM CHANGE

Clinicians who have a sound understanding of the developmental nature of executive function capacities are in a good position to advocate for system-level change that helps to bring educational practices in line with the growing body of knowledge about brain development. There are a number of things that communities and school districts could do to create school environments that reflect an understanding of the wide variations demonstrated in the rate of children's brain development. Many of these relate to school policies, and some to daily practices. For example, there is a growing body of research (Carskadon, 2002; Millman, 2005) that suggests that later start times for middle, junior, and senior high school students improves school climate, classroom productivity, and academic achievement. Clinicians realizing the benefits of later start times for reducing the effects of lingering sleep inertia symptoms on executive functioning during early day class periods can take an active role in advocating for later school start times.

Some school districts have homework hotlines and require teachers to post homework assignments, test scores, and the results of other assessments online where parents and students can easily access them daily. These systems greatly enhance home–school communication and make it easier for parents to assist with executive function cueing as the need arises. These systems also provide students with an effective tool for self monitoring. While the number of school districts offering these services is growing, there are still many districts, large and small, that do not see a need to invest in such systems. Clearly, this is an area where advocacy can be practiced by clinicians who realize the executive function-related benefits of these systems for students and parents.

In many sections of this book, the effects of maturation-related executive function difficulties on student production have been highlighted. Clinicians who understand these effects can take them into account when they are assessing students on an individual basis and advising on the development of individualized education programs. Just as importantly, however, clinicians can advocate for classroom-, department-, and school-level changes in assessment and grading practices and policies that overly penalize students whose brains simply are not ready for the demands placed on them. Policies such as assigning a failing grade or 0 points to students who fail to turn in homework on time, and then averaging these scores in with performance on tests and assignments designed to demonstrate skill mastery or acquisition of content knowledge serve no good purpose with students who are lacking in executive function capacity.

CASE VIGNETTES IN THE CONTEXT OF SCHOOL SETTINGS

In Chapter 7, we discussed intervention strategies that could be implemented for each of our case study children. In this section, we will revisit each case study and discuss how each student's executive function challenges were dealt with in the context of the school setting

Justin in the School Setting

In terms of school-based interventions, Justin's school did not offer study skills courses of any type for students such as Justin when the evaluation report was shared with parents and school staff. This situation changed after Justin's mother, an energetic community organizer, gathered a number of parents of failing students together and successfully petitioned the school board to provide a study skills course for students failing, or at risk of failing, courses in seventh grade. Since its inception, the study skills program at Justin's junior high school has grown significantly in terms of the numbers of students to whom the course is offered.

The study skills course provided Justin with a number of sorely needed skills that he has applied, with characteristic levels of inconsistency, to his courses. By the end of the seventh grade, Justin earned passing grades in all his courses, including a few B grades, and there was a noticeable improvement in his attitude toward school and toward himself. Justin still requires a great deal of assistance at home with getting organized and started on homework and long-term projects, and his mother monitors his class grades and assignments daily. With greater positive engagement in school, Justin began to express some interest in school subjects, especially English, after having a very charismatic and energetic teacher the second term of the seventh grade.

All has not gone as well as could be hoped for, however. Despite numerous discussions about executive functions and the difficulties resulting from an inability to effectively engage them at all times, some of Justin's teachers are committed to the idea that if Justin cannot perform up to their standards, he does not deserve to receive any accommodations that might assist him in performing better in their class. For some of these teachers, homework assignments handed in beyond the assigned date are graded as a 0 and averaged in with all other grades and assignments, with no exceptions. Justin's enthusiasm for English literature sparked a desire in him to enroll in an honors course, but this request was denied because of his academic history. It seems that in some schools, the sharing of knowledge is a reward dispensed only to the most deserving. The privilege of participation in a challenging course must be earned, not used as an incentive to strengthen the academic interests of those who are not already producing at the highest levels. On the positive side, Justin was scheduled for art in eighth grade (standard procedure for that grade) and was assigned an excellent teacher who was able to foster his talent and model more effective use of executive function capacities in relation to this strong area of interest for Justin. Through all the ups and downs of the school year, Justin has clearly begun moving in a positive direction. He will continue to require the assistance of his parents and school staff if this trend is to continue into his high school years.

Kevin in the School Setting

In terms of school-based interventions, attempts to involve Kevin's parents in intervention efforts proved to be too little too late. Having heard of the principal's edict, Kevin's parents were now extremely distrustful of the school staff and skeptical of any recommendations made by them. Although they initially refused to take Kevin to a physician to address the ADHD symptomatology, they did agree to a district-provided psychiatric evaluation. Unfortunately, the outcome only served to increase their ire, as the report provided by the psychiatrist indicated diagnoses of ADHD and conduct disorder and hinted at possible family dysfunction. Given the unfolding circumstances, parent involvement was nonexistent in a revised functional assessment and behavior support plan, and the parents resisted the idea of seeking counseling for Kevin or the family to help deal with the behavior problems at home even though they continued to consult with the psychologist, who completed the comprehensive evaluation about these problems and what they could do at home to reduce their occurrence.

While the revised behavior support plan did a much better job of addressing many of the antecedents associated with Kevin's explosive episodes, Kevin's classroom teacher was not able to effectively mange these antecedents in a consistent manner and was not very consistent in her attempts to implement the plan. It was apparent to school staff that the lack of parent involvement or support had greatly diminished her desire to put forth the significant effort required to externally control Kevin's behavior while attempting to deal with the other needs of her class. As a result, Kevin's behavior problems escalated and he was recommended for placement in a program for students diagnosed with emotional disturbance and conduct disorder.

The parents were initially hesitant to agree to this placement, but after meeting the teachers and observing them work with the students in the class, it became apparent to them that the structured environment of the program would provide the kind of external control needed to deal with Kevin's explosive behavior problems, at least during school days.

At the time of the writing of this book, Kevin is still receiving his education through the services of a full-time emotional support program. His behavior is effectively managed at school and his academic progress is good, but Kevin's teachers have to work hard at maintaining control in the absence of any medical intervention to help deal with Kevin's impulsivity and hyperactivity. Kevin's parents have noted some positive carryover into the home, but severe incidents still occur there on a fairly regular basis.

Caroline in the School Setting

Given Caroline's strong cognitive abilities and history of solid academic achievement, she was not considered as a student with a learning disability or as eligible for accommodations under 504, even though her self-regulation executive function difficulties are debilitating and there is a significant discrepancy between what she is capable of understanding and what she is producing academically. It is encouraging, however, that the high school she attends offers a course in study skills, which can be taken on a repetitive basis, and provides drop-in, regular education support centers in the four basic academic areas; even more encouraging is the fact that these services are well subscribed and hold little of the stigma often associated with support services. While Caroline may not need these services to understand course content, she does need them to develop organizational and task completion strategies. As accessible as these services are, however, Caroline has not made consistent use of them despite the strong encouragement from parents and friends.

Caroline is also likely to require significant mentoring within her high school community, not only in terms of providing her with encouragement and specific cueing to engage, initiate, plan, organize, monitor, and correct, but also in terms of helping her teachers to view her difficulties from a more accurate and, hopefully, sympathetic light, so that they may productively engage in the same cueing practices. To date, that form of mentoring has not yet materialized. Most recently, there has been some discussion at the high school of conducting weekly cognitive behavior therapy sessions with Caroline as part of an expanded counseling program.

Brett in the School Setting

Brett's parents took him to a specialist who prescribed psychostimulant medication to help treat his ADHD symptoms. In the school setting, the effects of the use of the medication were monitored weekly for 6 weeks and then monthly for 4 months using the ADHD-IV rating scale. Positive changes in ratings were noted within the first week of medication use and continued for 2 more weeks before leveling off well within the average range. A more specific behavior management program was implemented that helped to reduce incidents of "spontaneous escape" from the classroom or other areas of the school. The program made effective use of reinforcement of Brett for the desired responses when cued by school staff to inhibit impulsive actions or stop ongoing, undesirable activity.

Once medication was begun, there was an almost instant improvement in Brett's fine motor control, but his skills in this area were still well behind those of his same-age peers. As a result, Brett began receiving physical/occupational therapy three times a week for 30 minutes per session and is making slow but discernable progress in improving his handwriting and other fine motor skills. The guidance counselor at Brett's school has not yet started to work with him, but she has purchased materials on the ICPS program and plans to start a group with Brett and two other students once familiar with the program. Brett's parents are sleeping better at night now. A good thing, too, because they still need a lot of energy to keep up with Brett during the day. The use of medication, combined with a more consistent application of house rules and rewards for compliance with them, have made behavior management much easier. Most importantly, knowledge of executive functions and the recognition of the biological nature of Brett's problems have enabled them to deal effectively with the situation with much less uncertainty about their discipline methods or child-rearing philosophy.

Morgan in the School Setting

Overall, Morgan demonstrated difficulties with executive direction of her superior reasoning abilities when tasks were complex and/or required multitasking and coordination of visual and auditory processing. These difficulties were especially evident when she was engaged in reading comprehension and writing activities, including note taking and difficulties with maintaining a consistent work pace, with a tendency to slow down considerably when performing a task for more than 15 seconds.

Although Morgan has been well instructed in decoding rules and word analysis techniques, she demonstrated a lack of adequate use of word analysis techniques and decoding rules when attempting to read unfamiliar or less frequently encountered words. She demonstrated difficulty with rapid naming of letters, numbers, and words and with executive control of verbal production when required to inhibit or switch responses, and read both word lists and passages at a very slow rate. Morgan demonstrated difficulty with attending to the details of orthography (the visual features of letters and words), resulting in the misreading of many common sight words and a reduction in the ability to comprehend what was read. Morgan also demonstrated difficulties holding visual representations of words in working memory long enough to produce correct spellings of words despite her ability to read these same words and demonstrated difficulties with the proper use of punctuation, word spelling, and quantity and quality of production when required to write for extended periods of time.

The lead author of this book developed a format for psychoeducational assessment reports (see the two sample comprehensive psychoeducational reports provided on the CD) that always offers team-generated recommendations that specify what the child can do for himself or herself, what parents can do to help the child, and what school staff can do to help the child. The recommendations generated for Morgan are shown in Table 8.5. The complete report for Morgan is provided on the CD accompanying this book. Of particular note in the recommendations is the explanation of the nature of Morgan's producing disability and the maturational perspective needed to set the proper context for instructional efforts and parent and school staff expectations for progress. It is essential that all involved with Morgan take into account her severe executive function difficulties related to academic production. These difficulties are making it very hard for Morgan to demonstrate consistent improvement with individual reading and writing skill development as well as improvement in the integrated multitasking needed for effective reading comprehension and composition writing. While expectations for progress need to be adjusted, it is essential that Morgan's teachers persist in their efforts to provide good instruction for developing individual skills and integrating skills.

Morgan's severe problems with multitasking during the act of reading are not likely to disappear any time soon simply through exposure to good instruction. Despite the best teaching efforts, these difficulties are likely to persist, but their impact will gradually lessen over time as Morgan's neural system develops greater capacity for the self regulation and multitasking needed to fully integrate reading subskills, comprehend extended text, and to produce longer written compositions.

The recommendations in Table 8.5 also provided guidelines for specific alterations to an already excellent program of instruction in order to increase the likelihood of improved skill development and use. Critical to these adjustments was the addition of the use of books on tape to supplement reading instruction and enable Morgan to spend more time with her peers in the general education classroom during reading instruction. This adjustment enabled a significant alignment of internal desires (being with peers and fitting in academically) with external demands (use of the books on tape technology), providing a tremendous boost in motivation to Morgan. Also essential to the curricular adjustments was the increased use of strategies for helping to improve Morgan's attention to orthography when reading words from lists and in context.

As anticipated, progress since the time of the evaluation has been slow and inconsistent, but there is now a greater

Table 8.5 Recommendations Generated by the School-Based Team in the Case of Morgan

Recommendations
What needs to be done for Morgan (Recommendations for Educational Interventions) and who can do what needs to be done for Morgan?

Helping Morgan to reach her academic potential will require a collaborative effort involving Morgan's teachers, parents, and Morgan herself.

What Morgan can do for herself to improve mental functions and achieve academic success.

1. Morgan can continue to put forth the effort needed to improve her reading and writing skills.

2. Morgan can do guided or independent reading at home at least 30 minutes a day.

3. Morgan can become proficient at using the VIBE book player and make use of it to read books of her own choosing and the books that are being read in her class at school.

4. Morgan needs to continue to follow a good bedtime routine as directed by her parents to ensure that she gets plenty of rest each night. Lack of sleep can reduce the efficiency of cognitive processes. This means that some of the executive control difficulties Morgan experiences will be more pronounced and more disruptive of efficient learning when she has not had a sufficient amount of rest. Good nutrition is also necessary to help achieve optimum cognitive readiness for learning and production of schoolwork.

What Morgan's parents can do to help her improve mental functions and gain academic success.

1. Morgan's parents have already provided a copy of this report to Morgan's pediatrician and have discussed the possibility of pharmacological intervention for those aspects of Morgan's executive control difficulties that relate to inattention and distractibility. At the time of the writing of these recommendations, Morgan's parents are considering having Morgan begin a trial use of medication when she returns to school in the fall. If this decision is implemented, careful monitoring of Morgan's functioning should be done to determine if medication helps to improve her ability to focus and sustain attention for academic tasks both at home and in school. Once the impact of medication is known, a meeting should be held to discuss any needed revisions of Morgan's educational program to take into account how she functions when taking medication.

2. Morgan's parents can assist the school with the ordering of books on tape. Morgan's resource room teacher will send a list of the books that Morgan's fifth grade class is reading so that these can be ordered for use this year. Additional books that hold high interest for Morgan can also be ordered to encourage Morgan to use the VIBE audio player.

Table 8.5 (continued) Recommendations Generated by the School-Based Team in the Case of Morgan

3. Morgan's parents have been highly supportive of Morgan's efforts to learn and of the school's efforts to educate Morgan. Morgan's parents can continue to be supportive of Morgan's efforts to develop better reading and writing skills and continue to foster a positive attitude about school despite any difficulties and challenges that academic work might present.

4. Morgan's parents can continue to closely supervise and monitor Morgan's reading activities at home and continue to participate with her in the monthly book cub. Making reading a social process is important for helping to maintain Morgan's engagement with this important skill.

5. Similar to how Morgan's mother has been able to make reading a social process by joining the mother-daughter book reading club, any effort to make writing a social activity would also benefit Morgan. A club where each person writes briefly about a specific topic and gathers to read their essays to the group (e.g., Poetry Circles) would serve such a purpose.

6. Morgan's parents can continue to maintain consistent rules about homework and times for doing homework. If necessary, break homework tasks down into smaller parts and set a time limit for each part.

7. Although Morgan's reading and writing difficulties need to be addressed, most of the hard work in these areas needs to be done during the school day. Morgan has many social and recreational interests that she pursues with great enthusiasm. These are helping her to form her identity as a person and helping her to understand her personal strengths. It is important for Morgan to have some social and recreational outlets and to have time to spend with friends. Morgan should not be expected to spend more than an hour of any evening doing homework and reading tasks. As long as she is putting reasonable effort into her reading and homework tasks, her participation in extracurricular activities should not be overly limited.

8. It will be important to help Morgan maintain good sleep habits and a good diet in order for her to maximize cognitive efficiency.

What Morgan's teacher's can do to help her improve mental functions and achieve academic success.

Although Morgan will need to work hard and put her best effort into the process of demonstrating her learning in school, Morgan's reading, writing, spelling, and executive function difficulties will be evident to some degree even when Morgan is motivated to put forth her best effort, and these difficulties are likely to significantly impact the products of her efforts to demonstrate learning, such as reading assigned material and producing written material. In terms of general instructional practices, the following points were discussed at the team meeting:

1. The nature of Morgan's executive function problems compound her reading disability and create the condition of a "producing disability." Morgan's producing difficulties manifest in erratic, inconsistent application of the reading, spelling, and writing skills that she is being taught. In most ways, Morgan learns much

Table 8.5 (continued) Recommendations Generated by the
School-Based Team in the Case of Morgan

more than she is able to demonstrate. Patience on the part of all involved in Morgan's educational process (Morgan, parents, teachers, and other school staff) will be necessary in order to maintain the proper perspective on Morgan's educational progress. Morgan's executive function difficulties are primarily developmental in nature rather than caused by traumatic injury or a severely limiting neurological condition. This means that over time, Morgan is likely to gain greater use of the executive control neural circuits that are involved in reading and writing, although the gains made in the use of these capacities will lag behind those made by her more typically developing same-age peers. Although it may appear at times that Morgan is not benefiting from instruction because she does not demonstrate mastery of the skills that are being taught, or does not appear to be engaged enough with the instructional process, it is necessary for Morgan's teachers to persevere and continue to expose Morgan to the good instruction they have to offer. If Morgan is provided now with the exposure to skill learning that is needed for her to improve her reading and writing, then when her neural system matures to the point where she can perform more consistently, the skill base needed to do so will be in place. Without the needed instruction, no matter how ineffective it might seem to be at times, Morgan will not have the stored knowledge base needed to enable her to improve her reading and writing skills when she is neurologically more capable of doing so. The more practice Morgan gets now with these reading and writing skill routines, the more likely it is that they will be automatized at a later point in time, thereby enabling Morgan to become a much more proficient reader as an adult than she is as a child.

2. Attempts to assess the effectiveness of instruction with Morgan will need to take into account her producing difficulties; performance on progress monitoring measures is not likely to consistently reflect the real benefit of the time and effort that has gone into helping Morgan learn to read and write better. Because of the erratic nature of Morgan's demonstration of what she has learned, it is more reasonable to gauge her progress on the peak points in a series of progress monitoring assessments rather than to average across these assessments. If, at any point in the year Morgan can demonstrate a high level of proficiency with a skill, it should be acknowledged that she has learned that skill even though she might not consistently demonstrate it. Continued practice of the learned skill will be important, but intense drilling until consistent mastery is demonstrated would not be beneficial and risks Morgan's disengagement with the learning process. Most children need variety and change in order to stay motivated to learn. Morgan needs these things even more than the typical child. Without variety in the educational process, Morgan will start to tune out and instruction will have much less impact than desired. Specific instructional activities should be short, focus on one skill element or integration of two skill elements, and be repeated with reasonable frequency rather than long and spanning many different skill elements. It is true that the act of reading requires the simultaneous integration of multiple skills. Unfortunately, Morgan's executive function difficulties do not enable her to consistently integrate all these skills in the effective, seamless manner of a mature reader. Daily instruction should focus for a brief time on

Table 8.5 (continued)   Recommendations Generated by the
School-Based Team in the Case of Morgan

the integration of all reading skills. However, just as important, and possibly more important given Morgan's current executive control difficulties, will be the frequent repetition of short lessons focused on individual skills.

In terms of specific curriculum and instruction, the following points were discussed in the team meeting:

1. An excellent educational program has been designed for Morgan. This program currently consists of both regular and special education. Morgan's special education services and fifth grade regular education curriculum should continue with the minor changes mentioned below.

2. Instruction for improving reading fluency continues to be a goal of specialized reading instruction, and should continue to be addressed using the Great Leaps program.

3. Instruction for improving word recognition and word decoding skills continues to be a goal of specialized instruction and should continue to be addressed using the Sonday System. When Level 2 of the Sonday System is completed (likely some time during the next school year), decoding and encoding instruction should focus on a review of selected lessons from the Sonday System. The nature of Morgan's decoding difficulties are such that she will require continued instruction in the efficient application of decoding skills throughout her elementary, junior, and senior high school years.

4. Instruction for improving spelling skills continues to be a goal of specialized language arts instruction, and should continue to be addressed using the Sonday System. Use of the Stetson program should be discontinued to allow more time for instruction in reading and spelling through the Sonday System and other materials chosen by the learning support teacher.

5. Instruction for improving reading vocabulary and reading comprehension continues to be a goal of specialized instruction and should continue to be addressed through the Comp Plus program as well as the trade books that are being used in the regular fifth grade classroom. The trade books will be available on tape so that Morgan can use the VIBE player to assist with reading these books.

6. By using the VIBE player and recordings of the trade books being used in the regular fifth grade language arts program, Morgan will be able to participate in regular classroom discussions of these books when her schedule permits.

7. Given the nature of Morgan's learning and producing difficulties, it would be reasonable to consider reducing the number of science and social studies projects that Morgan is expected to complete. Exposure to content knowledge should be emphasized over demonstration of writing, planning, and organization skills through long-term projects.

A team meeting should be held shortly after the start of the sixth grade school year to make any necessary adjustments to instructional plans based on Morgan's record of progress and possible use of medication.

appreciation of the factors involved in Morgan's learning and producing difficulties and a renewed energy and commitment on the part of Morgan, her parents, and school staff to focus efforts on making as much progress as possible while adopting a patient attitude with Morgan's pace of neural development. If Morgan's parents choose to pursue the use of psychostimulant medication with Morgan in the fall, its use will be closely monitored for possible effects on attention and effort in general, and reading and writing production in particular.

Alex in the School Setting

The assessment work conducted with Alex revealed no executive function-related difficulties with academic production in reading, writing, or math, and Alex applied these skills effectively in his daily routines in the home. During 8 months of focused attempts to impose greater structure on Alex in an effort to help him move forward with life tasks, somatic incidents had not occurred, but nether had any meaningful results in terms of either work or education. Previous attempts with CBT and pharmacological intervention also were unsuccessful. Considering the severe nature of Alex's inertia and inability to plan for the future or generate goals, it became apparent that a more intensive form of external control intervention might be needed. In keeping with this line of thought, Alex's parents researched a number of residential treatment programs throughout the country. These programs involved living at a facility for an extended period of time, usually 12 to 18 months. The daily routine at the facility would be highly structured, and education and training experiences would be provided. At the writing of this book, Alex's parents had discussed these programs with him, but he was unwilling to commit to enrolling in one. By law based on chronological age, despite Alex's significant delay in brain functioning, Alex is considered a fully functioning adult capable of making his own decisions. In fact, Alex is much less than a fully functioning adult capable of making decisions. Alex, the chronologically defined fully functioning adult, remains at home, doing chores around the house and little else.

Some might suggest that Alex's parents are coddling him and what they should do at this point is require him to leave and find a job and a place to live on his own. Such a course of action is analogous to throwing a baby into the deep end of the pool as a way of teaching it to swim. The likely results would not be the desired ones, and could be potentially life threatening. In the lead author's experience with some cases similar to that of Alex, the only intervention that had the desired effect was that of time. It can be hoped that with the passage of more time, Alex's self-awareness and self-determination capacities, like those of these other cases, will mature to the point where he will truly be a fully functioning adult ready to contribute to society and care for himself. In the meantime, Alex's parents can remain a source of compassionate guidance and encouragement, with an eye to a future day when things will change.

SUMMARY

This chapter focused on how professionals reading this book can share their knowledge of executive functions with other school staff as well as how they can apply the concepts directly to their work in the school setting. As stated at the outset of this chapter, recognizing the wide variation in executive function maturation levels within same-grade students is the starting point for differentiating instruction in a manner that allows more children the opportunity to succeed in school. Students who must face the challenges of school with insufficiently developed self-regulation capacities will require the compassionate assistance of parents, teachers, and school staff as they strive to find ways to fit in with their peers and succeed academically. Clinicians who have a working knowledge of the executive function concepts presented in this book can play a significant role in helping school staff become more effective in providing the support that students with executive function difficulties need.

We have emphasized that the goal of efforts to share knowledge of executive functions should be an understanding of how these concepts can be integrated into existing ideas about instruction, assessment, and intervention rather than a wholesale replacement of existing ideas. We also emphasized the need to make all students aware of academic goals and behavioral expectations, noting that students who are consciously aware of goals and expectations are much more likely to find ways to engage executive function capacities to assist in achieving these goals and expectations.

In terms of assessment and intervention for social and emotional problems in the school setting, we contrasted the traditional functional behavior assessment and behavior support plan model with an executive function-driven functional assessment and intervention model. The advantages of an executive function-driven model were discussed with special emphasis on this model's capacity for providing explanations for the causes of social and emotional difficulties along with intervention planning that spans a continuum from extensive external control to minor assistance with self-regulation of perceptions, emotions, thoughts, and actions.

The issues of progress monitoring and response to intervention were discussed. It was noted that interventions that take into account, and program for, the effects of executive functions on social, emotional, and academic functioning will typically require progress monitoring and outcome measures that go beyond basic curriculum-based academic skills measures or standard behavior rating scales. To assist in developing appropriate measures for monitoring progress, clinicians were encouraged to consider the use of Goal Attainment Scaling methodology. We also discussed how clinicians familiar with the concepts presented in this book can advocate for system level change that helps to bring educational practices in line with the growing body of knowledge about brain development. In conclusion, we revisited our six case studies and discussed each in the context of their individual school settings.

Part 3

CONTEXTUAL APPLICATIONS

9

Detailed Case Study

To further illustrate the concepts and the assessment and intervention processes discussed in this book, this chapter will provide a detailed summary of a case study involving a student with executive function difficulties. The case is that of an older adolescent boy named Carter who was exhibiting behavior difficulties in a high school setting. The case involved an executive-driven functional assessment and the development of a behavior support plan. The case study will touch only briefly on some of the aspects of the assessment work done with Carter. The comprehensive psychoeducational evaluation report that was written when Carter was evaluated is provided in its entirety on the CD that accompanies this text.

A comprehensive psychoeducational evaluation is also provided on the CD for Morgan, a fifth grade student with learning and producing difficulties. This case has been included on the CD to provide readers with an example of applying knowledge of executive function assessment and intervention in the lower grades and for students whose problems are focused primarily in the symbol system arena of involvement.

CASE OF CARTER

Background and Context

Carter came to the attention of the psychologist through a request from his home school district for a comprehensive evaluation to help develop an appropriate educational program. The presenting problems included excessive truancy, frequent explosive emotional outbursts in the classroom, and fighting with other students. At the time of the referral, Carter was in the middle of what was being called his 11th grade year at the district's high school (Grades 10–12). His educational program at that time included a half day of instruction at a vocational technical program sponsored by the regional special education cooperative along with a half day of classes at the high school. These in-school classes included reading and social studies in a resource room setting for students with learning problems and general education classes for algebra and English.

At the elementary school level, Carter was referred to the child study team because of academic difficulties in reading and writing in second grade, and was provided supplemental instruction through the district's developmental reading and writing services program. Carter received these services for a year, but was still significantly behind peers in the development of skills at the end of that time period. As a result, Carter was classified as a student with a learning disability and received special education resource room support for reading and writing for the remainder of his elementary school years. Although some minor behavior problems were noted in late elementary school, academic difficulties remained the primary concern.

In junior high school, Carter began to exhibit significant behavior problems both in school and at home. His behavior became so unmanageable that he was admitted for several months to a residential program for students with emotional difficulties. An evaluation with a psychiatrist during seventh grade resulted in the prescription of a number of medications to control behavior. Although Carter's mother could not recall the names of all of the medications he was taking at that time, she did recall that the most effective seemed to be Depakote, which Carter took regularly for more than two years. The use of medication did help Carter maintain behavior control, but his academic production was still very poor and he failed multiple courses in the ninth grade.

Instead of starting Carter at the senior high school, his parents sent him to a military prep school for his 10th grade year, where things did not go well. Multiple rule infractions led to Carter amassing so many disciplinary punishments that they could not all be served. Additionally, Carter failed all of his academic courses. At the end of the year Carter was asked not to return to the school. Carter was then enrolled in his home district's high school to repeat the 10th grade. Although some behavior problems did surface that year, the major concerns returned to academic production as Carter failed two courses. Now in what was being considered his 11th grade year (with repetition of some 10th grade classes), Carter's academic problems were subsequently joined by a number of behavior difficulties that resulted in two in-school suspensions. With mounting course failures, Carter was falling further behind and his parents were becoming concerned that at age 18 he would drop out of school.

Although Carter's parents acknowledged the challenge that Carter presented as a student, they were beginning to feel that the school district had not done enough to help Carter succeed academically and behaviorally in the junior and senior high school settings. The school district administrators were uncertain of the best course of action to take with Carter, but were very interested in not having the situation escalate to a formal hearing or lawsuit. The district administrators were hoping that the consulting school psychologist could assist in developing an educational plan for Carter that would meet his academic and social/emotional needs and satisfy his parents.

Assessment Processes

Parent Interview

In an interview with Carter's parents, they expressed their frustrations with both Carter and the school district. While they appreciated the fact that the school district was trying to provide Carter with a program of studies suited to his needs, they still had concerns about some of Carter's course placements. For example, he was now repeating Algebra I for the third time. They were also very concerned about the increasing truancy problem. At home, Carter did not present behavior problems other than being argumentative about school issues when they were raised with him.

Carter's parents indicated that Carter got along well with the children and adults in the neighborhood and that he had a number of good friends with whom he spent most of his free time. They were certain that Carter's friends were "really good kids," none of whom had been in trouble in or out of school. They were aware, however, of the fact Carter and most of his friends smoked cigarettes and had used alcohol and marijuana at various times over the past year.

When asked about Carter's personal strengths and weaknesses, his mother responded that she really could not say what these were and would very much welcome any information about Carter's abilities that the psychologist could offer. Carter's father thought that Carter was good with his hands and had a knack for building and carpentry work and was interested in working on cars, something that he did often with his friends. Carter's mother indicated, and the school record confirmed, that although Carter had been receiving special education services since early elementary school, he had never undergone a comprehensive psychoeducational evaluation. At the beginning of the current school year, the school psychologist assigned to the high school had attempted to provide such an assessment for the first time, but Carter refused to work with the psychologist.

Carter's mother was not able to identify any specific factors in the home that might be specific triggers for Carter's truancy or explosive episodes in classes. She attributed Carter's lack of academic progress to his inability to complete the coursework he was being given, his lack of interest in school, and his inability to see the need to earn a high school diploma. In sum, Carter's mother expressed her greatest fear as being that Carter would not be able to graduate from high school or find employment once he left the school setting.

Teacher Interviews

Carter's general education teachers described Carter as a moody, temperamental adolescent and expressed concerns with his inability to control his temper in their classrooms. On some days in the larger general classroom setting, Carter could not resist responding to verbal taunts from other students, and the resulting altercations often escalated into an explosive episode. On other days, Carter would be withdrawn and refuse to talk to anyone. When in an agitated state, Carter would become disrespectful toward his teachers as well as toward other students. Carter's outbursts were handled by his general classroom teachers by sending him to the guidance office where he could cool down, regain his composure, and then return to the classroom. The guidance counselor developed a good relationship with Carter and was able to help him get control of his emotions and return to class most days. However, on some days, he remained agitated for one or more hours. Carter's small group instruction resource room teachers did not report the occurrence of explosive episodes in their classes but noted many cognitive inefficiencies in work habits.

Classroom Observations

During an observation of Carter in algebra class, Carter generally followed along as the teacher lectured on how to solve a set of problems, but 45% of the time, Carter did not appear to be engaged with the instructional process. No behavior incidents were observed and no other student said anything to

Carter during instruction that period. Observation of Carter in his social studies class revealed that the teacher mainly dealt with Carter by having him work alone at his desk on study guides and fact sheets. There was little interaction between Carter and the teacher and very little production on Carter's part, as he was on task in this class only 20% of the time. Observation of Carter during reading instruction revealed a much greater use of one-to-one direct instruction. The teacher and Carter appeared to have a very good rapport, and Carter responded very well to the personal interactions during direct instruction and was engaged with the instructional process almost 100% of the time.

Parent and Teacher Behavior Ratings

The BRIEF ratings provided by Carter's mother produced elevated scores on the Inhibit, Working Memory, Plan/Organize, and Monitor scales. The behavior descriptions of the BRIEF items Carter's mother endorsed as occurring often reflected concerns with the Modulate, Inhibit, Focus/Select, Sustain, Hold, Balance, Foresee/Plan, Organize, Monitor, and Correct self-regulation cues. Consistent with her interview statements, Carter's mother's BRIEF ratings did not reflect significant concerns with applying the Inhibit, Modulate, or Balance cues to maintain emotional control in the home. The ratings of both of Carter's teachers produced significantly high scores for all eight areas of the BRIEF. Analysis of the items rated "often" by the teachers reflected concerns with inadequate use of all 23 of the self-regulation executive function capacities.

Carter's mother and teachers also completed the Behavior Assessment System for Children rating forms. Consistent with the information gathered in the interviews, parent and teacher consensus concerns focused on conduct and learning problems, aggression and attention difficulties, and lack of leadership and poor study skills.

Interview with Carter

Individual work with Carter began with an interview intended to build rapport and serve as an informal vocational assessment. Upon meeting and shaking hands with Carter, it was apparent from his engaging manner that rapport was not going to be a problem. Without hesitation, Carter participated in conversation about his hobbies and interests and his difficulties with school work. Carter's manner of engagement and the quality of conversation were at a very mature level demonstrating an excellent capacity to engage an adult socially in a positive manner that allowed for a very positive impression and personal connection.

Carter's statements regarding his academic and behavior difficulties were frank and honest appraisals of his history and current situation and were consistent with the reports of Carter's parents and teachers and school records. Carter acknowledged his difficulties with reading and expressed confidence in his ability to do practical math. He also acknowledged that he often engages in behavior that is counterproductive to his goals, desires, and needs. Carter's comments and conversation revealed a superior capacity to verbalize a high level of self-understanding and self-awareness. It was apparent from these comments, however, that he experienced great difficulty with guiding his perceptions, feelings, thoughts, and actions effectively with this self-knowledge and awareness. From the descriptions of situations that caused him problems, it was apparent that Carter tended to get caught up in impulsive negative emotional responses usually triggered by misperceptions about a developing situation with no reflection on the possible consequences of his impulsive actions in the present moment. Carter explained that there are some students he has classes with who do not like him, and who know that he has a "short fuse." These students frequently taunt Carter during class, knowing that he will likely "explode." Even though Carter is aware of the situation, he saw himself as unable to control his reactions to the taunting.

When asked about his interests and after-school activities, Carter mentioned hands-on activities including building things with his friends, such as treehouses, and fixing cars. He mentioned spending a great deal of time with a few close friends, some of whom had already graduated from high school and who were working in the community. Carter admitted to drinking and smoking marijuana, mostly on weekends, with these friends, but added "We don't do anything crazy or out of control, we just drink and smoke a little."

Regarding the situation at the vocational-technical school, Carter stated "it's boring; they don't let you do anything there." When prompted for additional information, Carter offered: "We're already half-way through the year and we haven't touched a machine yet. We sit there and they talk at us for hours." Carter attributed his increased truancy to his lack of interest in what was going on in the classes at the Vo-Tech program.

Carter did not specifically mention reading as an activity of interest. When asked directly about reading, he indicated that he does like to read magazines such as *Handyman* and *Hot Rod*. From his extended discussion of this topic, it was clear that Carter did read these publications and gained much information from them. He agreed to bring a copy of one of these magazines to the next session to show the psychologist.

As the end of the school year was nearing, Carter was asked about plans for the summer. He stated that he and his friend intended to work for the friend's father's construction company. Regarding plans for after high school, Carter's response was somewhat surprising. He stated that he had not really given it much thought. When asked why that was the case, Carter expressed his frustration with his current situation, stating "with all the courses I've failed, I don't know how I am ever going to graduate."

It took some time to help Carter process his negative emotions about this situation and try to think past his current dilemma. To aid this process, the psychologist asked: "If we could arrange things so you could graduate next year, what would you want to do after graduation?" Just the mention of the possibility of graduating the following year had a visible effect on Carter, who immediately asked about the feasibility of such a situation. The psychologist asked: "Is that a goal you think you would want for next year?" Carter replied with an immediate "Absolutely." The psychologist offered Carter the following promise: "If you work hard and give me your best effort throughout the time we work together, I will do everything I can to get you into a program that will offer you a chance to graduate at the end of the next school year."

This proposition greatly energized Carter, and with the burden of school lifted from his shoulders, he allowed himself to consider the future. Now seriously engaged in conversation about what he would like to do after school, Carter returned to his current interests and hobbies, stating that he would want to work in the construction trades. At one point in the conversation, Carter reminisced that his most positive memories of interactions with his father and brother were of the times they spent working on construction work to finish the basement of their home.

Individual Assessment Work with Carter
Consistent with his stated interests, Carter demonstrated above average to superior performance with most tasks that required

him to apply reasoning abilities with nonverbal materials (e.g., WAIS-III POI Standard Score 121, 92nd percentile). Carter's visual and visuospatial capacities were very well-developed and he usually had no difficulty using these when initially registering, working with, storing, or retrieving nonverbal, visual information.

When engaged in conversation, Carter displayed no difficulties with clear communication of his thoughts and spoke in an articulate, easily understandable manner. Carter did not appear to have any difficulty understanding conversational speech or any of the directions that were given to him during the evaluation. Many of Carter's comments were humorous as he approached the evaluation tasks in a positive, sometimes playful manner.

In great contrast with his ability to converse naturally, Carter's receptive and expressive language skills were strikingly deficient when he was engaged in formal assessment activities. Although directions were clearly understood, Carter often asked for specific test questions to be repeated even in situations where he had been told that repetition of questions was not allowed. When providing answers to questions, Carter often responded in poorly stated phrases or short sentences representing partial thoughts, and these phrases and short sentences were sometimes grammatically and morphologically inaccurate. Carter's thinking with words tended to be very concretely oriented and tied to physical properties or features. He tended to avoid thinking with or expressing highly abstract concepts and ideas that would be difficult to tie to specific objects or events in the physical world. Reflective of these observed difficulties with language and abstract conceptual thinking, Carter earned scores in the low average to below average range on tasks that required him to reason with verbal information and/or provide specific verbal responses (e.g., WAIS-III VCI Standard Score 82, 12th percentile).

Carter's performance with basic measures of speed and fluency produced even poorer results with scores in the low to extremely low range. These difficulties with speed and fluency were not observed when Carter's language production was internally driven, that is, when Carter initiated conversation or responded to comments about things or topics he felt a need or desire to discuss. Verbal memory tasks were especially difficult for Carter, as he usually struggled to process and organize large amounts of verbal information, demonstrating much less efficiency than he was able to demonstrate with nonverbal, visual content. The more decontextual and random the presentation of verbal information (e.g., random series of numbers or numbers and letters for WAIS-III Digit Span and Letter-Number Sequencing), the poorer Carter's performance with the task (e.g., WAIS-III WMI Standard Score 82, 12th percentile).

Formal measures of reading produced extremely low scores for word reading, decoding skills, and reading comprehension. Considering Carter's stated interest in reading trade publications like *Handyman* magazine, and the fact that he brought a copy of the most recent, unread edition of the magazine to the assessment session on the second day to show the psychologist, an informal assessment of Carter's reading skills was conducted using his newly issued copy of *Handyman* magazine. Despite the low scores on the WIAT-II reading subtests, Carter was able to read sections of *Handyman* magazine silently and answer questions about the content of what he read with more than 90% accuracy. When reading orally from *Handyman* magazine, Carter read very slowly and struggled with the pronunciation of a number of longer, less familiar words. Longer, more familiar words were read slowly but with much greater accuracy. From Carter's production with *Handyman* magazine, it was clear that Carter possessed at least average facility when reading high interest technical material.

Carter demonstrated low average math reasoning skills (WIAT-II Math Reasoning Standard Score 93, 33rd percentile), but his production with basic calculations was very poor when these were assessed at the very end of the first assessment session (WIAT-II Numerical Operations Standard Score 77, 6th percentile). Given the fact that Carter incorrectly responded to many very simple basic calculation items, he was readministered the Numerical Operations Subtest during the first few minutes of the session on the second day. On this second attempt, Carter made far fewer of these basic calculation errors and increased his performance more than a full standard deviation (16 point increase) into the low average range (2nd administration Numerical Operations Standard Score 93, 33rd percentile).

Although Carter initially approached all tasks given to him with what appeared to be his best effort, his ability to sustain his attention and effort for the duration of a task was often very poor, although he usually was able to self-prompt and return to task performance after short "breaks" in effort. This pattern was most pronounced on verbal tasks and simple tasks that required sustained attention and effort. On complex tasks that required reasoning with nonverbal visual material, Carter was at his best and usually was able to sustain attention and effort for extended periods for these types of tasks with little difficulty. On many tasks, Carter's tendency to rush through a task without bothering to monitor or check his work cost him points as his final solutions were often correct in principle, but lacking in accuracy of details.

In contrast to the difficulties Carter experienced in directing effective use of language processes when engaged in academic-oriented tasks, Carter performed very effectively with the Wisconsin Card Sorting Test (WCST). Although he required three trials (13 trials to set completion) to grasp the concept underlying correct responding for the first set (11–16th percentile compared to the performance of same age peers), he was able to follow the shifts in task demands and sustain attention and effort for the next four sets, completing them in 14, 13, 16, and 11 trials respectively. For the final set, Carter's attention began to wane as he required 22 trials to complete the set. Carter's efforts reflected an above average level of conceptual engagement with the task (Percentage of Conceptual Level Responses Standard Score 110, 75th percentile).

Executive Function Summary

Consistent with the assessment model presented in Chapter 5, Carter's executive function capacities were assessed using multiple methods including records review, parent and teacher interviews, and rating scale responses, classroom observations, and an individual interview and direct formal and informal individual assessment work with Carter. Carter's history and the information gathered during the assessment strongly suggest that Carter does not experience any difficulties with self-activation and achieves an effective state of awareness relatively soon after waking. At the self-regulation level, Carter is demonstrating a number of difficulties. At home, Carter's parents report difficulties with the Inhibit, Modulate, Stop/Interrupt, Focus/Select, Sustain, Monitor, and Correct cues, mostly in relation to his emotional reactions to discussions of school issues or when trying to get Carter to complete homework assignments.

Teacher reports indicate significant difficulties with all 23 self-regulation capacities. In school, Carter's Inhibit, Modulate, Stop/Interrupt, Flexible/Shift, and Foresee/Plan problems are most evident in relation to his perceptions, emotions, thoughts, and actions involving interpersonal interactions with a specific group of peers who are antagonistic toward him. In terms of schoolwork and the symbol system arena, Carter's learning difficulties are exacerbated by producing difficulties that involve poor cueing of Inhibit, Modulate, Focus/Select, Sustain, Foresee/Plan, Organize, Hold, Manipulate, Store, Retrieve, Monitor, and Correct related to perceptions, thoughts, and actions.

Individual assessment work with Carter revealed specific deficits in control of language functions, especially the Retrieve, Organize, and Execute cues, and difficulties with focusing and sustaining attention, inhibition of impulsive responding, and lack of effective monitoring of work. These executive function difficulties had the greatest impact on Carter's performance of language-based ability measures and reading, written expression, and math achievement measures. In contrast to these difficulties, Carter demonstrated the ability to effectively engage many of these same self-regulation executive functions when performing ability measures that involved nonverbal visual materials including the WCST, a task designed to assess the use of executive functions in the direction of problem-solving efforts.

In terms of intrapersonal control during and after school, Carter's perceptions, emotions, thoughts, and actions are easily influenced, both positively and negatively, by others, especially his close peers. As a result, Carter does not effectively make use of the Inhibit, Modulate, Stop/Interrupt, Balance, Plan/Foresee, Organize, Monitor, or Correct cues when he is with peers who might not be making good decisions.

The environment arena is the one area where Carter is able to harness his capacities most effectively. When engaged in personal projects involving building or fixing things, Carter is able to minimize the effects of his academic skill deficiencies and engage many of the same self-regulation cues that prove so elusive in the other three arenas. As a result, Carter is much more productive in this arena. It should not be surprising, therefore, to find that Carter prefers to spend most of his time engaged with these activities rather than with traditional academic pursuits.

While the interview with Carter indicated that he has adequately developed capacities for self-awareness and self-analysis, his self-regulation difficulties often prevent him from using that knowledge to guide his perceptions, emotions, thoughts, and actions when he is with others. When free of the perception of school as a dead-end trap, Carter was able to express a higher level of self-determination and a greater capacity for vocational maturity and goal setting than he had previously exhibited. Given his previous reticence to extend planning into the future, it was not clear whether or not Carter possessed an adequate capacity for developing and implementing a plan to act on his stated career goals. At the time of the interview, Carter was showing no interest in exploring larger life questions associated with the self-generation level of executive involvement or exploring deeper meanings associated with the trans-self integration level.

From Carter's pattern of performance on symbol system measures and the information collected from the interviews, rating scale results and records review, it is difficult to determine the extent to which Carter's executive function difficulties are the result of lack of maturation of specific neural capacities or underutilization of existing neural capacities due to a lack of awareness of what capacities to cue and when and how to cue them.

Conclusions Based on Assessment Activities

Carter projects a very friendly and engaging self-image and makes a very good first impression. He is very comfortable talking with adults and has no difficulty effectively communicating his thoughts in a naturally flowing conversation. Carter is frank and honest in his self-appraisal and aware of many of his personal strengths and weaknesses. He possesses effective social skills but his use of these skills is often curtailed by his impulsiveness and other executive function difficulties related to emotional control. Although Carter experiences many difficulties with behavior control, he does not appear to be "mean-spirited" but rather seems to have a kind-hearted, warm nature that is often not expressed or seen in action and not perceived by others because of his executive control difficulties.

Carter demonstrates above average to superior reasoning abilities when he is dealing with visual nonverbal material. His tendency is to think very concretely about things that can be seen and focused on in the environment. This does not mean that Carter is lacking in reasoning abilities, but rather that he is much better at using his reasoning abilities when the problem is dealing with concrete information. Carter is much more capable of solving a problem involving "How do we build this?" than solving a problem that cannot be visualized or

handled, such as "How do we slow inflation?" Carter does his
best thinking when the elements of thought relate to physical
objects that can be manipulated in very concrete ways. Carter
also displays good visual memory skills for nonverbal visually
and kinesthetically perceived information and has learned the
concepts and procedures underlying basic math skills. Applying these skills consistently, however, is a problem for Carter
because of his impulsive response style and his tendency not
to check his work for errors. Even when Carter does check his
work, he is prone to overlook errors because his cueing of the
use of monitoring skills is not very effective.

Although Carter's everyday conversational skills are quite
good, Carter struggles greatly with academically oriented tasks
that involve a great deal of language. These struggles are rooted
in language processing problems that involve many aspects
of basic language ability. Carter is very slow with production
of language under conditions where specific language content
is being demanded. He has difficulties with auditory working
memory and segmenting sounds in a manner required for the
development of effective word reading skills. Carter also demonstrates difficulties with grammar and syntax and finds it
difficult to follow discussions that are complexly worded and
deal with abstract concepts that cannot be easily manipulated
concretely. The emphasis of the high school curriculum on
this kind of language processing has made it very difficult for
Carter to keep pace with his peers in the classroom. Although
it has been a tremendous struggle for him because of his language processing difficulties, Carter has managed to acquire
functional reading skills that he uses effectively to obtain
information in his areas of interest. Carter's reading abilities
for more academically oriented material such as prose writing
is very limited, however, making it difficult for him to succeed
in courses where reading of such material is required.

Carter often does not apply his cognitive skills as effectively as is possible, and this is primarily due to executive
control difficulties rather than to a lack of good intentions
or desire. Carter experiences a great deal of difficulty with
focusing and sustaining attention in situations that are not
perceived as being of immediate benefit. Carter also responds
impulsively to task requests and usually does not check his
work for accuracy, believing that his work is correct on the
first try.

Although it might appear that Carter is lacking in desire
and effort, the executive function difficulties that Carter

experiences are very real and they substantially affect his ability to sustain attention and effort for difficult tasks, to inhibit impulsive responding, to maintain emotional control, and to delay immediate gratification for more long-term rewards and benefits. With the kind of language and executive function problems that Carter is plagued with, it is not unnatural for an adolescent to withdraw and disengage from, or try to avoid altogether, activities and classroom demands that focus on the use of those skills that are lacking. Placed in situations where his lack of capacity will be evident to his peers, Carter's natural tendency is to try to avoid or deflect requests for performance in whatever way possible.

Like most students, Carter desires to succeed and thrive in life. When considering the underlying motives for Carter's undesirable behaviors a few questions come to mind: Why would any student want to continually take on tasks where the likelihood of success is extremely minimal? Why would any student want to subject himself continually to an environment where attention is most often focused on areas of weakness rather than areas of strength? One plausible answer to these questions is that there might be a long-term benefit—such as graduation from high school—that would outweigh the short-term humiliation and frustration. If Carter only had a language-based reading disability, he might be able to see the value in engaging school to the fullest despite the difficulties that would be encountered, but Carter's problems are not limited to severe difficulties with reading and language. Carter's problems extend into the realm of executive control processes where some of Carter's major difficulties include lack of effectiveness of cueing the inhibition of impulsive responding, the modulation of emotional and physical reactions, the focusing and sustaining of attention, the monitoring of performance for errors, and the correction of errors that occur.

In the current school setting, Carter is unable to effectively engage self-regulation capacities that would enable him to work toward reasonable goals. In addition, Carter does not believe that the current goal (i.e., earning all required course credits in order to graduate from high school) is attainable. Carter's lack of success in school is hardly a source of pleasure and it is not surprising to see behaviors that look like symptoms of depression along with his other difficulties. Failure does not form a good basis for happiness in the present moment or optimism about the future.

Socially, Carter possesses the skills necessary to interact with others effectively and meaningfully. He has friends and derives enjoyment from his social connections with others. Carter's social difficulties are not a result of poor social skills, but rather an inability to deal with frustration appropriately by inhibiting impulsive responding and maintaining emotional control so that the long-term consequences of immediate actions can be considered and can then influence how he chooses to behave. For Carter, the ability to inhibit impulsive responding and maintain emotional control in challenging social situations is very poorly developed and is at the root of most of his difficulties in the school setting. These executive function difficulties might be developmental in nature, reflecting a slower rate of growth rather than a total absence of capacity. Although Carter's executive functions are not on a par with his age peers, they are better now than they were a few years ago. Continued progress is likely to be observed, but the rate of growth of these executive function processes might continue to lag behind that of his peers so that Carter will continue to look deficient in these areas compared to peers despite his substantial progress relative to what his capacities were like in the past. It is possible that Carter possesses these executive function capacities, but is unaware of how to effectively utilize them in his social encounters in school and when working on academic material. Whether due to delays in maturation or underutilization, Carter's executive function difficulties will need to be addressed in the development of an appropriate educational program.

Carter's social nature, concrete thinking style, academically oriented language difficulties, and executive function limitations are a difficult mixture to deal with in a formal traditional academic setting. Because of his unique mixture of strengths and weaknesses, Carter responds best to a teaching style that is based on a high level of personal engagement and connection and is focused on activities that have obvious and immediate benefits. Forms of mentoring and individualized tutoring are likely to be most productive and beneficial for Carter.

Carter's particular cognitive and physical strengths appear to be in line with his strong interests in the building and construction trades. The remainder of Carter's high school education should focus on helping him develop the skills necessary to succeed in his chosen career path. With an effective educational program that integrates academic coursework with on-the-job work experience, Carter will have the best possible grounding for entering the workforce with skills that will help him obtain and maintain employment in his area of interest. Carter is most likely to succeed in the workforce when the external demands of the job are aligned with Carter's internal desires and when his coworkers are a mature group who can help Carter grow and develop greater emotional control and self-discipline.

Summary of Problems

Based on the information gathered from Carter's parents, Carter himself, and the school staff, the following problems were identified as the focus of concerns:

- Unexcused absences
- Temper outbursts in general education classes
- Lack of engagement with instruction during class time
- Lack of completion of class assignments
- Lack of participation in the Vo-tech program
- Failing grades
- High risk of dropping out of school

Post-Assessment Activities and Program Planning

The results of the assessment were shared first with Carter, his parents, the high school principal, and the director of pupil personnel services. Additional time was spent discussing the results individually with Carter, with special emphasis on his cognitive strengths and the career plans that he had articulated during the interview. As promised to Carter, the psychologist presented the idea of designing an instructional program that would enable Carter to graduate at the end of the following school year. The director of pupil personnel services and the principal both agreed that this seemed to be a reasonable and feasible option and agreed to convene a meeting prior to the start of the school year to discuss details with school staff.

In the interim, the psychologist and director of pupil personnel services met with the director of the regional special education cooperative's work experience program. As the director described the available work study positions, it was apparent that none of the placements involved direct experience in the construction trades, a fact that had the potential of complicating the design of an alternative program for Carter.

Prior to a meeting held near the end of August to plan for the upcoming school year, the psychologist contacted Carter's mother to inquire about Carter's summer activities. Carter's mother offered that Carter had truly been energized by the prospect of completing high school in one year and had taken very seriously the career goals he articulated in the interview with the psychologist. Any doubts about Carter's self-determination capacities in the area of planning, and implementing long-term goals were dispelled with what his mother related next.

As it turned out, the summer job with Carter's friend's father had not materialized. This fact, however, did not deter Carter from his intended goal. With no prompting from his parents, Carter cold-called all of the construction businesses listed in the local yellow pages to ask about the availability of jobs. Carter's efforts were rewarded quickly, as he was hired by a private contractor to assist with home improvement building projects that same week. Carter's mother stated that she had never seen him as engaged as this with anything else. He would be awake by five o'clock in the morning and on the job by six. He would come home, shower, eat, and then go to his boss's house to help him finish remodeling his own home family room. She indicated that this had been the routine for two straight weeks. Although she was dubious as to whether the enthusiasm would be maintained, she was happy to see it continue as long as possible.

Four weeks later, the psychologist contacted Carter's mother again to check on Carter's status. At this point, Carter had been on the job for six weeks and was still going strong. She was especially pleased with the relationship that Carter had formed with the contractor. Apparently, this successful tradesman had experienced school difficulties similar to Carter's and could sympathize with his plight. As the discussion progressed, it occurred to the psychologist that Carter might have solved the issue of the lack of fit of the intermediate unit's work experience placements. At the mention of the possibility that this contractor might be a good work experience supervisor for Carter, Carter's mother agreed and provided the psychologist with a phone number for a contact. To the psychologist's delight, Carter's work supervisor was very enthusiastic about the idea of helping out with Carter's work study program and agreed to attend the meeting in August to help design Carter's program for the upcoming school year.

In late August, a meeting was held with the director of pupil personnel services, the director of special education, the high school principal, the guidance counselor, two special education teachers who worked with Carter, a representative of the work experience program, and the contractor who was employing Carter. The program designed for Carter at this meeting included the following:

- Period 1: Reading with special education teacher; working on improvement of decoding skills with continued use of the Megawords program combined with instruction in sight word recognition and comprehension for construction trade-related words and reading material (the contractor agreed to provide several important trade manuals and other materials for Carter to use while working on reading skill development).
- Period 2: Mathematics with a special education teacher focusing on practical math that would be used in the construction trades. (Again, the contractor offered suggestions for the type of math that would be most useful.)
- Period 3: State-mandated history course required for high school graduation taught in a small group setting.
- Period 4: Technical electives (Robot-building first half of year; Small Engines second half of year).
- Period 5: Lunch.
- Periods 6–9: Work experience at contractor's work site.

At the meeting, the following goals also were established for Carter's educational program: Reasonable attendance would be maintained; standard disciplinary practices would be applied for any unexcused absences; the ideal goal here was no unexcused absences since the setting and antecedent conditions leading to absences in the past were being removed from the environment.

- Temper outbursts would be dealt with through the established time-out procedures, with the ideal goal being no outbursts in any week since the antecedent conditions thought to be triggering the outbursts were being removed from the environment
- Adequate engagement with instruction during class time; as measured by weekly teacher reports
- Adequate effort put into completion of class assignments as measured by weekly teacher reports
- Passing grades in all classes
- Improvement of reading skills as measured by weekly teacher reports

- Improvement in accuracy of math calculations and development of new math skills as measured by weekly teacher reports
- Educational work experience that would lead to employment after high school as verified by the on-site supervisor
- Graduation from high school at the end of the school year

Baseline data from the end of the previous school year related to these goals included the following:

- 18 unexcused absences during the previous school year
- 10 credits short of what is required for graduation
- 14 temper outbursts in last two months of previous school year
- Daily instances of disengagement with instruction
- Daily instances of lack of completion of classwork
- Failing grades in three of five classes

Program Implementation and Outcomes

Carter's specially designed educational program was implemented at the start of the new school year. Table 9.1 shows the initial baseline data related to problems, the program goals related to the problems, and the program outcomes related to each problem. As shown in the table, Carter achieved all of the goals of the program and graduated at the end of the school year. From the perspective of Carter, Carter's parents, the psychologist, school administrators, and many members of the school staff, Carter's specially designed educational program was judged to be a success.

While Carter's overall program produced the desired outcomes, it was not without its trying moments. After two very successful months of implementation, a critical juncture was reached in early November. At that time, the psychologist received a call requesting his presence at a meeting regarding Carter. As it turned out, Carter had arrived at school one morning in a disoriented state. When apprehended by a school security officer Carter admitted to having smoked marijuana that morning. A search of Carter found a small amount of the drug in his pocket. By school rules, Carter's behavior resulted in a week-long in-school suspension. The meeting was being convened to decide how to handle Carter's situation since he

Table 9.1 Outcomes of Carter's Specially Designed Instructional Program

Problem Baseline Data	Instructional Program Goal	Program Outcome
18 unexcused absences during the school year	Maintain reasonable attendance	Carter's record indicated 4 excused absences for the year and 0 unexcused absences.
14 temper outbursts in last two months	Temper outbursts would be dealt with through the established time out procedures, with the ideal goal being no outbursts in any week since the antecedent conditions thought to be triggering the outbursts were being removed from the environment	The counselor's log at the end of the year indicated no temper outbursts reported during the school year. Carter did not need to make use of the time out procedure at any time during the academic year.
Daily instances of disengagement with instruction	Adequate engagement with instruction during class time; as measured by weekly teacher reports	Teacher weekly reports reflected adequate levels of engagement throughout the school year.
Daily instances of lack of completion of classwork	Adequate effort put into completion of class assignments as measured by weekly teacher reports	Teacher reports reflected adequate effort and task completion levels throughout the school year.
Failing grades in three of five classes	Passing grades in all classes	Carter earned passing grades in all his classes during the school year.
Poor word recognition and decoding skills resulting in reading achievement scores in the 1st percentile	Improvement of reading skills as measured by weekly teacher reports	Teacher reports indicated improvement across the academic year. Work experience supervisors reported effective use of reading skills on the job.
Frequent errors in simple calculations producing scores in the bottom quartile	Improvement in accuracy of math calculations and development of new math skills as measured by weekly teacher reports	Teacher reports indicated improved accuracy of math calculations across the academic year. Work experience supervisors reported effective use of math skills on the job.

Table 9.1 (continued) Outcomes of Carter's Specially Designed
Instructional Program

Problem Baseline Data	Instructional Program Goal	Program Outcome
Failing Vocational Technical courses Excessive unexcused absences Disengagement with classes	Educational work experience that would lead to employment after high school as verified by the on site supervisor	Carter completed the work experience program, learning a number of valuable construction trade skills. Carter was hired full time by his original work experience supervisor at the end of the school year.
12 credits short of what is required for graduation. Unable to graduate unless failed courses are retaken and sufficient number of credits are accumulated	Graduation from high school at the end of the school year with standard regular education diploma based on participation in specially designed instructional program	Carter graduated from high school at the end of the school year.

had stated that he had gotten the marijuana from one of the
workers at the construction site where he was doing his work
experience. Realizing that this could jeopardize the entire
program, the psychologist called the high school principal to
discuss the situation and was greatly relieved when the principal started the conversation by stating: "This is just a bump
in the road for Carter; we'll manage to get over it."

The meeting was attended by the director of the work experience program, Carter's special education teachers, the principal, and the assistant principal in charge of discipline, the
director of special education, the psychologist, Carter, and his
parents. At the meeting, the principal explained that although
the construction job had been a very positive work environment in many respects, it was too open-ended to ensure that
appropriate controls of Carter's behavior could be maintained.
Since Carter could not return to the work site, an alternate
work site would be provided for him.

Prior to the meeting, the principal and the director of special education had spoken with the supervisor of the school
district maintenance crew and they had agreed that Carter
would work with the school district staff on various construc-

tion projects underway in district buildings. Thus, although Carter would lose his current position and the pay that he was receiving, he would not lose his opportunity to complete the work experience program and graduate at the end of the year.

While Carter understood that the change was necessary and a result of his behavior, his response to the situation was reflective of his difficulties with autonomous decision making. Carter offered a justification for his behavior, stating that marijuana really should be a legal substance, and that if it were, he would not be in trouble right now. The psychologist tried to help Carter realize the flaw in his argument, pointing out that the issue here was not whether marijuana is legal or illegal. By analogy, it was explained to Carter that while alcohol is legal, if he were to show up for work unable to perform because he was drunk, he could be fired for being drunk on the job. The issue was not the legality of the substance that Carter possessed; the issue was the impairment of mental capacities that he demonstrated while under the influence of the substance. It was also pointed out to Carter that while 10 people had been gathered to figure out how to help him maintain his opportunity to achieve his goals, next year if working a full-time job outside of school, it was likely that no such group would be convened to assist him if a similar situation should arise after his graduation from school.

Fortunately, the transfer of supervisory responsibilities to the school district supervisor of maintenance worked out well. Carter was able to establish a good working relationship with the supervisor and the older, more mature members of the district maintenance staff. Carter completed his work experience with no further significant incidents and was able to graduate at the end of the school year.

Immediately after graduation, Carter was hired by a local construction company and remains gainfully employed in the construction trades to date. Carter's path through the "real world" has not been without obstacles, however. Carter's strong self-determination capacity has been both his greatest strength and his greatest weakness. Carter's determination to make it on his own has enabled him to live independently from his parents and maintain employment. Consistent with his developmental profile, Carter continues to lag behind in the maturation of many self-regulation capacities, making it hard for him to control his everyday functioning in a manner that would enable him to fully realize his personal goals. This creates a tremendous amount of frustration for Carter, which fuels his use of marijuana and alcohol as a means of self-medicating to ease the psychological turmoil. Although his work ethic has always ensured employment, Carter has struggled to find the right fit in terms of employer, supervisor, and coworkers and has changed jobs several times as a result. These changes have never been triggered by lack of adequate production on the job (Carter's ability to stay focused on productive work in externally structured environments has been noted by many), but rather by a souring of relationships. Carter is a very gregarious individual who relates well to older adults. Unfortunately, he is drawn to older individuals who share his liking for marijuana and alcohol and who have self-control difficulties of their own despite their advanced age. Because he is easily influenced by others, Carter is drawn into a pattern of social drug abuse. At some point, he realizes the destructive nature of the relationships he has formed and handles the situation by making a complete break with his work and social environments. In his efforts to achieve greater self-control in the intrapersonal arena, Carter then engages in a period of complete abstinence as he begins a new job. Relying strictly on his own resources, Carter avoids the development of social ties in the new work place. Over time, however, the impulses become too strong, resulting in weekend binges, overspending, and deterioration of functioning outside of the workplace. On more than one occasion, Carter has resorted to living out of his car until he could regain his financial footing.

Although this cycle has been repeated several times, the length of time that Carter spends positively engaged in work and effectively engaged in adaptive self-control increases while the time that he spends negatively engaged self-destructive patterns of perception, emotion, thought, and action decreases. Not surprisingly, both Carter and his parents vacillate between states of optimistic joy and anxious fear. In moments of careful reflection, however, they all can see how Carter's overall trend is a positive one. Carter has developed a high degree of self-awareness regarding his personal strengths and weaknesses, but his insistence on complete self-reliance has resulted in his refusal to seek professional help in dealing with his problems. With sufficient energy and effort, Carter is likely to continue his positive growth trend of gaining greater self-control and applying it to good purposes. With luck, Carter will be able to avoid situations where his periods of poor self-regulation could produce long-lasting, extremely negative consequences.

Although Carter's executive capacity difficulties resulting from a slow rate of neural development continue to place him at risk, his situation is really not that much different from that of any of the rest of us. At any given time, a brief commonplace lapse of executive control at the wrong time could result in extremely negative consequences for anyone. In Carter's case, however, the period of time spent in a state of poor executive control is much greater, making the odds of a negative incident much greater. Carter is not a "bad person" consciously choosing to continually seek immediate self-gratification of his desires with no concern for others. Nor are his periods of highly adaptive positive functioning simply a deviously constructed veneer concealing his true evil nature until the façade can no longer be maintained and the "real" Carter shows himself in selfish disregard of others. Carter is simply a person with a less developed frontal cortex who is doing the best he can with the physical and mental resources he possesses.

Commentary on Carter's Case

The program designed for Carter utilized an executive-driven functional assessment to produce a broad-based behavior support plan that extended beyond the classroom into the community. In designing the overall program, it was understood by those involved in the process that Carter was making poor choices, but that these choices were being made with neural capacities that were either underdeveloped or with neural capacities that were adequately developed but that were not being engaged due to Carter's lack of understanding of how to engage them either nonconsciously or consciously.

The intervention plan incorporated many elements of a traditional behavior support plan, such as structuring the environment to produce antecedent conditions that would enable Carter to demonstrate the desired behaviors and specifying consequences for both positive and negative behaviors. These traditional elements were combined with several components designed to directly address Carter's executive function difficulties. These executive function-oriented components included strategies for maintaining external control as well as strategies for helping Carter develop greater internal self-regulation capacities as specified in Table 9.2. It should be noted that while the program design was guided by the psychologist, the executive function intervention elements were implemented by other professionals and individuals working with Carter, including the special education teachers, Carter's

Table 9.2 Executive Function Intervention Strategies
Incorporated in Carter's Behavior Support Plan

Strategies for Maintaining and Encouraging Increased Development and/or Increased Use of Internally Driven Self Regulation Capacities

Increasing Awareness of the Need for Increased Use of or Development of Executive Function Capacities

Prior to the start of the plan the psychologist assisted Carter in identifying realistic personal goals for the upcoming school year.

The psychologist also assisted Carter in understanding his personal profile of cognitive ability and executive function strengths and weaknesses and the kinds of executive function self regulation capacities that would be needed in order for Carter to achieve his stated goals.

Modeling

Carter's supervisor was selected because of his ability to connect with Carter on a personal level and because of the similarity of their high school experiences. As a successful tradesman and businessman, the contractor provided Carter with a model of the executive function capacities needed for success and how to overcome difficulties and develop and use these needed capacities.

Self-Administered Rewards

Carter quickly realized that the educational program being designed for him enabled him to satisfy school requirements while providing him with the opportunity to do things that were very satisfying to him personally.

Strategies for Maintaining External Control

Structuring the Environment

Carter's educational program was designed to structure his learning and work environments in ways that reduced the likelihood of negative perceptions, feelings, thoughts, and/or actions and increased the likelihood of positive perceptions, feelings, thoughts, and/or actions.

Structuring Time

Carter's educational program was designed in a way that maximized the effective use of time.

External Cues

Carter's teacher's and work supervisor were aware of the types of cues and prompts they would need to use to help Carter maintain control of his perceptions, feelings, thoughts, and actions and use his talents and skills in a positive, productive manner.

Table 9.2 (continued) Executive Function Intervention Strategies Incorporated in Carter's Behavior Support Plan

External Feedback
The one-to-one and small group instruction design of classroom experiences and the close supervision provided in the work experience setting provided increased opportunities for delivering positive feedback to Carter in a timely manner.
External Rewards
Carter's educational program was designed to enable him to attain highly desirable rewards including graduation from high school and employment in the field of his choosing.
Aligning External Demands with Internal Desires
Carter's educational program was specifically designed to align the external demands of the educational system with his internal desires to gain experience and employment in the field of his choosing.

work supervisors and more mature coworkers, the high school principal and vice principal, and the guidance counselor.

The success of Carter's specially designed instructional program was the result of the cooperative efforts of school administrators, teaching staff, service agency representatives, community members, the psychologist, Carter, and Carter's parents. There is no question that such a program could not have been developed without a firm commitment to the idea that Carter was capable of achieving the desired outcomes and that his failures in school were due to the lack of fit between Carter's abilities and skills and the demands of the educational system. The willingness to design such a program was also possible through all participants' understanding of the executive function difficulties that Carter was experiencing and that these difficulties were not of his own choosing, but reflected his current state of development of and/or ability to utilize his neural capacities. Most critically, this understanding was embraced by the high school principal. Without his strong leadership during the program planning process and his flexibility and creativity in considering options, Carter's program would not have been designed or implemented. Carter's program could easily have been sabotaged, if not from the outset, then certainly in November, by a principal who did not believe that students like Carter deserve a chance to prove themselves in educational programs that are geared to their mental, physical, emotional, and executive function capacities.

The way in which Carter's program was planned and implemented illustrates a very critical point about school-based interventions of this type; the success of the program is dependent on the beliefs of the individuals involved and their commitment to the goals of the program and to the student as much as, and possibly more than, the technical or scientific soundness of the techniques and methods used to implement the program. If any of those involved did not want to see Carter succeed, many opportunities were presented for them to assure failure. The commitment of all participants to the goals of Carter's program and their willingness to adjust the program to maintain the possibility of success was justified, rewarded, and reinforced by the long-term outcomes realized in Carter's case.

The specially designed program provided Carter with the clear message that the school administration was on his side and was prepared to help him achieve his goals rather than set him up for failure. With realistic goals established, the program allowed Carter to envision success and generate hope for an improved future. The collaboratively established program goals enabled Carter to tap into his internal desires and use these to effectively regulate his perceptions, feelings, thoughts, and actions in a manner consistent with what was being externally demanded by his parents and school officials.

The psychologist believes that more than anything else, it was this alignment of internal desires with external demands that enabled Carter to adapt so quickly to the program and demonstrate such dramatic shifts in perception, feeling, thought, and action. Discussions with the psychologist helped Carter realize what was needed in the way of self-regulation to achieve his goals. With the internal impetus so strongly in place and an increased awareness of what was needed in the way of self-regulation, Carter was able to begin to nonconsciously and consciously engage self-regulation capacities to achieve desired outcomes. The modeling of effective self-regulation that Carter observed in his work experience supervisors and special education teachers greatly enhanced Carter's effectiveness in using his own self-regulation capacities.

Carter's situation very effectively demonstrates many of the points we have attempted to make clear throughout this book, such as the importance of creating a sound executive function environment, assuring that it was possible for rewards to be attained and punishments to be avoided, the effects of maturation and underutilization on executive function use, and the need to ensure that consequences for unacceptable behavior (e.g., use of drugs in Carter's case) are proportionate to the offense and do not hinder intervention efforts. In Carter's case, it was essential that the case conceptualization was based on three keys discussed in Chapter 7. To develop Carter's educational program, it was assumed that: (1) Carter's executive function difficulties were associated with sub-optimal brain function due to lack of maturation of and/or underutilization of existing neural capacities; (2) Carter's brain function could be altered through intervention efforts; (3) the interventions used with Carter would enable and enhance the use of intact brain functions. As can be seen from the manner in which Carter's education program was implemented, those involved maintained and modeled attitudes of hope, perseverance, and patience with intervention efforts as well as reasonable expectations for behavior change and sensible and reasonable consequences for unacceptable behavior.

By giving Carter a chance to succeed rather than forcing him to "pay the necessary price for his failures," the school district staff enabled a student to begin the long process of turning his life around and becoming a gainfully employed contributing member of society. Had Carter not been provided with a reasonable opportunity to help himself, it is likely that Carter quickly would have become a burden to society, placing additional strain on the already overworked social and penal systems of the community.

It is extremely important to note that while the specially designed instructional program provided the structure for success, it was Carter himself who responded to the structure and took full advantage of the opportunity presented to him. Critics might argue that Carter did not deserve the opportunity he was given and that the specially designed program implemented for Carter sends the wrong message to children who are just too lazy and unmotivated and lack the desire to succeed in school.

A number of staff members at Carter's high school were initially skeptical of Carter's chances of completing the program and graduating. They believed that Carter's difficulties were a matter of choice and stemmed from deep character flaws that could not be altered with such program changes. They were certain that Carter would find a way to self-sabotage the school's efforts because, at the deepest level, he was committed to avoiding any form of responsibility or hard work and did not really want to succeed and become a productive member of the general community. They felt that Carter should be required to "play by the rules" and be held accountable for his actions. They believed that Carter had successfully manipulated the psychologist and the educational system into giving him a "free ride" through school. They were quite certain that Carter would eventually drop out of school because he lacked the motivation and desire to work hard and pass all of his courses as required, and that due to his poor character, he would end up in jail shortly after dropping out of school. This, after all, was the pattern that they had observed in other students whom they judged to be similar to Carter in character make-up. Why should Carter be any different? Many of these individuals extrapolated from Carter's situation to obtain their explanation of "what is wrong with America today." By making school easy for students, we are eroding the quality of education and producing a generation of young men and women ill-prepared for the rigorous demands of the workplace in a time of great crisis.

Some of the school staff members who were initially skeptical of Carter's chances for success were astounded by how quickly Carter altered how he regulated many of his perceptions, feelings, thoughts, and actions. It was very apparent to them that the strategy of providing Carter with realistic goals and an educational program that provided a reasonable opportunity to achieve those goals worked very effectively. For some of these individuals, Carter's success made them rethink the idea of how education should work for some students and enabled them to be more open to making accommodations for students who struggle with the production demands of the traditional one-size fits-all educational process that is often forced on them. For the most deeply jaded, however, Carter was simply an example of a student who got his way and was rewarded for the wrong reasons. His intervention was an example of how far some administrators will go to avoid facing up to their responsibility for enforcing the rules and regulations, how the educational systems of today are being eroded by weak-minded mental health professionals who pander to the lazy nature of today's youth, and how moving away from a one-size-fits-all approach to education will result in educational anarchy and generations of shiftless, unmotivated citizens.

It is clear from the highly polarized reactions to Carter's successful completion of his high school program that educational practices will never be fully based on considering the outcomes of evidence-based interventions, but rather will always involve the deeper philosophical beliefs of those involved in the educational process. The authors of this book hope that readers will be able to appreciate the positive impact that the intervention documented here had on Carter and his parents as well as the school and the general community. It is our strong belief that only through interventions of this type that deal with executive function difficulties in an informed, effective way will we be able to improve the educational outcomes for students like Carter and many others whose executive function-related problems are preventing them from succeeding in school. In our thinking, Ross Greene's time-tested adage is the best philosophy to adopt when working with children experiencing executive function difficulties: "Children do well if they can; if they can't, we need to figure out why so we can help" (Greene, 2001, p. 310).

10

Summary and Conclusions

The major goals of this book were to introduce the reader to the concept of executive functions as directive mental capacities, to address specific issues critical to a deeper understanding of executive functions, and to show how the concept of executive functions could be applied by practitioners to improve assessment and intervention work with children exhibiting a wide variety of academic, social, and emotional problems. The purpose of weaving case studies throughout the book was to assure that important points regarding executive functions would be related in the context of actual clinical practice. Readers who would like to review the cases in their entirety or who might wish to share them with colleagues for discussion will find the complete narratives of each case study on the CD accompanying this book. In this summary chapter, a recap is provided of the specific executive function issues the authors set out to address in this book. These issues are discussed in the context of four general topic areas: Conceptualization, Assessment, Intervention, and Knowledge Sharing.

CONCEPTUALIZATION OF EXECUTIVE FUNCTIONS

In Chapter 2, we spent time building a contextual basis for understanding what executive functions are, and what they are not. In our initial discussion, we defined executive functions generally as the directive capacities of the human brain, but we warned against oversimplification of the concept with clichés such as "executive functions are the CEO of the brain." Rather, we emphasized the complex, multidimensional nature of executive function directive capacities and noted how the various executive functions are best viewed as a set of independent but coordinated processes with amount, efficiency, and coordination of effort varying widely from person to person.

We also noted the importance of not thinking of executive functions as being synonymous with traditional conceptions of intelligence, especially those tied to IQs derived from standardized tests of intelligence. This important point was illustrated in our case studies where it was shown how children with superior intellectual abilities—like Justin, Caroline, Morgan, and especially Alex—could demonstrate severe difficulties in their attempts to effectively direct the use of these superior abilities. Proper consideration of the role of executive functions enables us to realize that success depends not just on the intelligences one possesses, but on how and when one cues the use of these intelligences. Thus, executive capacities are not abilities in the traditional sense; they are not responsible for carrying out specific mental functions such as reasoning, but rather are the directive processes that indicate what capacities need to be engaged, when they need to be engaged, and how they need to be engaged.

In Chapter 3, we presented the McCloskey Model of Executive Functions as a multidimensional framework for conceptual organization of the broad array of directive capacities of the brain that have been described and researched in the scientific literature over the past several decades. Additionally, we introduced the critical concepts of Domains of Functioning (Perception, Emotion, Cognition, Action) and Arenas of Involvement (Intrapersonal, Interpersonal, Environment, Symbol System) to more clearly understand the capacaties that executive functions direct, and the contexts within which they direct them.

Our case studies reflected the application of these concepts to describe the specific nature of the executive difficulties each child is experiencing. Differentiating executive control by domain of functioning and arena of involvement enabled us to see how self-regulation difficulties can affect functioning in some domains and arenas but not in others.

In Chapter 4, we addressed a number of important contextual factors to help increase depth of understanding of executive functions. The first of these related to the development of executive functions over time. It was pointed out that the development of the neural structures that enable executive functions is a process that begins shortly after birth and continues well into adulthood, with a noticeable growth spurt typically occurring during the early adolescent years.

The holarchical nature of the development of executive functions across the various levels of the model was also discussed. Holarchical development, unlike hierarchical development, involves a process of continuing to move on to the next levels of development without necessarily completing development within lower levels. Also, development at lower levels can continue at the same time that development is moving on to higher levels. Development of executive functions, therefore, is best thought of as a layered process where growth continues within layers even as new layers are added.

The discussion of development highlighted the problems caused for many children by the disparity between the natural biologically determined maturation of executive functions and the culturally imposed timelines for the use of executive functions in educational settings. For children whose executive capacities are maturing slower than cultural expectations for growth, unreasonable demands for increased use of executive functions can have many negative consequences. The cases of Justin, Morgan, Alex, and Carter all serve to highlight the importance of recognizing the role of maturation in developing executive function capacities. Special attention was given to the paradoxical nature of society's willingness to acknowledge and accommodate for differences in the rate of observable physical maturation, but complete lack of willingness to acknowledge and accommodate for differences in rate of unobservable internal neural maturation.

The important dimension of locus of control was discussed in some detail. This discussion related the difference between internal and external access to executive control of perceptions, emotions, thoughts, and actions, explaining that internally commanded access is much easier for children to achieve than externally demanded engagement. The difference in internal command versus external demand was used to explain why many children are much more capable of engaging executive control "when the spirit moves them" than they are when adults demand the immediate engagement of these capacities.

Given that executive functions are engaged to direct all aspects of functioning throughout the day, their centrality to any conception of mental health should be obvious. This is currently not the case, however, as the standard classification system of mental disorders embodied in the current version of the DSM fails to make any mention of executive functions. We do believe that this situation will be rectified in the next edition of the DSM, likely in the form of the addition of a specific diagnostic classification with a label such as *executive dysfunction*. Although such a classification will improve the capacity of mental health professionals to acknowledge the debilitating effects of executive function difficulties, it will not adequately address the ubiquitous nature of executive function involvement in regulating all aspects of perception, emotion, cognition, and action. We believe that, in addition to a separate *Executive Dysfunction* classification, the DSM-V should also include a new diagnostic axis—an *Executive Function Axis*. The purpose of this new axis would be to describe the specific executive function difficulties exhibited by any client in relation to the information offered on the other five axes. This axis would identify the number and degree of severity of the specific executive function difficulties that would need to be addressed in treatment planning.

Chapter 4 concluded with the general observation that executive function difficulties manifested in the symbol system arena result in what Martha Denckla has termed Producing Disabilities. These producing disabilities were contrasted with the more traditional conception of Learning Disabilities. The topic of producing disabilities was addressed in much more detail in Chapter 6 in the discussion of the assessment of executive functions in relation to academic skill production problems.

EXECUTIVE FUNCTIONS AND ASSESSMENT

In Chapter 5, we noted that although assessment of executive functions is not yet a standard part of all psychoeducational assessments, a number of instruments have been developed over the last decade to assess the executive functions of children. We observed that almost all of these measures are standardized, norm-referenced individually administered tests that share a common set of limiting characteristics: (1) they utilize only a formal direct approach to data collection from a single source—the child; (2) they focus assessment on executive direction of information processing capacities only within the domains of perception, cognition, and action; and (3) they focus only on directing the use of information processing capacities in relation to functioning in the symbol system arena.

To correct for this narrow focus, we proposed the use of a multidimensional, multi-method approach to assessment involving both formal and informal methods applied both directly with the child and indirectly with parents, teachers, and others who know the child well. We recommended starting assessment activities with interviews of parents and teachers (Informal Indirect) and the use of ratings scales such as

the BRIEF or the MEFS (Indirect Formal) and following with
assessment activities involving the child (Direct Informal and
Formal), including classroom observations, child interviews,
and standardized norm-referenced and process-oriented data
collection and interpretation.

Because of the almost exclusive focus on direct, formal
standardized, norm-referenced tests for assessing executive
functions with children, we devoted much of Chapter 5 to a
discussion of what can and cannot be effectively measured
with these direct formal measures. We pointed out the necessity of viewing executive function tasks as separate, independent measures and warned against the practice of combining
multiple executive functions tasks (subtests) to form a global
composite, likening this practice to that of creating the neuropsychologists' g. Despite this warning, however, it would not
surprise us to see traditional measures, such as the Wechsler
Scales, incorporate two or three executive function subtests
into the next revisions and offer an Executive Functions Index
(EFI) to go along with the other four indexes (VCI, PRI, WMI,
PSI) now offered on the WAIS-III and WISC-IV. In fact, such a
practice has already been enacted with the WISC-IV. Such a
move represents a step backward in the assessment of executive functions, as many less knowledgeable practitioners
would be prone to administer these few, very narrow measures
of a limited number of self-regulation capacities, aggregate the
results into an EFI score, and believe that they are adequately
providing a good summary of the child's "overall" executive
function capacities.

We do acknowledge, however, that although limited in
focus, individually-administered norm-referenced tests often
can play an important role in the assessment of a child's
executive functions when they are appropriately interpreted
for the context of classroom production. We also pointed out
that a number of tests not specifically developed for executive
function assessment could in fact be used very effectively for
that very purpose. We summarized these points in four principles that should be considered when attempting to assess
executive functions using direct formal methods:

1. All tasks identified as measures of executive function
   also measure other information processing capacities
   (e.g., language, reasoning, visuospatial, memory).
2. All tasks identified as measures of information processing capacity (i.e., process or abilities) and/or aca-

demic skills also measure executive functions to some degree.

3. All tasks are measures of multiple executive functions; no measure assesses the use of only one self-regulation executive function capacity.

4. The amount and nature of executive function involvement in an assessment task will vary greatly depending on the format, content, and complexity of the task.

Through the use of rational task analyses, we attempted to illustrate how to think about individual tasks in order to identify the specific executive functions they do or do not assess along with the information processing capacities those executive functions are directing during task performance. To assist in assessing in more detail the effects of executive functions on task performance, we offered three unique interpretation techniques referred to as *cascading production decrements, cascading production increments,* and *cascading production paradoxes* and provided illustrations of each.

In considering direct informal approaches to assessment, we provided a discussion of the process-oriented approach to observation of task performance and interpretation of results and how to apply the approach when assessing to identify the role of executive functions in task performance. We concluded Chapter 5 by revisiting our six case studies and providing a brief synopsis of assessment work completed with each.

Although the Wisconsin Card Sorting Test (WCST) was not discussed in detail in Chapter 5, discussion of results from the WCST were incorporated into the brief case summaries to highlight the variable nature of executive function task results even when executive function difficulties are clearly present. These discussions of the WCST results also helped to highlight the importance of applying a process-oriented approach to interpretation rather than simply relying on standard scores generated to summarize test performance. For those unfamiliar with the WCST, more detailed information about the test and how it is used was provided in the context of Carter's (Chapter 9 case study) psychoeducational report located on the CD accompanying the book.

The content of Chapter 5 and the brief assessment summaries at the end of Chapter 5, however, did not discuss direct formal and informal assessment of executive function involvement in the performance of academic achievement tasks. Rather, discussion of the assessment of executive functions in the context of academic skill production was discussed in detail in Chapter 6.

In Chapter 6, we discussed in depth the role that executive functions play in academic production. For each of the major basic academic areas of reading, writing, and mathematics, we deconstructed skill performance, showing the specific self-regulation executive functions likely to be used to accomplish each skill. These discussions were followed by suggestions of methods for assessing the impact of executive function difficulties on reading, writing, and mathematics. Many of these involved cascading production decrements and/or increments involving the combined use of ability and/or process measures with academic skill measures. Additional suggestions highlighted process-oriented observation and interpretation techniques primarily as they are applied to academic skill measures. We also briefly discussed how executive function difficulties impact academic performance in the upper grades. In concluding Chapter 6, we discussed academic assessment information related to each of our case studies focusing on the role of executive function difficulties, if any, in academic production.

The discussions of direct formal and informal assessment in both Chapters 5 and 6 focused specifically on how to interpret the role of executive functions in the performance of various types of individually administered, norm-referenced tasks. In reading these chapters, practitioners should keep in mind that while defining the role of executive functions in directing performance on measures of abilities, processes, lexicons, and skills is an extremely critical component of any comprehensive psychoeducational evaluation, they are not the sole focus of such evaluations. The case study discussion presented in Chapter 9 and the related comprehensive psycho-educational assessment reports provided on the CD enabled the reader to see how these important executive function elements are incorporated with all of the other elements of case conceptualization, assessment, and intervention work.

In Chapter 8, we discussed the use of modified functional behavior assessment techniques for evaluating behavior problems, noting that the traditional functional behavior assessment model does not provide a conceptual basis for understanding the root causes of why setting events and antecedents result in problem behaviors even when the negative consequences associated with the problem behaviors are completely undesirable from the student's perspective as well as that of parents and teachers.

As an alternative to the traditional approach, we advocated for the use of executive-driven functional assessment that makes it clear that the origin of the problem behaviors lies in brain functions over which the student does not presently have conscious control. In other words, the negative behaviors being exhibited by the child do not represent conscious acts of defiance, but rather are the result of inadequate activation of executive function capacities necessary for regulating perceptions, feelings, thoughts, and actions. We believe that this important insight engenders understanding and compassion rather than negatively biased attributions suggesting character flaws or poor parenting practices.

We proposed that whereas traditional behaviorally oriented functional assessment can be viewed as an A-B-C (Antecedents-Behaviors-Consequences) model, *executive-driven functional assessment* can be viewed as an A-[EF/PETA]-B-C (Antecedents-Executive Function miscuing of Perceptions, Emotions, Thoughts, Actions-Behavior-Consequences) model. In addition to clarifying the source of the problems, an *executive-driven functional assessment* identifies the specific executive function difficulties that must be addressed in intervention efforts through improving internal self-regulation and/or applying external control. The case of Carter in Chapter 9 offered a detailed example of the application of the *executive-driven functional assessment.*

EXECUTIVE FUNCTIONS AND INTERVENTION

In Chapter 7 we provided a general perspective on intervention for executive function difficulties and described various approaches that could be utilized in intervention efforts. We offered the premise that the goal of any intervention should be to increase the child's capacity for internally directed self-regulation, and emphasized that intervention efforts depend on an understanding of three key concepts:

1. Executive function difficulties are associated with suboptimal brain function.
2. Brain function can be altered through intervention.
3. Interventions can activate the use of intact brain function.

In the discussion of these three concepts, we attempted to clarify a general philosophy about conceptualizing the nature of the executive function difficulties and approaching intervention efforts.

Related to the first key concept, we emphasized that it is important for parents, teachers, and others not to attribute the particular production deficits they observe to character flaws or consciously chosen states of mind, such as laziness, lack of motivation, apathy, irresponsibility, or stubbornness. Rather, it must be understood that the observed behaviors are rooted in brain function, that the child's current state of brain function likely was not a matter of conscious choice, and that immediately changing these brain functions likely is not within the consciously controlled skill set of the child. Avoiding negative personal attributions while adopting a more appropriate conception of the nature of the executive function problems should lead to clear statements indicating behaviors that can be changed through intervention, with the ultimate goal being changing the behavior from negative to positive.

Regarding the second key concept, we pointed out that in the absence of clear evidence that a child was born with severe brain damage or has suffered a severe traumatic brain injury since birth, it is best to assume that a child possesses the neural capacity to alter current brain function states. We believe that this optimistic stance enables the clinician to develop an intervention plan with the goal of positive change rather than the goal of simply managing a sub-optimal state of functioning.

In relation to the third concept, we concluded that if the executive difficulties are the result of disuse of existing neural capacities, then an intervention plan focused on positive behavior change goals will be based on teaching the child how to activate these neural networks, either consciously or nonconsciously, to achieve the positive goals. We believe that the amount and rate of progress toward positive goals will be constrained only by other contextual factors such as maturation, the level of functioning of other cognitive capacities (e.g., the child's capacity to benefit from language-based learning), or significant biologically based conditions.

We also addressed five issues that help to provide greater depth of perspective to conceptualizing interventions. The first of these involves balancing the teaching of internal control with requirements for external control. Although the ultimate goal of intervention should be to increase the child's capacity for internally directed self-regulation, we recognize that initially children vary greatly in terms of how capable they are of benefiting from an intervention focused on developing internal self-regulation. Conceptualizing interventions, therefore, will likely require the need to balance external control substitution efforts with internal control teaching efforts. In many instances, intervention will need to start with the application of external controls and gradually move to teaching the child strategies and techniques that will affect internal change for improving self-regulation. Effective interventions require careful monitoring of progress during the intervention period to enable the practitioner, parents, and school staff to make the necessary decisions about the timing and extent of alterations made to external control contingencies and internal control teaching efforts.

The second issue addressed the environment in which interventions are implemented. It was noted that the effectiveness of any intervention attempt will depend greatly on the executive function capacities of the practitioner and those most closely associated with the child—family, friends, teachers, administrators, etc. These individuals create an executive function environment in which the child can increase skill development through the modeling and coaching provided to them in the environment.

The third issue pertained to the use of rewards and punishments in intervention efforts. It was noted that the use of rewards and punishment assumes, either implicitly or explicitly, that the child already possesses the executive skills required to achieve the desired goals, and that failure to achieve goals is simply a matter of conscious choice and lack of desire. As readers of this book now know, the executive function difficulties of many children make it difficult for them to sufficiently or consistently cue themselves to achieve goals, even when motivation to do so is high. In other cases, rewards and punishments can be very effective as they serve as a source of consistent, frequent feedback about the effectiveness of performance, thereby enabling engagement of the proper level of self-monitoring required for achieving goals.

If rewards or punishment are to be used as part of an intervention program, practitioners were advised to monitor progress closely and be prepared to make modifications and/or eliminate the rewards and punishments and redesign the intervention rather than concluding that the child is not capable of responding positively to intervention efforts. Most importantly, it was pointed out that externally administered rewards and punishments are still forms of external control. As such, they do not teach children to become consciously aware of, reflect on, and internalize control. While rewards and/or punishments can play a role in the external control phase of an intervention program, the ultimate goal of internally directed self-regulation will require the child to be consciously engaged in learning how to develop and use executive function capacities in the absence of external rewards and punishments.

The issue of maturation was revisited from the perspective of intervention efforts. We discussed the slowing effect that delays in maturation can have on progress toward intervention goals, and how the passage of time, in itself, can be a powerful intervention mechanism. We pointed out that for children faced with overly aggressive expectations for brain maturation, a little time may be all that is needed to achieve the desired levels of self-direction. Even in the case of children with more substantial developmental delays, the most effective intervention may simply be more time for maturation to occur.

We noted with equal emphasis, however, that recognition of the effects of maturation does not mean that practitioners and family members should adopt a wait-and-see approach to dealing with executive function-related problems. Rather, we acknowledged that energy and effort should be put into developing and implementing interventions in the present moment that attempt to produce positive behavior changes in the current areas of difficulty. By engaging intervention efforts, practitioners and parents are providing the child with knowledge of self-regulation processes that can be tapped when increases in neural development make increased use of executive capacities possible.

The final issue we addressed was that of consequences for unacceptable behavior. Here we argued that given the fact that the executive function difficulties children experience are not of their own choosing, some leeway is needed when applying consequences for behaviors that violate rules. Although we did not advocate that all rules be suspended when dealing with children with executive function difficulties, we do believe that the consequences should be of a reasonable nature and not overly harsh.

Consideration of maturation and consequences naturally leads to a discussion of retention policy in school. The research completed to date suggests that grade retention is beneficial only for a small subset of students. Although the characteristics of this subset are not well established, we strongly suspect that executive function difficulties are among the characteristic features of this group. In the absence of clear evidence regarding exactly which students would benefit from retention however, we believe that retention cannot be supported as a general intervention practice for students exhibiting executive function difficulties.

We concluded the discussion of issues relevant to conceptualizing intervention by offering general guidelines for planning and implementing interventions:

1. Provide the child with as rich an "executive function environment" as possible.
2. Initially adopt the position that the executive function difficulties are the result of nonconscious disuse of existing executive capacities that can be activated through intervention efforts.
3. Focus on making the child aware of the executive capacities needed to achieve desired behavior goals and on teaching the child how and when to activate the use of the needed executive capacities with the ultimate goal being internalization of the self-regulation routines needed for effective functioning.
4. Develop and apply, as needed, interventions involving external control. Monitor the use of these interventions closely to determine when to begin the gradual or complete withdrawal of external control so that internal control can be engaged and demonstrated.
5. Maintain and model attitudes of hope, perseverance, and patience with intervention efforts.
6. Maintain, and foster in others, reasonable expectations for behavior change and sensible and reasonable consequences for unacceptable behavior.

Turning to a consideration of specific intervention strategies, we noted that although there is a lack of evidence-based literature available addressing executive function interventions per se, there exists a wealth of data from various professional fields related to effective interventions for dealing with children exhibiting executive function difficulties. We discussed many of these sources in a general review of the intervention literature.

Of particular note for increasing internal self-regulation are a wide variety of intervention techniques based on the core principles of Cognitive Behavior Therapy. The literature based on the use of behavior management with children diagnosed with AD/HD was pointed to as the best example of the efficacy of the use of external control strategies for managing executive function difficulties. Academic instruction techniques emphasizing self regulation and self monitoring were also referenced. In our general review of the literature, we noted the relative absence of interventions geared to dealing with executive function difficulties exhibited in the environment arena, and pointed out that this is an area of great need. Readers seeking additional information on interventions may find the annotated bibliography provided on the CD accompanying this book to be a useful source.

This general review was followed by a summary of intervention strategies. These strategies were grouped according to the internal-external control dimension and included the following:

Intervention Strategies for Developing Internal Control
- Increasing Awareness
- Modeling Appropriate Use of Executive Functions
- Teaching Specific Executive Functions as Skills Routines
- Using Verbal Mediation
- Using Verbal or Nonverbal Labeling
- Teaching the Use of Internal Feedback
- Establishing Self-Administered Rewards

Intervention Strategies for Maintaining External Control
- Pharmacological Treatment
- Structuring the Environment
- Structuring Time
- Externalizing Cues for Effective Processing
- Providing Feedback
- Providing Rewards
- Aligning External Demands with Internal Desires

We included in Chapter 7 a discussion of how to apply these internal and external intervention strategies to the 23 self-regulation capacities, offering an example using the Modulate cue. The chapter included detailed discussions of the intervention approaches likely to be the most effective with each of our case study children.

In Chapter 8, we revisited intervention issues in the context of school settings. We emphasized that practitioners need to realize that executive function interventions involving academic skill production problems should not be viewed as stand-alone activities. For example, there really is no specific intervention for "academic executive function problems," but rather interventions that take into account the impact executive function difficulties may have on a child's ability to demonstrate academic skills. We also pointed out that many of the most effective academic intervention programs make implicit or explicit use of strategies designed either to provide external executive function cue substitutes or to encourage students to internally regulate the use of executive function capacities. For each of the basic academic areas of reading, writing, and mathematics, we discussed how the internal and external control intervention strategies could be integrated into academic intervention efforts in order to reduce the impact of executive function difficulties and improve production.

In addition to discussion of basic academic skills, we briefly addressed how executive function difficulties impact production in content area instruction, especially in the upper grades, and offered suggestions for intervention approaches designed to increase the effectiveness of executive function use or to compensate for lack of use.

In conjunction with the concept of executive-driven functional assessments, Chapter 8 discussed how incorporating an understanding of executive function difficulties and the intervention approaches for dealing with these difficulties can help to expand behavioral support plans beyond their current limited emphasis on external control substitutes. We noted that the expanded A-[EF/PETA]-B-C executive-driven model for interventions focuses not just on behaviors, but on the perceptions, feelings, thoughts, and actions that lead to the behaviors and the executive control capacities that cue and direct all of these. The model increases awareness of the brain-based nature of the difficulties the child is experiencing, likely leading to a more sympathetic approach to dealing with the resulting behavior difficulties.

We also noted that the executive-driven model also holds self-regulation rather than maintenance of external control as the ultimate goal of intervention efforts. We acknowledged however the fact that in school settings, children's executive function difficulties range from very mild to very severe, necessitating a full range of intervention options from increasing internal control through increased awareness and skill-building to maintaining strict external control through a carefully monitored behavior support plan within a very restricted educational setting. Whatever path intervention efforts take, and whatever the outcome, we believe that adopting an executive-driven model will ensure sensible and humane treatment of the child along the way.

Chapter 8 offered a discussion of procedures for evaluating the effectiveness and outcomes of intervention efforts. We pointed out that when considering the school setting context, appropriately identified executive function difficulties can be addressed in conjunction with intervention efforts focused on specific social, emotional, and/or academic problems. We noted that these types of intervention efforts will typically require progress monitoring and outcome measures that go beyond basic curriculum-based (i.e., research-based) academic skills measures or standard behavior rating scales.

We suggested that Goal Attainment Scaling (GAS) is a methodology well-suited to developing measures to evaluate interventions that incorporate executive functions conceptions in their design and implementation as it involves the construction of individual items designed to evaluate specific program objectives. We emphasized that setting goals for intervention efforts and sharing those goals with the child are critical components of any intervention plan. We also acknowledged the often exasperating nature of attempting to demonstrate progress with students who are experiencing producing difficulties. We advised that understanding the behaviors that result from students' executive function difficulties can greatly assist teachers and other school staff in developing the frame of mind needed to maintain intervention efforts with these students.

We stated that when attempting to monitor progress and the effectiveness of interventions with students exhibiting executive function difficulties, clinicians need to consider two key issues: (1) how should decisions be made about whether or not progress is being made, and (2) how long should intervention efforts continue without major modification if the student is not demonstrating progress.

We illustrated methods for answering these two questions through an example case using GAS techniques to develop appropriate goals for intervention and appropriate measures for evaluating whether goals were being attained. We noted that one of the strengths of the GAS technique is that it requires specification, beforehand, of what would constitute adequate, less than adequate, and more than adequate progress within a specified period of time.

In conjunction with a specific case example, we offered some important principles to keep in mind when developing, implementing, and evaluating interventions for students with executive function difficulties, including:

- Identify and describe the executive function difficulties exhibited by the student and their impact on behavior and/or academic production.
- Develop intervention strategies that take into account the effects of executive function difficulties on production.
- Make clear the distinction between learning and producing and the need to consider them as two distinct but integrated elements of a single intervention program.
- Develop program evaluation measures using GAS techniques that enable parents, teachers, and other school staff to evaluate the effectiveness of intervention elements designed to improve learning and elements designed to improve production.

In concluding the discussion on progress monitoring, we acknowledged the difficulty inherent in attempting to answer the question of how long intervention efforts should continue without major modification if the student is not demonstrating progress. Although no definitive answer can be offered to this question, we provided a framework with factors to consider in attempts to solve this riddle for each individual case. In concluding Chapter 8, we revisited each of our case studies and offered information about intervention efforts in the context of the school settings of each child.

KNOWLEDGE SHARING

In Chapter 8, we stated that practitioners who have acquired a good working knowledge of executive functions can share this information with parents, teachers, administrators, and other school staff to help increase awareness of this important concept and its application to instruction, assessment, and intervention activities. We emphasized the need to relate information about executive functions within the context of existing ideas about instruction, assessment, and intervention rather than advocating for it as a replacement for existing ideas. It is hoped that the information presented in the first four chapters of this book will provide practitioners with a solid basis for developing their own understanding and application of the concept of executive functions that can then be shared with parents and school staff.

An important goal of sharing information about executive functions should be to help teachers realize the extent of the executive function demands they make on students and how these demands can be overwhelming for children who are experiencing slower than average development of executive function capacities. We highlighted the necessity of making all students aware of the academic goals and behavioral expectations in place in the school setting as well as the executive function capacities needed to achieve goals and meet behavioral expectations. Most importantly, students who are consciously aware of goals and expectations are much more likely to find ways to engage executive function capacities to assist in achieving goals and meeting expectations.

In Chapter 6, we discussed in detail the concept of producing disabilities and their contrast with learning disabilities, noting that the difference between learning and producing disabilities is an important one because it helps to understand many of the dynamics related to educational support services. We pointed out that the learning disability of a child who possesses effective executive function capacities is less likely to be noticed by parents and teachers because the child's executive function strengths enable them to compensate for learning weaknesses and demonstrate adequate production.

In contrast, children who have both learning and producing disabilities are much more likely to be noticed, and noticed sooner, by parents and teachers due to their lack of adequate production. In other words, it is their producing disabilities that draw attention to their learning disabilities. Children who demonstrate only producing disabilities are also more likely to be noticed, but the absence of learning disabilities often results in attributing the producing difficulties to negative personal characteristics such as lack of motivation rather than to executive function difficulties.

We strongly emphasized that without appropriate identification of the source of the difficulties of these children and assistance through interventions aimed at improving the executive capacities of these children, this group faces the greatest risk of failing in school and being deprived of a valuable education that would enable them to learn how to overcome their producing difficulties. Sharing knowledge of the nature of producing disabilities and their association with, or dissociation from, learning disabilities can greatly improve an educational system's capacity for developing an appropriate perspective on dealing with students who exhibit production difficulties.

We believe that once knowledge of executive functions has been shared with teachers and a basis for meaningful dialogue about the concept has been established, practitioners can assist teachers in finding ways to incorporate this knowledge base into instructional practices. The ideal goal here is for teachers to apply their knowledge of executive functions to help students increase their use of self-regulation capacities in developmentally appropriate ways. We reminded practitioners that good teaching practices routinely incorporate many very effective methods for teaching increased self-regulation and for maintaining external control when necessary. We encouraged practitioners to be familiar with the literature on best teaching practices and understand where these intersect with executive function intervention strategies as a means of offering suggestions for helping a teacher improve the use of teaching techniques most likely to be effective with students experiencing executive function difficulties.

Finally, we proposed that practitioners who have a sound understanding of the developmental nature of executive function capacities are in a good position to advocate for system-level change designed to bring educational practices in line with the growing body of knowledge about brain development. We noted that there are a number of things that communities and school districts could do to create school environments that reflect an understanding of the wide variations demonstrated in the rate of children's brain development and discussed some of these.

CLOSING COMMENTS

Ultimately, this book is about the functioning of children's developing minds and how the children in possession of these minds can develop greater control of them. Conjointly, this book is about how others, in particular school-based practitioners, can assess these efforts and identify and implement strategies to help children develop increased mind control capacities or arrange for substitute sources of control when needed. We operationally defined these mind control processes as executive functions.

Some strict behaviorists may object to the use of the terms mind or executive functions. They may argue that there is no such thing as mind. Additionally, some strict empirical neuroscientists may argue that the model of executive functions presented in this book does not accurately represent how the brain really functions to regulate perceptions, emotions, thoughts, or actions. Although the concept of executive functions presented in this book represents a confluence of a number of lines of basic research on brain function, the essential points of such behaviorists and strict neuroscientists are well taken. Mind and executive functions are metaphors; they are not tangible structures or physical processes occurring in the brain; they are "as if" concepts introduced to help us make meaning out of our phenomenological experience of existence in the world and to help us communicate this meaning to each other and to ourselves. They serve as a functional map, not the actual territory the map represents.

On a deeper philosophical level, it could be argued reasonably that there is no real way that any human brain can ever truly understand human brains. Brain self-study, by its very nature, is solipsistic; the entity of interest must be used during the attempt to study it. The use of metaphors to describe brain function should not be surprising or viewed as an outrage or a sham even though it is equivalent to the wizard's curtain in Oz. We make extensive use of metaphor with great positive results. No one has ever seen, or knows exactly what, emotions or thoughts really are, but we use these metaphors to communicate about brain function effectively on a daily basis. Without such metaphorical constructs it would not be possible to implement effective interventions such as cognitive behavior therapy. In a more mundane example, it is really quite implausible that the terms fruit and vegetable are essential representations of the "true" nature of the things we label as fruit and as vegetable, but we make use of these terms all the time to effect clear communication and achieve desired results. The reality of our existence and the language we use to describe that existence is not about "what is," but about what we collectively accept and label as "what is." Metaphors for the mind, like all other mentally constructed aspects of reality, are subject to change as collective consciousness evolves.

It is important therefore, for practitioners to keep in mind that executive functions as discussed in this book represent an interrelated system of metaphors typically referred to as psychological constructs. The clinical utility of a psychological construct depends on the extent to which it provides explanatory power, can be easily communicated and understood, and can be effectively applied to achieve desired effects. In this book, we offered a comprehensive model of executive functions and related contextual dimensions that we believe have great explanatory power in terms of understanding why children (and adults) perceive, feel, think, and act as they do. We also believe that this model can be understood by lay persons as well as professionals, and that it can be used effectively by practitioners in assessment activities and in intervention planning and implementation for children exhibiting a wide range of problems due to what we have chosen to call executive function difficulties.

When a psychological construct is poorly defined and only vaguely understood, the likelihood is much greater that it will be misapplied and eventually discarded or otherwise devalued. In writing this book, we wanted to help ensure the viability of the executive function conceptual network. To achieve that end, we provided a detailed model and suggestions for how to apply the model in clinical practice. We also countered several misperceptions and answered several frequently asked questions that reflected sources of confusion about executive functions and their application to educational settings.

The model and our explanations were based on our understanding of the scientific literature and our clinical practice with children we believed to be exhibiting executive function difficulties. We have personally seen the positive results of the use of the executive function conceptual network, some of which were described in detail in Chapter 9. Professional colleagues who have adopted and employed the executive function conceptual network have frequently commented to us on the transformative nature of its use. In the words of one of these colleagues: "It completely changed how I think about assessment and intervention in the schools and my professional role."

Ultimately, the validity of the concept of executive functions and its application in psychology and education rests not in its essential truth, but in its functional utility. If the concept can be used to improve communication and understanding in ways that produce positive changes in perception, emotion, cognition, and action, then it deserves to be used; if it doesn't, then it deserves to be discarded as a half-baked notion or trendy fad. We believe that the information we have amassed in this book on the executive function conceptual network and its usefulness, however, suggest that its utility will be long lasting and transformative in many ways for those who embrace it and apply it knowledgeably in their professional practice, and we remain committed to advancing its use in clinical practice. Ideally, we hope that this book will encourage clinicians and laypersons alike to join us in the use of the executive function conceptual framework as a basis for helping children improve their daily functioning through improved control over their perceptions, feelings, thoughts, and actions.

REFERENCES

Althorp, H., & Clark, T. (2007). *Using strategy instruction to help struggling high schoolers understand what they read.* Washington, DC: Institute of Education Sciences.

Alvarez, J. A. & Emory, E. (2006). Executive function and the frontal lobes: A meta-analytic review. *Neuropsychology Review, 16*(1), 17–42.

American Psychiatric Association (1994). *Diagnostic and statistical manual of mental disorders* (4th ed.). Washington, DC: Author.

Antshel, K. M. (2005). Social skills training reconsidered: What role should peers play? *The ADHD Report, 13*(1), 1–6.

Arnsten, A. F. T. & Robbins, T. W. (2002). Neurochemical modulation of prefrontal cortical functioning in humans and animals. In D. T. Stuss & R. T. Knight (Eds.), *Principles of frontal lobe function* (pp. 31–50). New York: Oxford University Press.

Atwood, T. (2007). *The complete guide to Asperger's syndrome.* Philadelphia: Jessica Kingsley.

Avila, C., Cuenca, I., Felix, V., & Parcet, M. (2004). Measuring impulsivity in school-aged boys and examining its relationship with ADHD and ODD ratings. *Journal of Abnormal Child Psychology, 32*(3), 295–305.

Baldo, J. O., Shimamura, A. P., Delis, D. C., Kramer, J., & Kaplan, E. (2001). Verbal and design fluency in patients with frontal lobe lesions. *Journal of International Neuropsychological Society, 7*(5), 586–596.

Balkin, T. J., Braun, A. R., Wesensten, N. J., Jeffries, K., Varga, M., Baldwin, P., et al. (2002). The process of awakening: A PET study of regional brain activity patterns mediating the re-establishment of alertness and consciousness. *Brain, 125*(10), 2308–2319.

Barkley, R. A. (1997, 2005). *ADHD and the nature of self-control.* New York: Guilford Press.

Barkley, R. A. (2000). *Taking charge of ADHD.* New York: Guilford Press.

Barkley, R. A. (2006). *Attention-deficit hyperactivity disorder, third edition: A handbook for diagnosis and treatment.* New York: Guilford Press.

Bar-On, R., Tranel, D., Denburg, N. L., & Bechara, A. (2003). Exploring the neurological substrate of emotional and social intelligence. *Brain, 126*(8), 1790–1800.

Baving, L., Laucht, M., & Schmidt, M. H. (1999). Atypical frontal brain activation in ADHD: Preschool and elementary school boys and girls. *Journal of the American Academy of Child and Adolescent Psychiatry, 38*(11), 1363–1371.

Baxter, L. R., Clark, E. D., Iqbal, M., & Ackermann, R. F. (2001). Cortical-subcortical systems in the mediation of Obsessive-Compulsive Disorder: Modeling the brain's mediation of a classic "neurosis." In D. G. Lichter & J. L. Cummings (Eds.), *Frontal-subcortical circuits in psychiatric and neurological disorders* (pp. 207–230). New York: Guilford Press.

Ben-Hur, M. (Ed.). (1994). *On Feuerstein's instrumental enrichment: A collection.* Arlington Heights, IL: Skylight Training and Publishing.

Benson, H., Malhotra, M. S., Goldman, R. F., Jacobs, G. D., & Hopkins, P .J. (1990). Three case reports of the metabolic and electroencephalographic changes during advanced Buddhist meditation techniques. *Behavioral Medicine, 16*, 90–95.

Berlin, H. A., Rolls, E. T., & Kischka, U. (2004). Impulsivity, time perception, emotion and reinforcement sensitivity in patients with orbitofrontal cortex lesions. *Brain, 127*(5), 1108–1126.

Berninger, V. W. (1998). *Process assessment of the learner (PAL): Guides for intervention.* San Antonio: Psychological Corporation.

Berninger, V. W. (2007). *Process assessment of the learner (PAL-II): Administration and scoring manual for reading and writing.* San Antonio: Harcourt Assessment.

Berninger, V. W., & O'Donnell, L. (2005). Research-supported differential diagnosis of specific learning disabilities. In A. Prifitera, D. H. Saklofske, & L. G.Weiss. *WISC-IV clinical use and interpretation: Scientist-practitioner perspectives.* Burlington, MA: Elsevier.

Berninger, V. W. & Richards, T. L. (2002). *Brain literacy for educators and psychologists.* New York: Academic Press.

Berthoz, S., Anthony, J. L., Blair, R. J. R., & Dolan, R. J. (2002). An fMRI study of intentional and unintentional (embarrassing) violations of social norms. *Brain, 125*(8), 1696–1708.

Biederman, J., Petty, C., Fried, R., Fontanella, J., Doyle, A., Seidman, L. J., & Faraone, S. V. (2006). Impact of psychometrically defined deficits of executive functioning in adults with attention deficit hyperactivity disorder. *American Journal of Psychiatry, 163*(10), 1730–1738.

Blake, P., & Grafman, J. (2004). The neurobiology of aggression. *The Lancet, 364,* 12–14.

Boring, E. G. (1923). Intelligence as the tests test it. *New Republic, 35*: 36–37.

Borkowski, J. G. & Muthukrishna, N. (1992). Moving metacognition into the classroom: "Working models" and effective strategy teaching. In M. Pressley, K. R. Harris, & J. T. Guthrie, *Promoting academic competence and literacy in school* (pp. 477–501). San Diego: Academic Press.

Brown, T. E. (2005). *Attention deficit disorder: The unfocused mind in children and adults.* New Haven, CT: Yale University Press.

Brown, K.W., & Ryan, R.M. (2003). The benefits of being present: Mindfulness and its role in psychological well-being. *Journal of Personality and Social Psychology, 84*(4), 822–848.

Bunge, S. A., Ochsner, K. N., Desmond, J. E., Glover, G. H., & Gabrieli, J. D. E. (2001). Prefrontal regions involved in keeping information in and out of mind. *Brain, 124*(10), 2074–2086.

Cahn, B. R., & Polich, J. (2006). Meditation states and traits: EEG, ERP, and neuroimaging studies. *Psychological Bulletin, 132*(2), 180–211.

Cardillo, J.E., & Choate, R.O. (1994). Illustrations of goal setting. In Kiresuk, T. J., Smith, A., & Cardillo, J. E. (Eds.). *Goal attainment scaling: Applications, theory, and measurement.* Hillsdale, NJ: Lawrence Erlbaum Associates.

Carmichael, M. (2007, March 26). Stronger, faster, smarter. *Newsweek, CXLIX*(13), 38–46.

Carskadon, M. A. (Ed.). (2002). *Adolescent sleep patterns: Biological, social, and psychological influences.* Cambridge, England: Cambridge University Press.

Case, L., Pericola, H. & Karen, R. (1992). Improving the mathematical problem-solving skills of students with learning disabilities: Self-regulated strategy development. *Journal of Special Education, 26,* 1–14.

Clark, C., Prior, M., & Kinsella, G. (2000). Do executive function deficits differentiate between adolescents with ADHD and oppositional defiant/conduct disorder? A neuropsychological study using the six elements tests and Hayling sentence completion test. *Journal of Abnormal Psychology, 28,* 403–415.

Dagher, A., Owen, A. M., Boecker, H., & Brooks, D. J. (2001). The role of the striatum and hippocampus in planning: A PET activation study in Parkinson's disease, *Brain, 124*(8), 1020–1032.

Daw, N. D., Niv, Y., & Dayan, P. (2005). Uncertainty-based competition between prefrontal and dorsolateral striatal systems for behavioral control. *Nature Neuroscience, 8*(12), 1704–1711.

Dawson, P., & Guare, R. (2004). *Executive skills in children and adolescents: A practical guide to assessment and intervention.* New York: Guilford Press.

Dehaene, S. (1997). *The number sense: How the mind creates mathematics.* New York: Oxford University Press.

De La Paz, S., & Graham, S. (2002). Explicitly teaching strategies, skills, and knowledge: Writing instruction in middle school classrooms. *Journal of Educational Psychology, 94,* 687–698.

De La Paz, S., Swanson, P. N., & Graham, S. (1998). The contribution of executive control to the revising by students with writing and learning difficulties. *Journal of Educational Psychology, 90,* 448–460.

Delis, D. C., Kaplan, E., & Kramer, J. H. (2001). *Delis-Kaplan executive function system.* San Antonio: Psychological Corporation.

Demakis, G. J. (2003). A meta-analytic review of the sensitivity of the Wisconsin Card Sorting Test to frontal and lateralized frontal brain damage. *Neuropsychology, 17*(2), 255–264.

Denckla, M. B. (1996). A theory and model of executive function: A neuropsychological perspective. In G. R. Lyon & N. A. Krasnegor (Eds.), *Attention, memory, and executive Function* (pp. 263–278). Baltimore: Paul H. Brookes.

Denckla, M.B. (2001). Unpublished manuscript.

Denckla, M. B. (2007). Executive function: Building together the definitions of attention deficit/hyperactivity disorder and learning disabilities. In L. Meltzer (Ed.), *Executive function in education* (pp. 5–18). New York: Guilford Press.

Diamond, A. (2002). Normal development of prefrontal cortex from birth to young adulthood: Cognitive functions, anatomy, and biochemistry. In D. T. Stuss & R. T. Knight (Eds.), *Principles of frontal lobe function* (pp. 466–503). New York: Oxford University Press.

Diamond, M. & Hopson, J. (1998). Magic trees of the mind: *How to nurture your child's intelligence, creativity, and healthy emotions from birth through adolescence.* New York: Penguin.

Eliot, L. (1999). *What's going on in there?: How the brain and mind develop in the first five years of life.* New York: Bantam.

Elliott, S. N., & DiPerna, J. C., with Shapiro, E. S. (2001). *Academic intervention monitoring system.* San Antonio: The Psychological Corporation.

Ferretti, R. P., MacArthur, C. A., & Dowdy, N. S. (2000). The effects of an elaborated goal on the persuasive writing of students with learning disabilities and their normally achieving peers. *Journal of Educational Psychology, 92,* 694–702.

Feuerstein, R. (1980). *Instrumental enrichment: An intervention program for cognitive modifiability.* Glenview, IL: Scott, Foresman.

Fletcher, J. M., Lyon, G. R., Fuchs, L. S., & Barnes, M. A. (2006). *Learning disabilities: From identification to intervention.* New York: Guilford Press.

Frakowiak, R. S. J., Friston, K. J., Frith, C. D., Dolan, R. J., & Mazziotta, J. C. (1997). *Human brain function.* New York: Academic Press.

Frankl, V. E. (1984). *Man's search for meaning.* New York: Washington Square Press.

Freeman, W. J. (2000). *How brains make up their minds.* New York: Columbia University Press.

Friedburg, R. D., & McClure, J. M. (2002). *Clinical practice of cognitive therapy with children and adolescents: The nuts and bolts.* New York: Guilford Press.

Gaskins, I. W., & Elliott, T. T. (1991). *The Benchmark model for teaching thinking strategies: A manual for teachers.* Cambridge, MA: Brookline Books.

Gersten, R., Fuchs, L. S., Williams, J. P., & Baker, S. (2001). Teaching reading comprehension strategies to students with learning disabilities: A review of research. *Review of Educational Research, 71*(2), 279–320.

Gioia, G. A., Isquith, P. K., & Guy, S. C. (2001). Assessment of executive functions in children with neurological impairment. In R. Simeonsson & S. L. Rosenthal (Eds.), *Psychological and developmental assessment: Children with disabilities and chronic conditions* (pp. 317–356). New York: Guilford Press.

Gioia, G. A., Andrews Epsy, K., & Isquith, P. K. (1996). *Behavior rating inventory of executive function-preschool version: Professional manual.* Lutz, FL: Psychological Assessment Resources.

Gioia, G. A., Isquith, P. K., Guy, S. C., & Kenworthy, L. (2000). *Behavior rating inventory of executive function: Professional manual.* Lutz, FL: Psychological Assessment Resources.

Goldberg, E. (2001). *The Executive Brain: Frontal lobes and the civilized mind.* New York: Oxford University Press.

Goldapple, K., Segal, Z., Garson, C., Lau, M., Bieling, P., Kennedy, S., et al. (2004). Modulation of cortical-limbic pathways in major depression: Treatment-specific efforts of cognitive behavior therapy. *Archives of General Psychiatry, 61*: 34–41.

Goel, V., & Dolan, R. J. (2004). Differential involvement in left prefrontal cortex in inductive and deductive reasoning. *Cognition, 93*, B109–B121.

Goldman-Rakic, P. S., & Leung, H. C. (2002). Functional architecture of the dorsolateral prefrontal cortex in monkeys and humans. In D. T. Stuss & R. T. Knight (Eds.), *Principles of frontal lobe function* (pp. 85–95). New York: Oxford University Press.

Grace, J., & Malloy, P. F. (2001). *Frontal systems behavior Scale (FrSBE).* Lutz, FL: Psychological Assessment Resources.

Grafman, J. (2002). The structured event complex and the human prefrontal cortex. In D. T. Stuss & R. T. Knight (Eds.), *Principles of frontal lobe function* (pp. 292–310). New York: Oxford University Press.

Graham, S. (1997). Executive control in the revising of students with learning and writing difficulties. *Journal of Educational Psychology, 89*, 223–234.

Graham, S., & Harris, K. R. (2005). Improving the writing performance of young struggling writers: Theoretical and programmatic research from the Center of Accelerating Student Learning. *Journal of Special Education, 39*, 19–34.

Graham, S., Harris, K. R., & Troia, G. A. (2000). Self-regulated strategy development revisited: Teaching writing strategies to struggling writers. *Topics in Language Disorders, 20*, 1–15.

Gray, C. (2002). *My social stories book.* London: Jessica Kingsley.

Greene, J. D., Nystrom, L. E., Engell, A. D., Darley, J. M., & Cohen, J. D. (2004). The neural bases of cognitive conflict and control in moral judgment. *Neuron, 44*(2), 389–400.

Greene, J. D., Sommerville, R. B., Nystrom, L. E., Darley, J. M., & Cohen, J. D. (2001). An fMRI investigation of emotional engagement in moral judgment. *Science, 293,* 2105–2108.

Greene, R. W. (2001). *The explosive child: A new approach for understanding and parenting easily frustrated, chronically inflexible children.* New York: Perennial.

Greene, R. W., & Albon, J. S. (2006). *Treating explosive kids: The collaborative problem-solving approach.* New York: Guilford Press.

Gresham, F. M., Cook, C. R., & Crews, S. D. (2004). Social skills training for children and youth with emotional and behavioral disorders: Validity considerations and future directions. *Behavioral Disorders, 30*(1), 32–47.

Gresham, F. M, Van, M. B., & Cook, C. R. (2006). Social skills training for teaching replacement behaviors: Remediating acquisition deficits in at-risk students. *Behavioral Disorders, 31*(4), 363–378.

Guy, S. C., Isquith, P. K., & Gioia, G. A. (1996). Behavior Rating Inventory of Executive Function-Self-report version: *Professional manual.* Lutz, FL: Psychological Assessment Resources.

Hale, J. B., & Fiorello, C. A. (2004). *School neuropsychology: A practitioner's handbook.* New York: Guilford Press.

Hale, J. B., Fiorello, C. A., & Brown, L. L. (2005). Determining medication treatment effects using teacher ratings and classroom observations of children with ADHD: Does neuropsychological impairment matter? *Educational & Child Psychology, 22*(2), 39–61.

Hale, J. B., Hoeppner, J. B., DeWitt, M. B., Coury, D. L., Ritacco, D. G., & Trommer, B. (1998). Evaluating medication response in ADHD: Cognitive, behavioral, and single-subject methodology. *Journal of Learning Disabilities, 31,* 595–607.

Harris, K. R., & Graham, S. (1996). *Making the writing process work: Strategies for composition and self-regulation.* Cambridge, MA: Brookline Books.

Hartman, H. J. (2001). (Ed.). *Metacognition in learning and instruction: Theory, research, and practice.* Netherlands: Kluwer Academic.

Hayes, S. C., Follette, V. M., & Linehan, M. M. (Eds.) (2004). *Mindfulness and acceptance: Expanding the cognitive-behavioral tradition.* New York: Guilford Press.

Heaton, R. K., Chelune, G. J., Talley, J. L., Kay, G. G., & Curtiss, G. (1993). *Wisconsin Card Sorting Test.* Lutz, FL: Psychological Assessment Resources.

Herzog, H., Lele, V. R., Kuwert, T., Langen, K. J., Kops, E. R., & Feinendegen, L. E. (1990). Changed pattern of regional glucose metabolism during Yoga meditative relaxation. *Neuropsychobiology 23,* 182–187.

Hill, D. E., Yeo, R. A., Campbell, R. A., Hart, B., Vigil, J., & Brooks, W. (2003). Magnetic resonance imaging correlates of attention-deficit/hyperactivity disorder in children. *Neuropsychology, 17*(3), 496–506.

Hirshorn, E. A., & Thompson-Schill, S. L. (2006). Role of the left inferior frontal gyrus in covert word retrieval: Neural correlates of switching during verbal fluency. *Neuropsychologia, 44,* 2547–2557.

Hoeppner, J. G., et al. (1997). A clinical protocol for determining methylphenidate dosage levels in ADHD. *Journal of Attention Disorders, 2*(1), 19–30.

Howard, R. C. (2001). Bringing brain events to mind: Functional systems and brain event-related potentials. *Journal of Psychophysiology, 15*(2), 69–79.

Isquith, P. K., Gioia, G. A., & PAR Staff. (2002). *Behavior rating inventory of executive functions-Software portfolio.* Lutz, FL: Psychological Assessment Resources.

Jimerson, S. R. (2001). Meta-analysis of grade retention research: Implications for practice in the 21st Century. *School Psychology Review, 30*(3), 420–437.

Jitendra, A. K., & Hoff, K. (1996). The effects of schema-based instruction on the mathematical word-problem-solving performance of students with learning disabilities. *Journal of Learning Disabilities, 29*(4), 422–431.

Jitendra, A. K., Hoppes, M. K., & Xin, Y. P. (2000). Enhancing main idea comprehension for students with learning problems: The role of summarization strategy and self-monitoring instruction. *Journal of Special Education, 34*(3), 127–139.

Johnson, S.C., Baxter, L. C., Wilder, L. S., Pipe, J. G., Heiserman, J. E., & Prigatano, G. P. (2002). Neural correlates of self-reflection. *Brain, 125*(8), 1808–1814.

Jones, C. B. (1996). *Attention deficit disorder: Strategies for school-age children.* San Antonio: The Psychological Corporation.

Kabat-Zinn, J. (1994). *Wherever you go, there you are: Mindfulness meditation in everyday life.* New Haven: Hyperion.

Kabat-Zinn, J. (2005). *Coming to our senses: Healing ourselves and the world through mindfulness.* New York: Piatkus.

Kaplan, E. (1988). A process approach to neuropsychological assessment. In T. Boll & B. K. Bryant (Eds.), *Clinical neuropsychology and brain function: Research, measurement, and practice* (pp. 125–167). Washington, DC: American Psychological Association.

Kaufman, A. S., & Kaufman, N. L. (1983). *Kaufman Assessment Battery for Children.* Circle Pines, MN: American Guidance Service.

Kaufman, A. S., & Kaufman, N. L. (1993). *Kaufman Adolescent and Adult Intelligence Test.* Circle Pines, MN: American Guidance Service.

Kaufman, A. S., & Kaufman, N. L. (1993). *Kaufman survey of early academic and language skills.* Circle Pines, MN: American Guidance Service.

Kaufman, A. S. & Kaufman, N. L. (2005). *Kaufman test of educational achievement,* 2nd ed. Minneapolis, MN: Pearson Assessments.

Kelly, B, & Carnine, D. (1996). Unpublished manuscript. http://www.cldinternational.org/PDF/Initiatives/MathSeries/kelly.pdf

Kiresuk, T. J., Smith, A., & Cardillo, J. E. (Eds.) (1994). *Goal attainment scaling: Applications, theory, and measurement.* Hillsdale, NJ: Lawrence Erlbaum Associates.

Klin, A., Volkmar, F. R., & Sparrow, S. S. (2000). Asperger syndrome. New York: Guilford Press.

Knopf, H. M. (2002). Best practices in personality assessment. In A. Thomas, & J. Grimes (Eds.), *Best practices in school psychology IV* (pp.1281–1302). Bethesda: National Association of School Psychologists.

Knoster, T. P., & McCurdy, B. (2002). Best practices in functional behavioral assessment for designing individualized student programs. In A. Thomas, & J. Grimes (Eds.), *Best practices in school psychology IV* (pp. 1007–1028). Bethesda: National Association of School Psychologists.

Koestler, (1964). *The act of creation.* New York: Dell.

Korkman, M., Kirk, U. & Kemp, S. (1998). NEPSY: *A developmental neuropsychological assessment.* San Antonio: Harcourt Assessment.

Korkman, M., Kirk, U., & Kemp, S. (1998). *NEPSY—Second edition.* San Antonio: Harcourt Assessment.

Krasnegor, N. A., Lyon, G. R., & Goldman-Rakic, P. S. (Eds.) (1997). *Development of the pre-frontal cortex: Evolution, neurobiology, and behavior.* Baltimore: Paul H. Brookes.

Kratochwill, T. R., Elliott, S. N., & Callan-Stoiber, K. (2002). Best practices in school-based problem-solving consultation. In A. Thomas, & J. Grimes (Eds.), *Best practices in school psychology IV* (pp. 583–698). Bethesda: National Association of School Psychologists.

Kurtz, B. E., & Borkowski, J. G. (1987). Development of strategic skills in impulsive and reflective children: A longitudinal study of metacognition. *Journal of Experimental Child Psychology, 43*, 129–148.

Levine, M. D. (1999). *Developmental variations and learning disorders.* Cambridge: Educators Publishing Service.

Levine, B., Robertson, I. H., Clare, L., Carter, G., Hong, J., Wilson, B. A., et al. (2000). Rehabilitation of executive functioning: An experimental-clinical validation of goal management training. *Journal of the International Neuropsychological Society, 6*, 299–312.

Levine Rubell, B. (1999). *Big strokes for little folks.* San Antonio: PsychologicalCorporation.

Lichter, D. G., & Cummings, J. L. (Eds.). (2001). *Frontal-subcortical circuits in psychiatric and neurological disorders.* New York: Guilford Press.

Luria, A. R. (1973). *The working brain: An introduction to neuropsychology.* New York: Basic Books.

Luria, A. R. (1980). *Higher cortical functions in man* (2nd ed.). New York: Basic Books.

Lyon, G. R., & Krasnegor, N. A. (Eds.). 1996. *Attention, memory, and executive function.* Baltimore: Paul H. Brookes.

MacMaster, F. P., Carrey, N., Sparkes, S., & Kusumakar, V. (2003). Proton spectroscopy in medication-free pediatric attention-deficit/hyperactivity disorder. *Biological Psychiatry, 53*(2), 184–187.

Marlowe, W. B. (2001). An intervention for children with disorders of executive functions. *Developmental Neuropsychology, 18*, 445–454.

Marzano, R. J. (2003). *What works in schools: Translating research into action.* Alexandria, VA: Association for Supervision and Curriculum Development.

Marzano, R. J., Marzano, & Pickering, D. J. (2003). *Classroom management that works: Research-based strategies for every teacher.* Alexandria, VA: Association for Supervision and Curriculum Development.

Marzano, R. J., Pickering D. J., & Pollock, J. E. (2001). *Classroom instruction that works: Research-based strategies for increasing student achievement.* Alexandria, VA: Association for Supervision and Curriculum Development.

Mastropieri, M A., & Scruggs, T. E. (1991). *Teaching students ways to remember: Strategies for learning mnemonically.* Cambridge, MA: Brookline Books.

Mayberg, H. (2001). Depression and frontal-subcortical interactions. In D. G. Lichter & J. L. Cummings (Eds.), *Frontal-subcortical circuits in psychiatric and neurological disorders* (pp. 177–206). New York: Guilford Press.

McCloskey, G. (2004). Unpublished manuscript.

McCloskey, G. (2007). *McCloskey Executive Functions Scales.* Unpublished manuscript.

McCloskey, G., & Maerlender, A. (2005). The WISC-IV Integrated. In A. Prifitera, D. H. Saklofske, & L. G. Weiss (Eds.), *WISC-IV clinical use and interpretation: Scientist-practitioner perspectives.* Burlington, MA: Elsevier.

McGinnis, E., & Goldstein, A. P. (1984). *Skill-streaming the elementary school child: A guide for teaching prosocial skills.* Champaign, IL: Research Press.

Mednick, S., & Ehrman, M. (2006). *Take a nap! Change your life.* New York: Workman.

Meltzer, L. (Ed.) (2007). *Executive function in education: From theory to practice.* New York: Guilford Press.

Mennutti, R. B., Freeman, A., & Christner, R W. (Eds.) (2006). *Cognitive-behavioral interventions in educational settings.* New York: Routledge.

Mesulam, M. M. (2002). The human frontal lobes: Transcending the default mode through contingent encoding. In D. T. Stuss & R. T. Knight (Eds.), *Principles of frontal lobe function* (pp. 8–30). New York: Oxford University Press.

Meyers, J. E., & Meyers, K. R. (1995). *Rey complex figure test and recognition trial.* San Antonio: Harcourt Assessment.

Miller, E. K. (2001). An integrative theory of prefrontal cortex function. *Annual Review of Neuroscience, 24,* 167–202.

Miller, B. L., & Cummings, J. L. (Eds.) (2006). *The human frontal lobes, second edition: Functions and disorders (science and practice of neuropsychology series)*. New York: Guilford Press.

Miller, W. R., & Rollnick, S. (2002). *Motivational interviewing: Preparing people for change* (2nd ed.). New York: Guilford Press.

Millman, R. P. (2005). Excessive sleepiness in adolescents and young adults: Causes, consequences, and treatment strategies. *Pediatrics, 115,* 1774–1786.

Miranda, A., Villaescusa, M. I., & Vidal-Abarca, E. (1997). Is attribution retraining necessary? Use of self-regulation procedures for enhancing the reading comprehension strategies of children with learning disabilities. *Journal of Learning Disabilities, 30,* 503–513.

Montgomery, P. C., & Connolly, B. H. (Eds.). (2002). *Clinical applications for motor control*. Thorofare, NJ: Slack.

Morin, A. (2004). A neurocognitive and socioecological model of self-awareness. *Genetic, Social, and General Psychology Monographs. 130*(3), 197–223.

Nagahama, Y., Okada, T., Katsumi, Y., Hayashi, T., Yamauchi, H., Oyanagi, C., et al. (2001). Dissociable mechanisms of attentional control within the human prefrontal cortex. *Cerebral Cortex, 11*(1), 85–92.

Nagahama, Y., Okina, T., Suzuki, N., Nabatame, H., & Matsuda, M. (2005). The cerebral correlates of different types of perseveration in the Wisconsin Card Sorting Test. *Journal of Neurology, Neurosurgery, & Psychiatry, 76,* 169–175.

Naglieri, J. A., & Das, J. P. (1997). *Das-Naglieri cognitive assessment system*. Itasca, IL: Riverside.

Newberg, A., Alavi, A., Blaine, M., Mozley, P. D., & D'Aquili, E. (1997). The measurement of cerebral blood flow during the complex task of meditation using HMPAO-SPECT imaging. *Journal of Nuclear Medicine, 38,* 95.

Newberg, A., Alavi, A., Baime, M., Pourdehnad, M., Santanna, J., & d'Aquili, E. (2001). The measurement of regional cerebral blood flow during the complex cognitive task of meditation: A preliminary SPECT study. *Psychiatry Research: Neuroimaging Section, 106,* 113–122.

Newberg, A., D'Aquili, E., & Rause, V. (2001). *Why God won't go away: Brain science and the biology of belief*. New York: Ballantine Books.

Nezu, A. M., & Perri, M. G. (1989). Social problem-solving therapy for unipolar depression: An initial dismantling investigation. *Journal of Consulting and Clinical Psychology, 57*(3), 408–413.

Olsen, J. Z. (2001). *Handwriting without tears.* Potomac, MD: Author.

O'Neill, R. E., Horner, R. H., Albin, R.W., Sprague, J. R., Storey, K., & Newton, J. S. (1997). *Functional assessment and program development for problem behavior: A practical handbook.* (2nd ed.) Pacific Grove, CA: Brooks/Cole.

Oosterlaan, J., Scheres, A., & Sergeant, J. A. (2005). Which executive functioning deficits are associated with AD/HD, ODD/CD, and comorbid AD/HD+ODD/CD? *Journal of Abnormal Child Psychology, 33*, 69–85.

Pennington, B. F. (1997). Dimensions of executive functions in normal and abnormal development. In N. A. Krasnegor, G. R. Lyon, & P. S. Goldman-Rakic. (Eds.), *Development of the pre-frontal cortex: Evolution, neurobiology, and behavior.* Baltimore: Paul H. Brookes.

Pennington, B. F. (2002). *The development of psychopathology: Nature and nurture.* New York: Guilford Press.

Pennington, B. F., Bennetto, L., McAleer, O., & Roberts, R, J. (1996). Executive functions and working memory: Theoretical and measurement issues. In G. R. Lyon & N. A. Krasnegor (Eds.), *Attention, memory, and executive function* (pp. 327–348). Baltimore: Paul H. Brookes.

Pennington, B. F., & Ozonoff, S. (1996). Executive functions and developmental psychopathology. *Journal of Child Psychology and Psychiatry, 37*(1), 51–87.

Petrides, M., & Pandya, D. N. (2002). Association pathways of the prefrontal cortex and functional observations. In D. T. Stuss & R. T. Knight (Eds.), *Principles of frontal lobe function* (pp. 31–50). New York: Oxford University Press.

Piaget, J. (1972). Intellectual evolution from adolescence to adulthood. *Human Development, 15*, 1–12.

Picton, T. W., Alain, C., & McIntosh, A. R. (2002). The theatre of the mind: Physiological studies of the human frontal lobes. In D. T. Stuss & R. T. Knight (Eds.), *Principles of frontal lobe function* (pp. 109–126). New York: Oxford University Press.

Picton, T. W., Stuss, D. T., Alexander, M. P., Shallice, T., Binns, M. A., & Gillingham, S. (2007). Effects of focal frontal lesions on response inhibition. *Cerebral Cortex, 17*(4), 826–838.

Posner, M. I., & Cohen, Y. (1984). Components of attention. In H. Bouma & D. Bowhuis (Eds.), *Attention and performance X: Control of language processes* (pp. 531–556). Hillsdale, NJ: Erlbaum.

Posner, M. I., & Petersen, S. E. (1990). The attention system of the human brain. *Annual Review of Neuroscience, 13,* 25–42.

Posner, M. I., & Raichle, M. E. (1994). *Images of mind.* New York: Scientific American Books.

Posner, M. I., & Rothbart, M. K. (1991). Attentional mechanisms and conscious experience. In M. Rugg & A. D. Milner (Eds.), *The neuropsychology of consciousness* (pp. 91–112). London: Academic Press.

Posner, M. I., & Rothbart, M. K. (1998). Attention, self regulation and consciousness. *Philosophical Transactions of the Royal Society of London. Series B, Biological Sciences, 353,* 1915–1927.

Posner, M. I., & Rothbart, M. K. (2000). Developing mechanisms of self regulation. *Development and Psychopathology, 12,* 427–441.

Posner, M. I. & Rothbart, M. K. (2007). *Educating the human brain.* Washington, DC: American Psychological Association.

Pressley, M., & Afflerbach, P. (1995). *Verbal protocols of reading: The nature of constructively responsive reading.* Hillsdale, NJ: Earlbaum.

Pressley, M. & Woloshyn, V. (Eds.). (1995). *Cognitive strategy instruction that really improves children's academic performance.* Cambridge, MA: Brookline Books.

Quinn, M., Kavale, K., Mathur, S. R., Rutherford, R. B., & Forness, S. R. (1999). A meta-analysis of social skill intervention for students with emotional and behavioral disorders. *Journal of Emotional & Behavioral Disorders, 7*(1), 54–64.

Ratey, J. J. (2002). *A user's guide to the brain.* New York: Vintage Books.

Reid, M. K. & Borkowski, J. G. (1987). Causal attributions of hyperactive children: Implications for teaching strategies and self-control. *Journal of Educational Psychology, 79,* 296–307.

Roid, G. (2003). *Stanford-Binet Intelligence Scale,* 5th Ed. Itasca, IL: Riverside.

Rolls, E. T. (2002). The functions of the orbitofrontal cortex. In D. T. Stuss and R. T. Knight (Eds.), *Principles of frontal lobe function* (pp. 354–75). New York: Oxford University Press.

Rosenshine, B., & Meister, C. (1997). Cognitive strategy instruction in reading. In S. A. Stahl & D. A. Hayes (Eds.), *Instructional models in reading* (pp. 85–107). Hillsdale, NJ: Lawrence Erlbaum Associates.

Salmon, D. P., Heindel, W. C., & Hamilton, J. M. (2001). Personality and behavioral changes with frontal-subcortical dysfunction. In D. G. Lichter & J. L. Cummings (Eds.), *Frontal-subcortical circuits in psychiatric and neurological disorders* (pp. 114–150). New York: Guilford Press.

Saltus, R. C. (2003, August 26). Lack direction? Evaluate your brain's C.E.O. *The New York Times.* Retrieved December 28, 2006, from http://www.quietmindfdn.org

Salvia, J., Ysseldyke, J.E., & Bolt, S. (2006). *Assessment in special and inclusive education.* Boston: Houghton Mifflin.

Scheid. K. (1993). *Helping students become strategic learners: Guidelines for teaching.* Cambridge, MA: Brookline Books.

Schraw, G. (1998). Promoting general metacognitive awareness. *Instructional Science, 26,* 113–125.

Schunk, D. H. (1989). Social cognitive theory and self-regulated learning. In B. F. Zimmerman & D. H. Schunk (Eds.), *Self-regulated learning and academic achievement: Theory, research, and practice.* New York: Springer-Verlag.

Schwartz, J. (1996). *Brain lock: Free yourself from obsessive-compulsive behavior: A four-step self-treatment method to change your brain chemistry.* New York: Harper.

Schwartz, J. & Begley, S. (2002). *The mind and the brain: Neuroplasticity and the power of mental force.* New York: Harper.

Scruggs, T. E. & Mastropieri, M. A. (1992). *Teaching test-taking skills: Helping students show what they know.* Cambridge, MA: Brookline Books.

Segal, Z. V., Williams, J. M. G., & Teasdale, J. D. (2002). *Mindfulness-based cognitive therapy for depression: A new approach to preventing relapse.* New York: Guilford Press.

Seidman, L. J., Biederman, J., Faraone, S. V., Weber, W., & Ouellette, C. (1997). Toward defining a neuropsychology of attention deficit/hyperactivity disorder: Performance of children and adolescents from a large clinically referred sample. *Journal of Consulting and Clinical Psychology, 65*(1), 150–160.

Shaywitz, S. (2003). *Overcoming dyslexia.* New York: Alfred A. Knopf.

Shure, M. B. (1992). *Cognitive problem solving program.* Champaign, IL: Research Press.

Siegel, D. J. (2007). *The mindful brain: Reflections and attunement in the cultivation of well-being.* New York: W. W. Norton.

Singer, B. D. & Bashir, A. S. (1999). What are executive functions and self-regulation and what do they have to do with language-learning disorders? *Language, Speech & Hearing Services in Schools, 30*(3), 265–274.

Singh, N. N., Lancioni, G. E., Winton, A. S., Adkins, A .D., Wahler, A. G., Sabaawi, M., et al. (2007). Individuals with mental illness can control their aggressive behavior through mindfulness training. *Behavior Modification, 31*(3), 313–328.

Springer, S. P. & Deutsch, G. (2002). *Left brain, right brain: Perspectives from cognitive neuroscience.* New York: W.H. Freeman.

Sternberg, R. J. (2003). *Cognitive psychology.* Belmont, CA: Thomson/Wadsworth.

Stoiber, K. C. & Kratochwill, T. R. (2001a). *Outcomes: Planning, monitoring, evaluating.* San Antonio: Psychological Corporation.

Stoiber, K. C. & Kratochwill, T. R. (2001b). *Functional assessment and intervention system.* San Antonio: Psychological Corporation.

Stuss, D. T. & Alexander, M. P. (2000). Executive functions and the frontal lobes: A conceptual view. *Psychological Research, 63: 289–298.*

Stuss, D. T. & Knight, R. T. (Eds.). (2002). *Principles of frontal lobe function* (pp. 109–126). New York: Oxford University Press.

Stuss, D. T., Levine, B., Alexander, M. P., Hong, J., Palumbo, C., & Hamer, L., et al. (2000). Wisconsin Card Sorting Test performance in patients with focal frontal and posterior brain damage: Effects of lesion location and test structure on separable cognitive processes. *Neuropsychologia, 38,* 388–402.

Taylor, J. G. (1998). Towards the networks of the brain: From brain imaging to consciousness. *Neural Networks, 12* (7–8), 943–959.

Teeter, P. A. (1998). *Interventions for ADHD: Treatment in developmental context.* New York: Guilford Press.

Temple, C. (1997). *Developmental cognitive neuropsychology.* East Sussex, UK: Psychology Press.

Terman, L. M. (1921). Intelligence and its measurement, part II. *Journal of Educational Psychology, 12,* 127–133.

Torgesen, J., Wagner, R., & Rashotte, C. (1999). *Test of word reading efficiency (TOWRE).* Lutz, FL: Psychological Assessment Resources.

Troia, G. A., & Graham, S. (2002). The effectiveness of a highly explicit, teacher-directed strategy instruction routine: Changing the writing performance of students with learning disabilities. *Journal of Learning Disabilities,* 290–306.

Vaitl, D., Gruzelier, J., Jamieson, G. A., Lehmann, D., Ott, U., Sammer, G., et al. (2005). Psychobiology of altered states of consciousness. *Psychological Bulletin, 131,* 98–127.

Voeller, K. K. S. (2001). Attention-deficit/hyperactivity disorder as a frontal-subcortical disorder. In D. G. Lichter. & J. L. Cummings (Eds.), *Frontal-subcortical circuits in psychiatric and neurological disorders* (pp. 334–371). New York: Guilford Press.

Wagner, R., Torgeson, J., & Rashotte, C. (date). *Comprehensive test of phonological processing (CTOPP).* Minneapolis: Pearson Assessments.

Watson, S. M. R., & Westby, C. E. (2003). Strategies for addressing the executive function impairments of students prenatally exposed to alcohol and other drugs. *Communication Disorders Quarterly, 24*(4), 194–206.

Webster-Stratton, C., & Reid, M. J. (2003) Treating conduct problems and strengthening social and emotional competence in young children: The Dina Dinosaur Treatment Program. *Journal of Emotional and Behavioral Disorders, 11,* 130–147.

Wechsler, D. (1997). *Wechsler Adult Intelligence Scale—Third Edition.* San Antonio: The Psychological Corporation.

Wechsler, D., Kaplan, E., Fein, D., Morris, R., Kramer, J. H., Maerlender, A., & Delis, D. C. (2004). *The Wechsler Intelligence Scale for Children—Fourth Edition Integrated.* San Antonio: The Psychological Corporation.

Wechsler, D. (2001). *Wechsler individual achievement test—second edition (WIAT-II).* San Antonio: Harcourt Assessment.

Wilbur, K. (1979). *No boundary: Eastern and Western approaches to personal growth.* Boston: Shambhala.

Wilbur, K. (2006). *Integral spirituality.* Boston: Integral Books.

Wilbur, K. (1995). *Sex, ecology, spirituality: The spirit of evolution.* Boston: Shambhala.

Wilbur, K. (1997). *A brief history of everything.* Boston: Shambhala.

Wilbur, K. (2000). *Integral psychology.* Boston: Shambhala.

Wilson, B. A., Alderman, N., Burgess, P., Emslie, H., & Evans, J. J. (1996). *Behavioral assessment of the dysexecutive syndrome (BADS).* Lutz, FL: Psychological Assessment Resources.

Wood, S. J., & Murdock, J. Y. (2002). Self-monitoring and at-risk middle school students: Academic performance improves, maintains, and generalizes. *Behavior Modification, 26,* 605–627.

Wood, E., Woloshyn, V. & Willoughby, T. (1995). *Cognitive strategy instruction for middle and high schools.* Cambridge, MA: Brookline Books.

Woodcock, R. W., McGrew, K. S., & Mather, N. (2001). *Woodcock-Johnson Test of Cognitive Abilities (3rd ed.) (WJ-III).* Riverside Publishing.

Ylvisaker, M. (Ed.) (1998). *Traumatic brain injury rehabilitation: Children and adolescents.* Woburn, MA: Butterworth-Heinemann.

Ylvisaker, M. & Feeney, T. J. (1998). Everyday people as supports: Developing competencies through collaboration. In M. Ylvisaker (Ed.), *Traumatic brain injury rehabilitation: Children and adolescents* (pp. 429–464). Woburn, MA: Butterworth-Heinemann.

Ylvisaker, M., Szekeres, S. F., & Feeney, T. J. (1998). Cognitive rehabilitation: Executive functions. In M. Ylvisaker (Ed.), *Traumatic brain injury rehabilitation: Children and adolescents* (pp. 221–269). Woburn, MA: Butterworth-Heinemann.

Zang, Y. F., He, Y., Zhu, C. Z., Cao, Q. J., Sui, M.Q., Liang, M., et al. (2007). Altered baseline brain activity in children with ADHD revealed by resting-state functional MRI. *Brain Development, 29*(2),: 83–91.

Zimmerman, B. J. (1990). Self-regulated learning and academic achievement: An overview. *Educational Psychologist, 25,* 3–17.

Zimmerman, B. J. (1989). A social cognitive view of self-regulated academic learning. *Journal of Educational Psychology, 81* (3), 1–23.

Index

fluent, 141
habits, interviewing about,
  149
learning disabilities, 152
model, 141
producing disabilities, 152
production, executive
  function self-regulation
  cues in, 142
self-regulation executive
  functions and, 140
Retrieve cue, 144, 145, 166
Rey Complex Figure (RCF), 94

S

SB-V, *see* Stanford-Binet Scale
  of Intelligence—Fifth
  Edition
School
  behavior support plan, 221
  executive function
    development and,
    78–81
    classroom exercises, 78
    demonstration of learning,
    79
    educational transitions,
    79, 80
    extreme developmental
    delays, 80
    production demands, 79
    skills learned, 78
  lack of positive feedback
    from, 217
School Neuropsychology,
  135
School setting, executive
  functions in, 233–272
  Academic Intervention
    Monitoring System
    Guidebook, 246
  academic problem assessment
    and intervention,
    243–245
  advocating for system
    change, 259–260
  A-EF/PETA-B-C executive-
    driven model, 243

Alex in school setting,
  270–271
  delay in brain functioning,
  270
  inertia, 270
  parents, 271
  self-determination
    capacities, 271
applications of executive
  function knowledge,
  233
behavior support plans, 238
Brett in school setting,
  263–264
  ADHD symptoms, 263
  biological nature of
    problems, 264
  fine motor control, 263
  ICPS program, 264
  physical/occupational
    therapy, 263
Caroline in school setting,
  262–263
  cognitive abilities, 262
  mentoring, 263
  organizational strategies,
  263
  self-regulation executive
    function difficulties,
  262
classroom-wide behavior
  management
  techniques, 242
cues, 253
decoding skill production,
  254
distinction between
  producing and
  learning, 249
emotional functioning,
  248–249
enhancement of group and
  individual instruction,
  235–236
executive-driven functional
  assessment model, 240
Executive Function
  Classroom Observation
  Checklist, 236